GOING GRAND

GOING GRAND

a novel by

Jack MacLeod

McClelland and Stewart Limited

Copyright © 1982 by Jack MacLeod

The Canadian Publishers
McClelland and Stewart Limited
25 Hollinger Road
Toronto M4B 3G2

Canadian Cataloguing in Publication Data

MacLeod, Jack, 1932-
   Going grand

ISBN 0-7710-5563-3

I. Title.

PS8575.L4587G64   C813'.54   C82-094038-0
PR9199.3.M258G64

Printed and bound in Canada

For Heather

With an affectionate doff of the cap
to Genni and Jeff,
the Saskatchewan Connection,
and my friends of the P.O.E.T.S. Corner

"It is ordained in the eternal constitution of things that men of intemperate minds cannot be free. Their passions forge their fetters."
                                        Edmund Burke

"University – [a] centre where one has the right and duty not to make up one's mind."
                                        The Idea File
                                        Harold A. Innis

PROLOGUE

The university stood, quiet, gravid, a reproachful sentinel opposite the vulgar buildings of the provincial government. Chiliast U. was located near, but aloof from, the slick restaurants and fashionably garish boutiques of Yorkville and Bloor Street. The campus lay north and west (the directions of adventure and hope), from the bank towers and gilded temples of Bay Street where fortunes were made and lost in minutes. The city surged and scuffled around it, but the university remained unhurried. Many of its open spaces had been paved over, asphalt lapping at the base of stubborn oaks and a resolute remnant of unblighted elms; a few tranquil islands of greenery, hedged quadrangles and lush playing fields, recalling long lost pastoral origins. These few verdant oases amid the desert of the city's concrete congestion gave solace to lounging students and ruminant professors in the warm autumn sun. Perversely, contrary to all natural rhythms and astronomical chartings, the campus came to life not in the spring but in the fall, when boisterous young people returned to it and the faculty grudgingly re-emerged from summer hibernation.

Along the few remaining shaded walks, students burnished by vacation sun smiled indolent greetings at pallid Professors, who were to be pitied or even pardoned for being old. Professors, extending themselves only to the limp reciprocity of mute salutation, nodded preoccupied acknowledgements to unformed and aimless young clones who possessed more enthusiasm than experience, more will than wit. The generations mutually indulged, tolerated, and misunderstood one another, each with the placid certainty that it knew a truth denied its counterpart. Their cheerfully counterpoised confidence ensured that the jostling of conflicting convictions in the classroom would remain benign and harmless. Students enthused about anything and everything fresh and unfamiliar, while their teachers pondered ruefully that under the sun nothing was new. Each generation gently rejoiced that reflection and criticism, if not wisdom, could find sanctuary within the university, even if they led to strangely opposite conclusions of easy change and stubborn changelessness. Amid turmoil and contradictions, the university persisted, as institutions do and individuals do not.

Carillon bells pealed from above an empty chapel. The corridors of the main Arts and Sciences Building echoed with the bleats of innocent, harassed freshmen in beatific beanies, who were herded by first-initial-of-surname line-ups for class allocations to courses which would be shifted or cancelled tomorrow. In the bowels of the Administration Building incontinent computers whirred and emitted little dotted-slotted cards that "verified" the existence of persons and imposed impersonality. Crowds of leather-jacketed, gum-gnawing youths wandered in and out of the square, squat, ugly Engineering Building, which hunkered monstrously behind a forlorn tuft of shrubbery at the southern end of the campus. And in the library, astonishing seminal books, untouched for years, waited patiently for a chance opportunity to swim upstream into the womb of any unwary receptive mind.

Teachers of English Literature left their office doors avidly ajar, but seldom did any student walk in. Undergraduates in fetid cafeterias vehemently argued the merits of John Nichols and Tom Robbins, Richard Wright and Robert Coover, but none of these appeared on a curriculum. No one read Fitzgerald anymore or remembered Hemingway's sneering rejoinder as to why the rich are not like you and me.

10

Just missed. Everything was so orderly, so pleasantly enviable, and just missed.

Over the portal of one of the college buildings was carved the inscription "The Truth Shall Make Ye Free." On the wall of a washroom cubicle was scrawled "The Truth Shall Make Ye Angry." That the truth might cause only perplexity, or even sorrow, occurred to very few.

On the north side of the circular drive that encompassed the front campus, Burke College glowered in haughty gothic dignity. Its fierce and grotesque gargoyles had been carved out of limestone by immigrant masons a hundred or more years ago; its worn plank floors creaked under the feet of a second century's scholarly supplicants. The stern greystone tower of the college loomed above the campus and watched imperiously over the careers and hopes of the fleeting generations. A narrow twisting staircase gave access to the top of the tower, although scarcely anyone had climbed it in years. There were those who said that after midnight a ghost walked the tower stairs.

But then, in any university, there are always some who will believe anything.

1

"It's driving me crazy-pushing me 'round the twist and up the spout!" muttered J.T. McLaughlin to the world in general and no one in particular. "Absolutely crazy. It's all just too much." McLaughlin suffered acutely from copelessness, the inability to cope, a condition he had once seen identified in a learned sociological treatise as one of the principal maladies of our times. In scholarly jargon, this pervasive contemporary affliction was called "Emotional and Nervous Dysfunctional Maladjustment to Prevailing Social Mores, Interstitial Institutional Patterns, and Interpersonal Relationships." A fancy name, of course, for neurotic.

By any name, J.T. McLaughlin was neurotic. If a madman is one who denies that two and two are four, and a neurotic is one who knows that two and two are four but can't stand it, McLaughlin could add, but could not accept the minimal results of his irksome addition. He was an uptight, twitchy, chainsmoking bundle of jangled nerves. A raw nerve in search of a protective coating. Like a tree without bark, a peeler crab without its shell. A typically bedevilled and bewildered product of hectic, pressurized, fuming urban industrialism, dependent upon the system yet chewed up by it.

J.T. McLaughlin was a Professor at Chiliast University, Toronto. A highly educated person, one who had swilled from the public trough of bursaries and scholarships for several academic degrees and a privileged teaching position, he could cope with intellectual abstractions and general theories well enough. It was the ordinary things of life, the social security cards, the personnel numbers, the carburettors, batteries, deadlines, bra snaps, bill collectors, bosses, and wives of the world that threw him. Particularly the wives and bosses. He had one of each, and could no more understand them than why some men volunteered for perilous combat missions in the jungle, why his neighbours voted Liberal, or how to repair his own jumpy and decrepit television set. Life's little imponderables and niggling insupportabilities.

It was not as though he did not try. The mundane mechanisms and vicissitudes of ordinary living produced in him a lively curiosity and a hopeful eagerness to deal with them, but the do-it-yourself projects he embarked upon never got done, the machinery and appliances he took apart wilfully resisted his best ham-handed attempts at reassembly.

McLaughlin, in short, was not a practical man. He was the sort who could grind the gears of an automatic transmission. But secretly he regarded himself as another Juan Fangio at the wheel of a car, with a negligent, natural brilliance for darting in and out of the tiniest gaps in the careening traffic around him. While driving he frequently engaged in shouting curses and imprecations at the less imaginative motorists who threatened him, yearning for hair-pin turns in the Grand Prix de Monte Carlo, and simultaneously chatting himself up, taking both sides of an earnest, solitary debate as he wandered from lane to lane in the heavy morning crush of Detroit iron, causing brake-slamming chaos and foul-mouthed consternation behind him. He often talked out loud to himself in urgent and expostulatory terms, which was what he was doing on this glowing autumn morning on the way to work.

"I'm forty-three years old," he reminded his impatient audience of one, swerving to avoid an errant lampost. "I have a house, a beautiful wife, three wonderful children, a Ph.D., a secure salary, an almost new car, group life insurance, five suits, a four-track stereo tape recorder, a power lawn mower, innumerable credit cards, snowblower, an electric toothbrush–and I can't stand it."

He emitted a grunt of non-resignation as he considered the tawdry inventory of his material possessions. It amounted to a fairly decent standard of living. Not entirely bad, he acknowledged, compared with what some poor buggers could call their own. But somehow–not adequate, not satisfying. Merely a catalogue of the orthodox bourgeois trappings, the predictable, let's face it, inevitable impedimentia of sparse borderline white-collar status. The subsistence level of the middle-class existence. The caboose on the gravy train. Surely proud poverty would be better than being only at the margin of solvency. He shuddered. He didn't really want to know.

At the next stoplight he glared resentment at a smooth-looking fascist in a new XJ-S Jag and mournfully recalled that ominous dappled orange scars of rust were already appearing on his own fenders. Sighing as the light turned green, he returned to his melancholy stock-taking of worldly goods.

The heavily mortgaged house of Mr. and Mrs. J.T. McLaughlin was old, small, and narrow. It had been quainted up with the addition of phoney shutters and carriage lamps that looked about as appropriate as an Indian feather headdress on the Mona Lisa. No amount of architectural masquerading could conceal the facts: the house had only one bathroom, a kitchen that fairly squealed for renovation, a sagging front stoop, and the whole fiasco was in desperate lack of paint.

His tape deck worked only in spasms. Last night a favourite Billie Holiday reel had broken just as Lester Young handed off the riff to Teddy Wilson, and resisted J.T.'s eleven-thumbed efforts to splice it back together. Four of his five suits were out of fashion, and the power lawn mower out-smarted all sweaty attempts to start it until his knuckles were skinned and well greased. The damned lawn would need re-sodding next year.

Possessions are a drag. They tie you down. Who needs them? J.T. McLaughlin, that's who. There was that nagging necessity (much encouraged by his wife) to acquire and display, to remain unsquelched by the rivalrous neighbours and to keep up with the snotty Joneses, all wallowing in the gim-micky luxuries of the technological society. All bound to the system by steel links of cacophonous T.V. blandishments, supercilious repairmen, and interminable time payments. Tidal waves of clamorous advertisements importuned from every quarter. "Be the first in your neighbourhood to own and rejoice in the New Improved Super-Deluxe chrome-plated Lulu computerized food processor with Q.R.S. and nine Fun Attachments! It will absolutely solve all your household problems. It will weave cloth, make porridge, paint the garage, wash dishes, cure halitosis, mind the baby, and put out the cat." (Do everything, in fact, except prepare food.) "Only twenty dollars down and four ninety-nine per month for twenty years or until your will is probated, whichever comes first."

I guess I could manage the four ninety-nine per month, McLaughlin reflected. It's the twenty dollars down in cold cash that raises the difficulty. Which reminded him that this week he just *had* to see that smiling imbecile of a bank manager about the overdraft. Damned embarrassing. Cheques bouncing like kangaroos in heat. Not Sufficient Funds: NSF. Surrounded and put upon by stark, impersonal initials, that was the problem. Little prickly letters that meant nothing but posed a constant threat to his existence: NSF, CIA, RCMP, OPEC, NATO, RRSP, PLO, IBM, RIP. Fearful little twits of initials, tiny but menacing. He yearned for solid and flavourful bouillabaisse, and the world slipped him a bowl of diluted alphabet soup. Meaningless soup and thin gruel made from plastic envelopes of dehydrated offal. Merely add water, hold nose, swallow hard, and pretend that it's real nourishment. Shake 'n Bake, Stir 'n Chill, Heat 'n Serve, Gulp 'n Barf. That's what our brave new world is made of: reconstituted food, artificial flavouring, intimidating initials, rebounding cheques, and mounting debts.

"Not that I'm poor," McLaughlin insisted as he shot a yellow traffic light. "It's only that I'm – unrich. My salary is warm centigrade, but my debts are hot Fahrenheit, or however they measure heat these days in millilitres per kilogram

16

Zoroastrian. I earn in kilometres and spend in miles." The odds on getting out of debt, never mind becoming wealthy, seemed steep. Everyone knows that only the top five per cent of the population is rich. A mere minority. But did they all have to live in his neighbourhood? Why had they all gone to school with his wife? The rich were so damned visible, so obtrusive. The welfare cases, on the other hand, tended to fade modestly into the background.

Where do they hide, these colourless poor? Shit, he knew the answer to that one. He taught economics, and he knew. Statistically, and in the abstract, he could quantify and locate them, but he didn't *feel* them, didn't notice them in the street. Funny how the old ass-out-of-the-trousers set never popped up at the parties he attended. Seldom did you trip over poor folks in airports or in the Park Plaza Hotel. Damned decent of them to stay out of the way, if you think about it. Riffraff recessant, and quite proper too. Eases the bourgeois conscience. Maybe poverty renders one limpid, like fried onions, discreetly transparent.

Millionaires, by contrast, seemed meddlesome and multitudinous. Maybe only five per cent, the affluent, but ubiquitous. Patricia, his wife, was blissfully unacquainted with almost anyone else, and constantly reported on whomever she'd met that day in Creeds or Holt's scattering C-notes like Kleenex. The crêpy Caribbean tans of the idle opulent glistened gloatingly at him all winter, not least the golden hides of students who took winter breaks in Fort Lauderdale. Vivid, these rich, and smug, omnipresent. He was surrounded by them like General Custer by the Sioux. His beleaguered mind slipped and swirled. "Custer. Now there's a guy I can relate to." Intrepid, suddenly filled with Mittyesque courage, McLaughlin gripped the steering wheel like a musket and eyed the rampaging redskins narrowly. "Clear off, you lot! You're only a statistical minority, and I got no wampum." If only the rich would stay on their reservations, he could tolerate them.

But they impinged. Made him squirm at the shortcomings

of his condition. McLaughlin got more bills than Santa Claus got letters. Like a Riviera playboy, he would always wonder if there wasn't some income beyond which he could not live.

And you can't pay your grocer with academic qualifications. He'd gone to school longer than any public relations huckster who topped eighty grand per year, as long or longer than any physician who ripped off Medicare for a hundred grand per annum. He could string three university degrees after his name and often did: B.A., M.A., Ph.D., plus L.W.T. and T.D.S.–these latter being solemn honorary degrees which he had awarded himself, "Leader of Western Thought" and "Trapped Debtor Slob." Credentials like these, together with one-fifty, would buy a toasted Danish. With all the imposing letters and qualifications, how come the slick commercial society deigned to poop on him only a measly thirty-four thou per year? Hell, some guys spill more than that.

Grinding his teeth and driving angrily, semi-consciously, McLaughlin twisted the wheel and spurted around a Buick on the inside, then made an abrupt left turn from the right-hand lane, oblivious to the screeching brakes and outraged bellows behind him. A damned lecture to give, if only he could get there on time and riffle through some old notes. Where had he left off on Friday with that class? They were only freshmen, eager to accept anything, and the autumn term was only a few days old. Economics 1A was a bore, but there would be two hundred green students numbing their earnest bottoms on the university chairs, two hundred closed minds and open mouths into which he had somehow to insinuate a few crumbs of learning. Whatthehell. Might as well repeat his opening lecture of last week and see whether anyone noticed. But what had he said in that introductory lecture? Couldn't remember. Never mind. Throw in some Marx or some Thorstein Veblen to get their attention, and sham it from there. Give them an impossible reading assignment, secure in the knowledge that the library would have only four copies for the entire class of two hundred. Set them to scrambling. Next week would be time enough to get organized.

"I care, really care about my teaching," he reassured himself with dazzling self-delusion. "Tomorrow I must prepare—but, holy leaping Jesus, just look at the snoobs on that brunette." Neck swivelling, eyes straining, he almost drove up the tailpipe of an Oldsmobile. Stomped on the brake at the last second. What an incredible pair of jugs. "Thank God, I'm a leg man, or my mind would snap." Those damnable, marvellous, braless females are more of a hazard to traffic, more of a death threat, than all the drunken drivers in North America. "Light a cigarette, lad, and calm down. Bloody cigarettes are killing me. Positively must stop smoking—maybe during the next summer holidays."

That had been his solemn intention only two months ago and his fervent vow of each summer holiday for the past three years. Tried almost everything; pipes, cigars, gum, fingernails, nipples, toothpicks, but there was no apparent substitute. "Why did God give us this hole in our faces if he didn't intend us to stuff things into it? If only I'd been born an anal type instead of oral. If only I'd been born with a silver spoon in my gob instead of my thumb up my ass.

"Ah ha, caught you in a contradiction there, my boy, an illogical and infelicitous inconsistency with your previous statement about anal-oral." He took a wry glee in catching himself out in such solecisms. These internal verbal sparring matches occasioned him some delight, for he generously regarded himself as an intellectual foeman worthy of his own steel. Wordy in his own stealth, by damn, discovering himself in a crude error of ratiocination, his logic all wet. "Moist on my own petard," he chuckled. "Drippy." But consistency, after all, is a virtue of small minds, and he could at least find some solace in the fact that his brain was still ticking over. A playful intellect, a dirty mind, and a warped imagination ranked high, most mornings, among the meagre satisfactions available to an impecunious academic. Just as well, too, because he'd forgotten to bring lunch money.

"And I've still got my health," he proclaimed into the rearview mirror with a defiant grimace. McLaughlin's six-foot frame was the fairly trim and compact body of a man whose nervous energy burned off a lot of his extra calories. His expressive hazel-green eyes had deep crinkles around their edges; his sandy-brown hair was combed straight back from a high forehead. On his chin a russet Van Dyck, well trimmed, offered a reddish counterpoint to his pallid skin. He cherished the only half-mistaken thought that he resembled a younger Jack Lemmon, plus beard. He had an iron gut that could hold its liquor, and frequently had to, for if pressed he would confess that his mental health might be less than robust, some days providing only a fingernail grip on reality. In this wigged-out world you had to be a bit mad in order to preserve your sanity. The threatening world impinged upon him more than he cared to admit. What was that line, "reality is for those who can't handle drugs"? No problem. He was old enough to be of the alcohol generation, those who were fond of saying that "reality is an illusion brought on by an insufficient ingestion of booze."

Illusions. Forty-three isn't *old*, for kristsake. Middle age is still years away, and I don't look a day over–well, only a couple of days over. Still tolerably sound of wind and limb, though. Slightly myopic, of course, even if too vain to wear glasses, but that was nothing. Hardly any real ailments at all. Bit of post-nasal drip. Bunion on left foot. Might admit to such trifling afflictions as thinning hair, thickening waist, and persistent erections at socially inconvenient times. There are worse things than satyriasis; helps no end with the old horizontal gavote. Horny is a synonym for healthy, isn't it? Although there *is* that tendency toward bronchitis. Bit of smoker's cough. A touch of bursitis, too, in the shoulder last winter. And dandruff. "I've got dandruff like Kellog has cornflakes. Also flatulence, and frequent heartburn. It does add up to a fair list. My God, I'm falling apart!"

Clenching his teeth and probing with his tongue for cavities, J.T. McLaughlin twisted the wheel of his Camaro, swooping and darting through the traffic with the grim resolution of an octogenarian fleeing a convention of morticians. Steady, now. It's all in the mind. Mental health, that's the thing to cultivate, he decided. Question is, how to do it? Advertisements for Mental Health Week conjured up notions of rows and rows of cheerful idiots squirting douches in one ear and out the other. Not efficacious, on the whole. Tidal waves of Rinso and Ivory Snow sudsing up the cortex to make the grey matter Borax white. A sound mind in a healthy body and all that crap. A numb and well-rinsed brain in a saggy body on a skateboard to hell was more like it. A salacious mind in a sin-soaked bod seemed more appealing than sanctimonious slogans of pseudo-salubrious psychowhammy and bothersome blither. "And if that blonde on the corner has such impossibly long and stupefyingly sensuous legs, why's to worry about emissions of encomiastic empyrean emotional enemas and egregious entropic epiphanies of an epiphenomenal nature?

"Hah. My vocabulary is now limbered up for lecturing," McLaughlin chortled, like a card-shark flexing his fingers and riffling the deck in preparation for dealing off the bottom. "I am ready to face the classroom. I think my banal boodle of braggadocio is ready to ramble, hot to trot. Do I know 'The General Theory of Employment, Interest and Money'? No, but hum a few bars and we'll see whether I can fake it." He permitted himself a dry chuckle.

Now, where to park. The major problem of western civilization clearly is where to find a hitching post for the iron monster. Dropping a generous dollop of cigarette ash on his tie, he spun into the already crowded parking lot of Chiliast University. Most students walked, but alarming numbers of them had wheels. In the lot you could usually identify the students' cars, which tended to be shiny great monsters, laid on by Daddy, or impertinently expensive sports models with bumper-stickers from Florida. Faculty cars, on the other hand, mainly ran to Volvos and Volkswagens speckled with rust. Dr. Thornton P. Naugle, President of the university, regarded any segregation of student and faculty cars as "undemocratic"; thus there was no separate area for faculty heaps–except "Reserved" spots for senior administrators –with the result that any Professor who arrived on campus later than eight forty-five found few, if any, places left to park.

Signs proclaiming "Reserved Parking Only" bristled at him from all along the line nearest Smyton Hall, the main Administration Building, the Kremlin. Large and imperious "Reserved" placards bore the names of President Naugle, provost G.R. Fine, Dean Lang, Dean Simpson, Deans without number from Dimbulb to Dimwitty, and even a *Mr*. Wall. This worthy (widely but unaffectionately known as "Stone" Wall) had been parachuted in from a failed career in a major brewing corporation, and basked in the title of Vice-President in Charge of Computer Operations, Public Relations, Research Grants, Paving and Tree Removal, and Acting Head of the Department of Classics, just another ornament in the bureaucratic firmament of aparatchik meatballs who did the big thinking for Chiliast U.

Couldn't find a more stunned array of dummies in Madame Tussaud's, thought McLaughlin as he swung past a miraculously empty unreserved space, grinned, and swerved instead into a slot marked "Reserved–Mr. Reinkind–Vice-President, Administrative Services." With a smirk of satisfaction he set his emergency brake and locked up. A glance at his watch revealed that he had only four minutes before he was due to begin his nine-o'clock lecture. No time to trot to his office in search of frayed lecture notes. Have to ad lib it again this morning. And he'd forgotten to stop for cigarettes.

2

After the lecture, which did not go well, McLaughlin retreated to his office, a wounded rat seeking its hole, only to find the Chairman of his department lurking in the corridor waiting to intercept him.

"Ah, it's you, McLaughlin." (Was he expecting Adam Smith? J.T. wondered.) "Good to see you. How was your lecture?"

"Went fine, Mr. Chairman, just fine, thanks." He couldn't admit otherwise. "Come in and sit down, sir. What can I do for you?"

Dr. L.T. Wright, Chairman of the Department of Economics, a short, bald man with slightly bulging eyes and a more than slightly bulging middle, hunkered his not inconsiderable expanse of well-upholstered rear into the most capacious chair in the room, made a little praying mantis steeple with his fingers, and eyed his junior associate narrowly. "Tell me, didn't you teach the Labour Economics course for us two or three years ago?"

"No, I've never taught Labour Economics. It's not my line at all."

"Must have confused you with someone else. Doesn't matter. Must have been a filbert of my imagination."

McLaughlin never knew whether such lines from the Chairman were unconscious slips, which he should ignore, or feeble attempts at humour at which he was expected to laugh immoderately. He chose the coward's way out, flashing a nervous half smile, and at the same time biting at a fingernail. Amiable silence is a defence mechanism much favoured by people who feel desperate. He knew there was more coming.

"Old Kirkup is down for the labour course this year, but

he's just fetched up in hospital with a tumour. We all hope it's beneficent, of course, but we must find replacements to cover his classes. Labour isn't your line of country, you say?"

"Not at all. I'm sorry."

"No matter. Just a small class anyway. I'll cancel it. Early enough in term that the fuddled students can take something else."

"But–but we can't just strand the students that way," McLaughlin expostulated. Too late, he saw the jaws of the trap he was walking into.

"Glad you see it in that light," murmured the Chairman. "The fact is, Kirkup was also down for a section of Eco. 1A with the engineers. A noon-hour class. Introductory Principles. Sort of thing you could handle easily, I'm sure. Two hundred and fifty students, quite a mob, but I've arranged to give you a Teaching Assistant to help with the marking. Miss Mott. Mildred Mott. Oh, don't thank me, the budget can stand it, and I've thought it all through. I'm sure you'll be able to pick up the slag."

"Slack," J.T. muttered involuntarily.

"Yes, it has been a bit slack around here, but I'm sure we can all buckle under and make a go of it."

"Well, just a minute now. There must be alternatives. Finstad, for example. Finstad has only small senior seminars, no big freshman classes; he could do it, and I already have a first year section of two-hundred students, plus my two senior courses. Or Grimsby. There's another one who could do it. God knows his classes are notoriously–" (he was going to say unpopular)–"small."

"Finstad is no use," said the Chairman. "He mumbles and is inaudible in big classes. Besides which, deep down he's shallow. Not the sort of thing for the engineering sections at all. Should have been put out to pasture years ago. Even to graduate students, his credibility is not believable. A dab hand with the equations, is Finstad, but no good at all with jokes. That's what you need with engineers, amusing illustrations and jokes. Superficial people simply aren't funny."

McLaughlin ruefully reflected that Finstad was younger than himself, but had been born antique. It was also apparent that trying to talk to Dr. Wright was like watching two parallel lines fading into infinity, seeming to get closer, but never meeting. Still, he decided to try again.

"What about Grimsby?"

"No," replied the Chairman, "wouldn't do. Bert Grimsby is not cut out to deal with engineers. Oh, he's good at supervising Ph.D. thesis work, and adequate with small classes, but in the big lecture theatres he isn't worth a pinch of coon feathers. Getting worse all the time. Very unco-operative these days, Grimsby, and sullen. Moody. Morose. Sometimes he seems to be dragging his heels like a snake in the grass."

"Like a snake wearing spurs on each foot, I suppose you mean."

"What? Oh, exactly. Spurs that drag. Just so. Pity about Grimsby. Used to be a good chap. Anyway, McLaughlin, I'm giving you the engineers and you'll want to pitch in for the sake of team and do the necessaries, I'm sure. No problem for you, I take it?"

Trapped, but one more run at it. "Actually, if you want me to take on that extra class, the students in my fourth-year seminar may get less of my time. You wouldn't want our own senior students in the department to suffer, would you?"

"I'm glad you brought that up," purred the Chairman, one jump ahead. "That might be a blessing in sheep's clothing. In these serious times of cut-backs and budget restraints, a penny saved is a penny not yearned. Awrrumph-umph-umph," he chortled. "You see what I mean, don't you?"

"Not clearly. No."

"I'll spell it out for you, then, in paragraphs of one syllable. The computer print-out of registration indicates that you have only thirteen students in that fourth-year class. Great thing, President Naugle's new computer system. And you do remember the new administrative understanding, McLaughlin? Any course with fewer than fifteen students enrolled may be given by the instructor if he wishes, but will not be regarded as a full course on his normal teaching load. You could cancel that course, you see, or you may decide to give it on your own time, but it would not be counted as a regular course by the computer. Better to cancel, I should think."

Yes, you should, thought McLaughlin, but stifled the urge to say so. Bloody hell. Faced with the prospect of trading off a jolly little piece of cake like that senior seminar for a dirty great mob of two hundred and fifty engineers, he realized that he was in a serious corner. Sweet reason was his only hope.

"Look, Dr. Wright, I realize you've got to set up some sort of sacrificial lamb in front of that engineering lot. In general, I'm willing to help the department in any way I can, but–"

"That's the spirit," said Wright.

"But that fourth-year seminar has thirteen of our very best senior undergraduates in it, because they *chose* to take it, *plus* six graduate students, who are taking it as an extra, overload course. The computer simply didn't pick them up. They want it. They need it. They should not be deprived of it. I mean, they've decided that my course is important to their intellectual development."

"So you agree to continue teaching that course for the good of the department, not as part of your normal load, and to take on the engineers as I suggest?"

"No–er, yes. No! Damn it, just because the computer isn't programmed to recognize initiative. . . ." He made a strangled noise. "I mean, I very much want to keep that class alive."

"Splendid. I knew you'd see it that way."

"Now wait a minute. What I'm trying to say is–"

"I fully understand what you're saying, my boy. Decent of you, too, I must say. You're asking, in effect, for permission to continue an extra fourth-year class on a voluntary overload basis without remuneration. Very good of you, indeed. Laudable. Permission granted. It's irregular, of course, but I see no reason to deprive you of the opportunity to do what you think best. I'm a flexible man. I'll bend to that. Just so long as you realize that this extra seminar must not be allowed to interfere with your publications."

"Publications?" His voice became squeaky.

"Naturally our general departmental policy on salary increments and promotions will continue to depend on the output of your published research. It would not be a good idea, career-wise, to permit your self-imposed teaching arrangements to interfere with the anticipated flow of your professional publications. When did I last see you in print, McLaughlin? I can't seem to remember."

"My book on Innis came out last year."

"Ah, yes. Rather a slight little volume, just a reworking of your earlier Ph.D. thesis, wasn't it? Hmmm. Pity the reviews weren't better. Still, it saved your bacon with the Promotion and Tenure Committee, if I recall, and kept you from being, ah, terminated. But that was last year, and altogether a horse of a different persuasion, eh? Awrrumph-umph-umph. Important to press on with new work, McLaughlin. I trust you won't permit your commendable zeal in the classroom to interrupt more–ah–serious matters."

"But–but you just this moment lumbered me with an extra–"

"Speaking of lumbered, I'm afraid we may have some additional dead wood around our necks this year. That new fellow, Nalorian. There's a peculiar one."

"Just the ticket. I'll bet *he* could handle the engineering section."

"No, no. That's all settled now. Anyway, I hired this Nalorian chap to do all the money and banking courses. Just for one year while Wilson is away on sabbatical. A heavy enough load. Nalorian will find he has to sweat a bit for his salary, which luckily isn't much. Got him cheap because he was between jobs. A foreigner you know, some sort of a wog or other. I hope his English is up to snuffle. Never can tell with these D.P. wanderers, can you?"

"That's the man I met last week at the departmental

meeting. His English is–" (he was going to say, better than yours, you stunned turnip) "–more than adequate. I had a very favourable impression of him, actually. Lively type."

"Possibly. But he'll bear watching. If you hear anything on him, keep me informed."

"My gawd, Mr. Chairman, I've got *quite* enough problems of my own without riding herd on my colleagues. I wouldn't–"

"Just asking you to keep an eye on him, that's all. Something not quite right about him. Seldom wears a tie like a gentleman. He has a wee tiny spoon and some other weird symbol on a chain around his neck; maybe some kind of religious nut, do you think? And the sod has an easel."

"An easel?"

"For painting. Right in his office, if you please. Says he daubs a bit. Can't be an altogether sound chap, can he?"

"Interesting. But look, Dr. Wright, about these engineers, I want you to know–"

"Think nothing of it. Not at all." Wright could be quick with the interruptions when it suited him. "I know you'll thank me for Miss Mott. She'll be more than satisfactory as a marker, I'm sure. Well, I must be off."

So must I, to have got into this mess, thought McLaughlin. "But I really must ask you about a larger room for my third-year class. There are forty-two students, and the room seats only thirty-five."

"Mere housekeeping. No problem. Have a word with my secretary. She'll know what to do. Now I really must push along. An administrator's work is never done, you know. Good day to you."

3

Good day. In a pig's patoot. What else could go wrong? J.T. wondered.

Muttering to himself that Chicken Little was probably right, McLaughlin walked down the corridor to see whether Cutty was available to share his miseries.

George Cuttshaw had been his friend and best buddy this side of the Saskatchewan border ever since they were in graduate school together. Cuttshaw was from Edmonton, McLaughlin from Saskatoon. From the beginning they had mutual interests in jazz, antique automobiles, coeds, and single malt whisky when they could afford it, plus a shared wonderment that people in the wicked east were so markedly different from good lovable westerners like themselves. Cuttshaw disliked the name George, and none of his friends had called him anything but Cutty for years. McLaughlin equally hated the name Jack, which smacked too much of the sleazy used-car salesman, but could never persuade anyone to call him John – he didn't much look like a John – so most people, including his wife, called him by his initials.

Cutty's door was open. His shortish frame was more thick than lean, but his manner was youthful and his grey eyes twinkled with humour. He wore an appealing smile, a careful, dark three-piece suit, and closely trimmed dark-brown hair. Crisp, solid, and competent were words applicable to Cuttshaw, and yet he was always indulgent of the more intense and erratic McLaughlin.

"Hi, J.T. I gather you've had a visitation from our improbable Chairman, old buggerlugs Wright himself. I heard him awrrumphing when I passed your door."

"Jeez, Cutty, it was a proper whizbang sumbitch of an interview, let me tell you."

He told him. Cuttshaw was sympathetic, if amused.

"Come on down to the cafeteria for a coffee. In honour of your new duties, I'm buying."

"You'd better be. I'm broke again."

"You're always broke, J.T. Haven't known you when you weren't. I guess that's why you went into economics in the first place."

"To make money? Not really."

"No, I mean so that at least you could fully understand *why* you're always broke. Might be as good a reason as any to study the subject, I suppose. You must be the best informed pauper in town. Or perhaps you were merely an early victim of the Heywood Broun theory of economics."

"Heywood Broun? I don't remember that."

"Course you do. Broun worked at *The New Yorker* with Woolcott, Benchley, Dorothy Parker, and all that lot. They could never figure out why Broun came back from the race-track most Friday afternoons with a smile on his kisser. Never seemed depressed, never seemed to lose money. When they asked him, Broun said he had a system. 'Simple,' he said. 'I put my stake in one pocket, my winnings in the other, so when both pockets are empty, I know I've broken even.'"

"Aw, come on, Cutty. Let's get that coffee."

As they walked down the corridor, McLaughlin persisted with his tale of woe. "And then, on top of the goddam engineers, I tried to tell Wright that I needed a bigger room for my third-year class. But would he even listen? Fobbed me off on his secretary."

"Hard to get through to him, I agree."

"Hard? That isn't the half of it. Him and his goddam garbled homilies. I think he's a few straws short of a full bale. Can't he get anything right?"

"Obviously he outsmarted *you*, friend genius."

"That's not the point. He just bulldozed me."

"Bull shat you, more likely. The Chairman is much renowned for his skill in ladling out el toro poo-poo."

"This is serious, Cutty. The man's a con artist and a threat to us all. Economics he may know, and paper shuffling and how to manipulate people, but he doesn't know common sense, human nature, or his buttock from his belly button. How did he ever get to be an administrator?"

"Precisely because of those qualities, I suppose."

"The man's dippy."

"But he manoeuvred you into doing the dirties. By the sound of it, even Trish couldn't have played you better, you trout. Hook, line, and sinker, he had you."

McLaughlin ground his teeth.

"I really put it to him, Cutty. I told him there are forty-two students in that course, and the bloody computer has given me a room that seats thirty-five. Can you believe it? That mindless menace of a computer will be the ruination of this university, I said, and damned if he-"

"May I be of service, Professor McLaughlin?" cut in an unexpected voice.

"*Jeez*! You startled me. I didn't hear you coming up behind me, Mr. Zukowski."

"Did I overhear you to say, young sir, that you required a larger classroom?"

"I did. You did. That is, yes, I was telling Cutty here that I need a larger-"

"A larger room suitable for forty-two students at four p.m. on Tuesdays and Thursdays. Would that be correct, sir?"

McLaughlin could only stare at him blankly.

"I believe I may be able to accommodate you. If you would be so good as to direct your students tomorrow to number 267A, I think you will find that room satisfactory."

"Yes, well, that's very helpful of you, Mr. Zukowski, but isn't the room in use?"

"The room is not as yet assigned for use at those times, Professor McLaughlin. Be assured that I will arrange it."

"I thought the Space Allocation Office and the computer attended to all that," said Cutty.

"There are certain things in this college, Professor Cutt-shaw, which remain unknown even to the computer. Some of us older, er, functionaries of the college make it our business to know things which may occasionally be of assistance. But don't bruit it about, mind. No sense in calling undue attention to minor–irregularities. Just ask me, and consider it done."

"That's awfully helpful of you, I must say. Would you come along with us for coffee?"

But the recipient of his gratitude had already padded off quietly.

"A bit of luck, that, Cutty. Remarkable old geezer, isn't he? I wonder how in the world he knew about that? 267A, he said."

"Zukowski has been keeping things sorted out around here since long before you and I were students, J.T. Unobtrusive, but quite a guy. Totally devoted to the college, it seems. Even the Principal can't remember when Zukowski wasn't around."

"I'd be hard put to guess his age. Must be an awfully old geezer. What's his story?"

"Oh, I don't know. We've all just used him for years, and been glad of him, but nobody asks many questions about an old crutch, just leans on it."

"I suppose so. He does sort of sneak up on you, though, doesn't he?"

"Only when you need him. I've gone months, even a couple of years, without seeing him, until there was some little matter to put right. The students call him 'The Zook.' They regard him as a helpy-elf sort of codger and laugh at his old-world manners. Grimsby tells me that Zukowski retired as caretaker years ago, before he can remember, but that he lives on a cot behind some packing cases in the boiler room, and after he retired no one had the heart to put him out. Does no harm, I guess."

"Did me some good, by the looks of it. I must go and look at that classroom."

"Later. Come on and we'll get our coffee."

4

"Did you have a nice day, dear?"

"Rotten. Perfectly appalling."

"That's nice."

Patricia, usually called Trish, better known to the credit manager of every department store in town as Mrs. J.T. McLaughlin, much preferred talking to listening. Pert and perky, very sassy, with a nimble and unpredictable mind much quicker than J.T.'s clanking academic apparatus, Trish had an infuriatingly high I.Q. on those infrequent occasions when she bothered to use it, but her brain was almost totally untrained and undisciplined. This led innumerable leches on the cocktail party circuit to mistake her for a chowder-head and to get zapped for their troubles. Her flippy manner and lambent up-your-kilt-Charlie attitude were reinforced by a full arsenal of feminine wiles. She had a very casual, even reckless style, but inwardly remained as cool and contained as a cocktail shaker of vodka martinis, which was her first choice of weapons at the moment for a cheerful domestic assault. The target for tonight, as so often, was the inconvenient imbalance in the family budget, and her husband's habitual neglect thereof.

For these familial tussles, Trish was the more formidably armed of the two combatants. What she lacked in heavy firepower, she more than compensated for with devilish diversionary tactics, the persistence of a wet puppy, and an alarming flair for fingernail-slashing infighting that would do credit to a Gurkha guerrilla. Apart from a darting and resolute mind, her other small-arms and advantages included luminous blue eyes, a curly towsel of strawberry-blonde hair, an arresting twitchy-assed figure, and the fact that her husband utterly adored her.

Initially, when they were first sparring and courting, he had come on as the high-minded intellectual who could discourse enthrallingly on the eternal verities, while she played off him demurely as the fluffy flibbertygib who used her private-school accent of Rosedale-ese to talk of nothing more weighty than proms, sports cars, and field hockey. A few years of marriage, however, disabused him of all illusions as to which of them had the more steely, if off-beat, common sense. In their abnormally happy connubial tennis match, the score was most often carded as 15-love, to Trish's advantage.

Since she was very much the best wife he ever dreamed of having, even if she kept him off balance at times in these days of marital demolition derbies, she seemed indestructible and he was determined to keep her. But it wasn't always easy. The style to which she was accustomed was not inexpensive. Still more troublesome than her natural propensity to spend was his relative inability to earn, plus his inclination to make occasional financial splurges on things like books and penny stocks and vintage automobiles. These latter peccadilloes he readily excused in himself, while remaining raucous in his denunciation of her clothing bills. But his slick economic theorizing was by no means matched by his fumbling practice. Much as he hated to admit it, his Punch had to scuffle hard to keep up with her Judy.

"Thanks," said J.T., accepting the proffered martini greedily. "What a bitch of a day."

"Didn't go well?"

"That imbecile boss of mine slugged me with an extra class. Wright hands out the shit jobs with the benign self-satisfaction of a Maharaja giving alms. What gripes me is that I'm supposed to *like* it. He condescends to me like a plummy Polonius lecturing the deranged Hamlet. Jeez, how I'd like to skewer him behind the arras."

After letting him talk it out, only half-listening, and waiting for him to get his nose into the second martini, Trish wheeled to her priority topic.

"Nancy Riddle next door had me simply in *fits* today, talking about her problems with her car." Trish spun out the story with verve, then delicately slid in, "Which reminds me to ask you whether you remembered to mail this month's cheque for the payment on our heap?"

"It's not a heap, Patricia, it's an only slightly second-hand Camaro. And, no, it slipped my mind. The envelope is probably still on my desk."

"Ought to be attended to."

"Tomorrow."

"Uhmmm. All right, dear. But the thing is, we might be falling behind in some of these payments. The bill came today for the roofing, and we'll just *have* to pay that, aside from the overdraft at the bank, I mean, and the man came this afternoon to give an estimate on what it will cost to shape up the furnace. It'll come to six hundred or more. Do you want to see his estimate?"

"No, not right now. No. Basically it's these interest rates on the mortgage that are doing us in. But if we're so broke, why are we drinking martinis?"

"Well, certain things are basic."

"You're right. Maybe we should cut back on some frivolous items like food and heat. Whatthehell. We may be dragging some payments, we may be what your family would call shabby genteel, but I'm damned if I'm ready to be sober genteel. I guess we have some appearances to keep up, if only to ourselves."

"Speaking of which, Nancy Riddle asked me if we'd like to go skiing with them at Christmas."

"Might be nice, sure. Where do they want to go? Beaver Valley or some place close?"

"They had Gstaad in mind."

"*Gstaad*? Jeez, gimme a break, will you? The furnace isn't paid for and they want us to go to bloody Switzerland?"

"It was only a thought. I told her we might be busy. Anyway, there's a bit left in the shaker. Give me your glass."

"Yeah. Easy now, not so much. Well. Thanks."

"Whatever we decide to do over Christmas, we've simply got to get on top of these bills. Seriously, honey."

"Aw, Trish, pack it in. We'll figure this out later. Today wasn't my favourite day of the century. It'll keep."

"You're right, J.T., but these little things are on my mind, you know? We've got a *lot* of bills this month. We don't want things to get out of hand."

"I just don't know. At the moment, I just don't know."

"But we've got to figure it out. Soon we'll have to defecate or shift off the potty, wouldn't you say? I mean, what do we pay first? It's all so *tire*some."

"So let's go at it calmly and rationally, Trish. If we were to be logical about this we'd order our priorities. On the one hand, we could pay off that roofing debt, although I think he'd wait, and on the other hand, we should get the cheque in for the car payment, and tell the man to go ahead with the furnace on the firm expectation that next month – you see?"

"What I see is on the one hand, on the *other* hand. God, what I wouldn't give for a one-handed economist!"

"Now wait, Trish, what I'm saying is, if we can hold these demons off for another month until that trust fund your Dad set up for you pays the dividend, or at least until I get the royalty cheque for that textbook Cutty and I did last year, we might be able to handle the overdraft and juggle these payments, until – the end of the month isn't far off, after all – until then? Don't you think?"

"Until. Maybe. Perhaps withanyluck and couldbepossibly if and depending *upon*. What is this, J.T.? What *is* this jiggledyjog? All I'm trying to say is, we've got to pay the ever-loving brown-eyed *bills*, for Pete's sake."

"I know, Trish, I know. Believe me, we're not far apart on this, but let me handle it, okay? I'll go into the bank tomorrow. I promise. Couldn't we eat now?"

"You shouldn't go *in*to the bank, J.T., you should *rob* the flipping bank. Otherwise we'll end up in debtors' prison."

36

"Nah. It'll work out. Would you bring me cakes in prison, Trish, if I heisted a bank?"

"I'd bring you blueberry pie and angel dust and caviar and clean socks and frozen daiquiries, not to mention a book on Household Accounting Made Easy."

"You're a doll, Bonnie."

"Any time, Clyde."

*   *   *

Later that evening, J.T. sloped up the stairs to read a bedtime story to Davie. Usually this was something that McLaughlin enjoyed, one of the nicest parts of a day, but tonight he felt weary and short on patience. Is there anything more exhilarating than little tads when you're ready for them, or anything more enervating when you're not?

His youngest son, being four years old, displayed only limited taste in literature, and loudly demanded the two hundred and eighty-sixth reading of *The Three Little Pigs*. "Okay," said J.T., with less than electric enthusiasm, but he managed a smile as Davie curled up beside him in gleeful anticipation of the happy familiar. They turned the pages together in warm coziness, and McLaughlin declaimed the housing formulas of the little porkers with as much drama as he could muster. Inhaling the bath-fresh fragrance of his son's hair, his mind wandered.

"You skipped a line, Dad."

"Sorry. 'So the third little pig built his house of *bricks*, and-'"

"Good thinking, third pig!" Davie exclaimed.

"Right, son. 'And then the Big Bad Wolf came along, saying if you don't let me in, I'll-'"

"What's our house made of, Dad?"

"Our house? Well, wood, sort of."

"Wood?" Davie persisted.

"Yeah. Clapboard, actually."

"Why, Dad?"

"I'm not sure. I guess that's just the way it was built."

"Oh."

"But it's strong enough, don't you worry."

"If you say so, Dad."

"Sure. Now off you go to sleep."

"All right. But when I grow up, I may go into the brick business."

"You do that, son. Good night."

McLaughlin shambled down the stairs wondering whether he'd ever regain the simple good sense of a child.

5

The next morning, on the way from the parking lot to his office, McLaughlin encountered Professor Bert Grimsby. A large and somewhat shapeless man, Grimsby measured six feet two inches, if he ever stood straight, which he seldom did. He slouched when he stood, trod heavily when he walked, and sagged and slumped when he sat. Grimsby's broad frame carried two hundred and forty-five pounds of ill-distributed flesh. His lumpy body could have been constituted mainly of mashed potatoes. His remarkably rumpled and extravagantly stained tweed suits all looked like remnants from a rummage sale in an impecunious neighbourhood, and gave him a strong resemblance to an only slightly animated bean bag. Small, yellowish teeth and rather dull staring brown eyes behind thick glasses did little to enhance his solemn, fleshy face. Very round and protuberant ears extended from either side of his balding head, framed by errant tufts of uncombed hair, which resembled divots from a neglected golf course during a drought. He appeared older than his forty-eight years. He looked used, abused, tired. All in all, Grimsby might have been mistaken for a dispirited koala bear mourning its last friend.

"How are you, Bert?"

"Not too well. Only fair-to-middling. Things are a bit bleak with me at the moment. Don't you just hate the beginning of term?"

"As a matter of fact, I rather like it. Fresh faces, fresh start, and all that. It would be better, I think, if only it was less hectic."

"Ah, J.T., I do find it discouraging that the same lot of louts and layabouts, whose skulls I couldn't penetrate last year with an idea or a sledge hammer, are turning up again for more punishment. It's all so melancholy. They'd be better off driving trucks or washing cars. Why do they want to study economics anyway, can you tell me? Rows and rows of tiresome young people fussing about a tiresome subject. I try, God knows I try, to deflect them into something easier and harmless, like sociology, but what can you do? Gluttons for punishment, they seem. I guess we all are, or we wouldn't be here."

"Come on, Bert, things can't be that bad." J.T. cast about frantically for another topic. No matter how draggy or desperate he felt, his friend Grimsby always seemed worse, and in greater need of encouragement. Somehow Bert's extremes usually rallied the boy scout in McLaughlin. "How's the writing going? Smacking away on the typewriter, are you? You must be nearing the end of that textbook. It will make your fame and fortune, I'll bet."

"No, no, I'm sorry to say that isn't going well. I can't seem to sleep nights, worrying about how to improve it and make it clearer. Then I get up again at three a.m., after tossing and turning, and pace the floor for a while before adding a paragraph or a long footnote, which only seems to make things worse. This causes me to worry even more, and makes sleep out of the question. Can't seem to pin the bloody material down. The only sleep I get is just after dawn until the wretched alarm clock rings. Most days, you see, I can't write because I'm groggy from not writing adequately the night before. Most nights, I can't seem to sleep because of the guilt about not getting more on paper the previous day. Nightmares, you understand, and constant pricks of conscience. If only I could simplify the damned thing."

"Aw, I'll bet it will be good, Bert. You certainly know your stuff. Just let it roll."

"No, it's not that simple. I don't seem to have the light touch of the popularizer. Fourteen reservations and exceptions and qualifications occur to me for every sentence I type.

It may all prove impossible to get down. I despair of it. Sometimes I think I should chuck it all."

Jeez, what do you say? thought McLaughlin. He decided to go the whole route. "So, all right, chuck it. If that's the worst that could happen, pitch it, or at least back off and leave it for a while. You don't need it. You've got full professorial rank, tenure, and respectability in the profession. What more could you want? Ditch it."

"What more could I want? I'm not sure. Years ago there was something else I wanted, but I've almost forgotten what it was. Fame, perhaps, or peace of mind. Something elusive. Whatever it was, it didn't much matter. It's so easy, J.T., just to keep on going through these motions, but I wish I could remember what these motions were supposed to be in aid of. It's all so senseless."

McLaughlin groaned. "Krist, but aren't you the Cheerful Charlie of a Tuesday morning. You really give me a lift, Bert, you know that?"

"Is it Tuesday morning? Odd. I'd have sworn it was Thursday. Doesn't matter. I have the same classes Tuesday morning as I have Thursday. Things repeat; things blur. But will this week never end?"

"It's only the beginning of the week, Grimmers, and the beginning of term. You've got to pull yourself together."

"I suppose. I'm sure you're right. Still, there are days when I'm not sure any of this is worth while. Teaching, writing, working. Is any of it worth doing? It's all so easy, and all so pointless. Maybe I'm just tired, or disillusioned. I'm not sure."

"Look, Bert, you just got out of bed this morning on the wrong side of the alarm clock. Don't be so goddam solemn. Tell you what, come and have lunch with me at the Faculty Club at one, okay? We'll have a beer and talk about all this; maybe I could be of some help with your book. I'll get Cutty to join us – he's always full of ideas. Lunch will perk you up. What do you say?"

"That's very kind of you, J.T., but I think not. I have a sandwich in my briefcase, and I should be dieting anyway. Trying to avoid the beer, you know. And I do have a scholarship committee report to write up, as well as my two-o'clock lecture to prepare. No, I think I'll pass on lunch for today, but thank you. I'll be better off at my desk. The beginning of term makes me fretful. I keep dwelling on how relatively little work I got done during the summer, how I let myself get behind with things."

"We're not in a race, for kristsake. It's easy to catch up. There's lot's of time, and time is free."

"Free? I wonder. There's always a price to be paid, somehow. Who said that the wise man grieves most for wasted time? Probably Dante. I'm not sure."

"If any of us were sure, we'd be geniuses, and we'd be laughing."

"Possibly. It seems a long time since I've found anything to laugh about."

"Aw, Bert, *please* get off that. This whole academic thing is a privilege and a lark. The ivory tower is far better than a nine-to-fiver or a padded cell. Not to worry."

"Maybe you're right. By the way, J.T., I saw the posters yesterday for your public lecture. Brave of you to volunteer for that sort of performance. I'm not at all sure I could handle such a chore."

"Public lecture? *Me*? What the flaming hell do you mean?"

"The public lecture on Innis. Posters are up all around. I wish you well of it. Not the sort of thing I'd like to tackle. Big thrashes and ceremonials like that intimidate me."

"Oh, that. For a minute there you had me going. It's nothing much. Last winter when my book on Innis finally appeared I was asked by the Students' Economics Club to talk about it, but I begged off till the autumn, pleading prior commitments."

"It's autumn now."

"Yes. Well, I suppose they've remembered, and may want

to hold me to it, but it's just a chat to the club. All very informal. Not a public lecture at all."

"I hesitate to contradict, but the poster I saw leads me to believe they may have snuck one over on you. Check the main bulletin board. It definitely says, 'Public Lecture,' in the Outreach and Fund-raising series, co-sponsored by the Alumni Association."

"Alumni? Fund raising? But that's out of the question. That's terrifying! Nobody told me about this. You *must* be wrong, Bert."

"Don't think so. Why else would they bother to print up such flashy posters?"

"My gawd. Ohmygawd! Look, apart from ruining my day, you may have told me about the ruination of the term. I've got to go and find out about this. I'd forgotten that I'd agreed months ago to play with matches, and suddenly you're telling me that I'm to be a prime cut of sacrificial lamb on the innermost circle of the Inferno. If you're right, I'm in deep shit."

McLaughlin shuddered, as Kafka must have shuddered when they came for him to stand trial. No bail. No warning. No sense to it all. "I've gotta run now. Sorting this out may be a bit of a chore, you know? I'll see you later. But if you're right, holy suffering saintly Q. Moses, if you're right. . . ."

McLaughlin turned and fled.

6

A hasty interview with the Chairman's secretary confirmed his worst fears. He was for it. Committed. With his mind reeling and his brain turning to yogurt, McLaughlin gave another sick glance at the poster that sealed his doom, hitched up his trousers and his droopy soul, and straggled off toward his office like an old horse plodding down the chute to the glue factory.

On the stairway, there stood the new man, Professor Nalorian, beaming.

"How are you, McLaughlin? Isn't this a fine, lively morning!"

"I guess so. Yeah. It'll have to do. How's it with you, Nalorian?"

"Going grand. Going just grand. I've been looking forward to talking with you again. There were several things you mentioned at the sherry party after the departmental meeting that I'd like to learn more about."

"Oh? Such as what? Come on in, then. I'm preoccupied as hell, but I don't have any appointments till a bit later."

"Your office is nicely set up. Very pleasant. This is a photograph of your wife, I take it?"

"Patricia. Yes."

"Lovely looking woman. Charming. You can always tell about men from the look of their wives. I see I wasn't wrong about you."

"Wrong?"

"No. I had you pegged right away for an unusual fellow. Out of the ordinary. Your wife is a beauty, obviously, but in addition to the conventional glamour, I see character and wit. Oh, yes. She'll do. You'll do."

"Do? Do what? Just what the hell are you saying, Nalorian? We've only recently met, and are you bloody well making judgements and giving out grades? What is this shit? I've got some other things on my mind, and I'm not sure I much like this conversation."

"Merely trying to accelerate things, McLaughlin, getting down to it, you see? Ordinarily it might take us a year or so to know one another, but I'd rather take the leap and cut through a few months. I might be mistaken, but I have the feeling we'll get along. Whenever I join a new department in a new place, it's my habit to take stock and to be selective. You are not yet a discard."

"I'm not? Jeez. Thanks a bushel, Nalorian."

"That's all right. And is this a photograph of Sidney Bechet? There you are. I knew there'd be something unusual in your office. Finest clarinet of the century. The Jelly Roll Morton of the sweet stick. Your walls speak volumes."

"The walls hold up the ceiling. But I'm glad you recognized Bechet. Not many do."

"Of course. Now here, I believe, is a painting of some merit. By whom, may I ask?"

"Teitelbaum. Mashel Teitelbaum. He's a friend of mine. We grew up in the same place."

"No! Incredible! Then you must be from Saskatchewan."

"Yeah."

"But that's marvellous. Everyone knows that Teitelbaum is one of the best painters in this country."

"You're kidding. He's just a guy I happen to know."

"Happen to know? Don't give me that evasive Canadian crap. We're talking of giants, monsters! Why, Teitelbaum is a legend, and one of the few originals of recent decades. I ask you, who is as good?"

"Oh, I don't know."

"You don't know. You should know! You Canadians tear my ass. What is this defeatist complex you lug around with you? You're all in love with failure, terrified of success because it might not be 'respectable.' You produce great artists, great individuals, like Jon Vickers and Maureen Forrester, Margaret Laurence, Riopelle, and Northrop Frye, Alice Munro and Glen Gould, yet you don't know what to make of them, scarcely recognize them until some second-string idiot journalist-critic in London or New York tells you it will be 'acceptable' to pay attention to them. By the time you begin to realize that you have produced internationally renowned talents or genuine geniuses, it's too late–they've either died or emigrated. Then you sit around wringing your hands about the lack of an indigenous culture. Baffling. And here you are telling me that you are actually acquainted with Teitelbaum."

"Well, yes, acquainted. I sort of like his work. How is it that you know about him, Nalorian?"

"Because I keep my eyes open. Because I've travelled around and observed. When I arrive in a new place, naturally I try to find out about it, what it's like and what kind of creativity it harbours. I paint a bit myself, so I quickly plug in to what's happening. Now, tell me about Teitelbaum. Could I meet him?"

"Why not? He's a good sort. A bit eccentric, but just a guy you meet at cocktail parties."

"Just a–hold it, McLaughlin. Surely you're not dismissing such a talent as merely 'eccentric'? Hold it right there and see whether I've got this straight."

Nalorian stopped pacing the floor and leaned against the wall. The two men looked at each other with mutual interest and surprise. Few things are as arresting as opening doors onto new people, or even opening new doors onto familiar people, and neither man seemed certain what to make of the other.

Nalorian eyed McLaughlin like a curious specimen seen through a microscope. What he saw was an intelligent if slightly neurotic specimen of *homo canadiensis*, six feet of turtle-necked sweater and unpressed trousers, sensible enough but guarded, unwilling to hazard a positive opinion, reluctant to take a chance that he might be right. McLaughlin, for his part, tried to offset his antipathy to being scolded or prodded, and to see this newcomer more clearly. Nalorian was not tall, perhaps only ten inches over five feet, but seemed taller because of his wiry stand of thick black hair and his erect, spare frame. He carried no fat and seemed to vibrate with intense energy; his hot cobalt eyes dominated a sharp nose above a large, toothy, full-lipped mouth, and his slender, tapered hands were constantly in motion. There was a fleck of scarlet running through the cloth of his well-cut glen-checked suit worn over a bright-red waistcoat. Nalorian's total appearance was that of a careful dandy of indeterminate age, whose understated flamboyance caught your attention before you were fully aware of why. He always spoke rapidly, and when his face came infrequently to rest it was in the position of an insistent smile.

Under J.T.'s quizzical gaze, Nalorian extracted a long and slim Monte Cristo panetela cigar from a Spanish leather case, lit it, puffed contentedly, and beamed. His smile was incandescent, like the warm glow of a summer sunrise. When he focussed it on a selected target, his smile conveyed irresistibly the assumption that the recipient was a fascinating person – and yet that same ingratiating beam could be turned off as rapidly as it was turned on, leaving the careful observer with the disquieting sense that the burnished grin was just possibly too strong, or even smug. Here was a man possessed of boundless confidence, and no stranger to vanity. Nalorian had that quality of force, of raw vitality, that made him the natural pivot of any group and the source of a laser beam of contained zest in any single encounter. This was not a simple or transparent man. McLaughlin judged that not far beneath the sleek patina of the boulevardier's charm there lurked the razor's edge of the wily street-fighter. Nalorian's laugh was quick, and his low, understated voice exuded the kind of authority that made one want to lean forward to catch every word. But did that intensely luminous smile reveal hot emotions or conceal cool depths of cunning?

"What was it you wanted to ask me about?" J.T. inquired.

"Teitelbaum. But let's leave that painting business for now. I'll press that subject with you another time. I wanted to tell you how much I liked my first impressions of this university, and to ask you a bit about the staff. Yesterday I had long talks with some of them. Remarkable people."

"Which ones have you met? Cuttshaw? Finstad? Wright, certainly, and maybe Grimsby?"

"No, no, I've met most of the *faculty*, of course, but I was talking about the staff. The caretaking staff. The cleaners."

"Oh, I see." He didn't see.

"If you want to learn about a place, I've found that it's useless to talk to the President, or the Vice-Presidents, or even your immediate colleagues. It's the ordinary folks of the cleaning staff who can give you the picture."

"Really. I hadn't thought of that."

"Clear as noon. The administrative executives know, or are supposed to know, a bit about everything. Consequently, they know nothing. The technicians in any institution–that's chaps like you and me, McLaughlin–know their own subjects, but they must specialize, know more and more about less and less, and usually go around in a rarified fog. But a caretaker sees everything that's going on. Always begin with the cleaning staff."

"Uh-huh. So what have they told you?"

"They tell me that you must be a decent sort of a guy because you usually remain after class to answer students' questions, and often have students in your office arguing about everything, which is a good sign. They tell me that our Chairman, Wright, usually leaves by three p.m. and always has a clean desk, which suggests he's more organized and in control than he lets on. The word is that Professor Grimsby spends most of his time clipping his fingernails and staring out the window, seldom has students in his office, and has very little paper in his waste-basket. Professional journals un-opened on his desk for weeks, which suggests he's half asleep. Forgets to water his plants. Often leaves for the night with his lights still on and the door left unlocked."

"Doesn't prove a thing, Nalorian."

"Maybe. But the cleaners get a sense of these things, I think. They say Grimsby's distracted, loses things, and doesn't realize they're lost. That might be all right if he were writing or publishing, maybe absorbed in creative work, but they say he hasn't had a new pad of paper in months, so he couldn't be writing much. Grimsby's in bad shape, I'd judge, from these reports."

"Grimsby's an odd man, I'll grant you, and maybe a bit morose. But he gets by."

"He does. I've looked up some of his work, and it's uncommonly good. But he's published nothing in the last four years."

"Maybe lying fallow."

"Maybe. But why does he read junk magazines and the local tabloid, which the cleaners say they find in his wastebasket, if his mind is on economics?"

"Damned if I know. Why are you cross-examining charladies if you're so keen on economics? This whole conversation seems to me a bit–raw."

"Research, McLaughlin. Getting the feel of the place."

"I'm beginning to think you've infiltrated a real spy network, Nalorian. Do the cleaners also intercept mail and take retainers from the RCMP or the CIA?"

"It's not to joke about the caretakers, McLaughlin. Very aware people, these. My father always told me that one of the first rules for a gentleman is always to be more than courteous to your inferiors and never more than courteous to your superiors. The head janitor is remarkably useful. He told me where to find a genuine leather couch under a stairway, a couch which has not been used in years, and helped me to move it into my office. You know as well as I do that if I'd gone through channels and asked for a couch it would have been months, years, before I had any hope of getting anything at all, never mind a leather one. I don't see a couch in your office here."

"No."

"There you are. Always approach any situation from the bottom, is my advice."

"You may be right."

"Oh I'm right about that sort of thing, you may depend on it. Is Niagara moist? I've bounced around enough places and worked in enough universities to have discovered how things go."

"Where did you last teach, Nalorian?"

"South Dakota. That's another story. I'll tell you all you need to know about me after we've become friends, which we will. No, don't wave and sputter at me; we will. What I want to know is, where does Mr. Zukowski fit in? There's a rare old bird."

"Jeez, Nalorian, I wouldn't have believed that you were going to hold a grand inquisition on the cleaners in your first week here."

"Second week."

"Whatever. Well, Zukowski retired years ago, I'm told, long before my time, but still lives in the college, behind the furnace room or somewhere in the bowels of the building, I think."

"Interesting. The old fellow is pretty canny. He found me an easel for my office. I just mentioned my need to him one day, and when I opened my door the next morning, there it was. But what I really need now, McLaughlin, is a loft."

"A what?"

"A loft, a studio with lots of light for my painting."

"Will you have time for that sort of thing? I mean, I thought you had the whole load of the three money and banking courses."

"Child's play. I can handle that with one hand tied behind the Chairman's secretary, write two academic articles with the other, perform card tricks when neither hand is looking, and still find time to get in a bit of painting in the late afternoon. It's all a simple matter of organizing your days, of course. First one decides, then organizes, then accomplishes. No problem. All a matter of will."

50

"Krist. You make it sound so simple."

"Certainly. Don't you know the ropes, McLaughlin, don't you understand the tricks? No? You amaze me. I took you for quicker than that. There are no secrets. Coping with life is merely a series of tricks. You master them. You use them. Got to know your stuff, of course, and then merely keep on pushing before the bastards get a chance to shove back. No big thing. Dale Carnegie was right. All of life – personality, professional status, success – it's all a matter of tricks and confidence. I firmly believe that I can do it, and therefore it's easy."

"What is?"

"Anything."

J.T. smiled uncertainly at that, and took a few seconds to consider whether he'd just been the recipient of a lesson on the basics, or whether he was being had. He flipped a mental coin that landed unbelievably on edge, shrugged, and sighed. "Maybe you'd let me in on a few of those tricks, Nalorian."

"Why not? It would be my pleasure."

"The thing is, at the moment I'm in a bit of a bind. I've just learned that our Uncle Wriggly Chairman has committed me, without my realizing it, to a big thrash of a public lecture that has me in fits, tied in knots."

"Why?"

"My gawd, because I have only three weeks to prepare, because I didn't know about it, or had forgotten about it, because I thought it was just a minor diddley-ass chat to the students in the Economics Club, because I thought the audience might be twenty or thirty people, and they've reserved a hall that holds fourteen million; because it's advertised and *public*, for kristsake, and I could make a horrible spectacle of myself and embarrass myself and the department and the university and never live it down, and oh dear sweet leaping Jesus, how will I get out of this mess?"

Nalorian tossed his head and laughed. "I knew I liked you, J.T. – may I call you J.T.? – because I was sure you had some genuine emotion somewhere under all that uptight self-

51

conscious dourness. Not only are you afraid, but you actually admit it. Delicious. I love it. A Canadian WASP with *feelings*, however base and self-protective. I must tell this to Mrs. Nalorian. If you prick them, do they not bleed? Just like real human beings. Marvellous! I was beginning to think that all English Canadians were bloodless and gutless from the ankles on up. All ice-water and playing it safe and bucking to be Vice-Presidents. Not true?"

"Now just a goddam minute. After two weeks, how did you get to be such a big-assed expert on WASPs and Canadians? Not all of us are overjoyed, let me tell you, to be called bloodless and gutless by a wise-aleck immigrant who crossed the border a few hours ago and thinks he's qualified to pass judgement on the Canadian character from some simplistic perspective of arrogant misunderstanding. I don't have to listen to this sort of crap."

"There you go again, McLaughlin; betraying emotion. You icebergs are not all tip, eh? The fact is, I taught at McGill for two years back in the sixties, and I do have some notion of Canadians. I must fill you in on my background some day. I've lived and worked in sixteen cities and five countries since I left Armenia – but that too is another story."

"I'd be interested. Shoot."

"Some other day. Meanwhile, I'll be glad to give you advice about your dreaded lecture. See here, you've written a book about Innis, not true? So you know more about your subject than any clown in the audience. No one could challenge you from the floor, no one would dare say you are wrong. You are in control. They're in the palm of your hand. It's a golden chance to say what you want to say and to spread truth and enlightenment, to bring them fresh understandings and the snap and flash of new insights. They positively yearn for authoritative views. You'll be made, McLaughlin, you'll be a celebrity – don't you see? This lecture is your heaven-sent opportunity to fulfil yourself, to launch yourself as a meteor into the academic firmament. Lord, how I envy you!"

McLaughlin gulped. For a moment he could almost see, almost believe. . . . But cold fear and self-doubt will douse the brightest fireworks. McLaughlin blinked and sighed. "Nice of you to try that, Nalorian, but I'm still up against it, still with my ass a matter of inches from the buzz saw."

"I wasn't trying anything, J.T., I was merely telling you a truth."

"Uh-huh. Sure. But let's get back to ordinary reality. You were asking me earlier about a loft or a studio. What I could do would be to give you Teitelbaum's phone number and see whether he could put you onto the right sort of person." He fumbled with a flip-card index and wrote out the desired digits.

"Many thanks. But you know, you're a hard man, J.T., a tough nut to crack. You have that Canadian tortoise shell of resistance even to dreams of excellence. If you want to persist in going through life apologizing for yourself in the usual Canadian manner, go ahead, don't mind me. I find it a bore, and unnecessary, but go right ahead. Be a klutz. Be a victim. Be my guest."

"Thanks a lot. I may."

"Well, then, the other thing I wanted to ask you about is the ghost."

"The what?"

"The college's ghost. A lovely idea. One of the cleaners told me that the college has a resident spirit left over from the previous century, an apparition that sometimes walks the tower."

"Oh, that old yarn. I've heard about it, but I've never shaken hands with any ghost."

"Do you know anyone who has actually encountered it?"

"Not for a certainty, no. The head janitor says that he's seen a strange light in the tower on occasion, and he tells tales about hearing footsteps behind him when there's been nobody there, but you know how these people are. Imagine anything, and then embellish it. Wright once said that a big man in a black hat walked through his door when the door was locked, but I assume that the Chairman is having me on half the time. So what are we talking about? Fairy tales?"

"Probably. But I do like a good story, and this legend seems persistent."

"Really, Nalorian, this has been the most bizarre conversation. From caretakers to painters, from insults to psychological hype and con to ghosts. What are you playing at? If it's all the same to you, I'd like to get on with some work."

"Yes, yes, but first just tell me what you know of the ghost story."

"Well, it's one of those things where you don't remember who first told you which version he allegedly heard from some other colleague who is now retired or dead, with nothing clear or agreed, and still less verified. It's scarcely worth the telling. But my recollection of the yarn, Nalorian, is—"

"Call me Nobby."

"What?"

"Nobby. Nubar Armand Nalorian. Most of my friends call me Nubby, or Nobby."

"Okay, but do you want to hear this story or not?"

"I do. Definitely I do."

"Yeah, well—uh—Nobby, the story goes that when the college was built, in 1858, I think, the architect hired a group of stone masons to execute his designs and to carve some gargoyles."

"I've looked at some of the carvings. Remarkable."

"Yeah. So one of the stone masons was called Reznikoff, Ivan Reznikoff. He was dating or 'walking out with' a girl named Susie. But Susie, although she said she was saving up the money Ivan gave her so that they could get married, was also seeing one of Reznikoff's co-workers, another stone mason named, what was it, Paul something, Paul Diabolos. She was two-timing Ivan. When Reznikoff learned about this, he attacked Diabolos with an axe, right by the door of the Croft Chapter House—the axe gash can still be seen on the door - and then a chase up the stairs of the tower ended with Diabolos sticking a knife into Reznikoff and throwing poor Ivan's body down the stairwell.

"Reznikoff's bones weren't found until the fire of 1890, which destroyed part of the building. The report is that during the reconstruction of the college, the bones were discovered and buried in an unmarked grave in the northeast corner of the quadrangle."

"But the ghost walks?"

"Well, so the story goes. Reznikoff's ghost is said to appear from time to time in the college tower."

"That's all?"

"That's all I know. That's all I remember."

"There you are again, McLaughlin. A masterpiece of unimaginative Canadian understatement."

"Meaning what?"

"I mean that you Canadians have many odd and sometimes unique stories to tell, stories which in any other country would be the stuff of great tales or even legends, but you fail to make a full or good drama of them. You brush them aside, almost with apology. In dismissing your own stories, you dismiss yourselves. It's perplexing."

"Oh, come off it, Nobby. It's just a yarn - a bit of folklore; improbable, and of no consequence."

"That's where you're wrong. Stories are of great consequence. Stories define people, and give their existence some colour and texture. Without stories, you have no past, and therefore no basis for a future. You are spiritually impoverished. I wish I could understand what makes you Canadians want to appear so bloody dull. If you only knew it, or would admit it, you're one of the more gutsy and flamboyant peoples in the world."

"Look, if you want to believe in ghosts, it's fine with me, all right? But now maybe you'd let it go at that, and let me get on with some work. I have things to do, really."

"Really. Myths are real. Do you know what's 'real,' J.T.?"

"I guess I do, yeah. I know I have some lectures to prepare. And that public presentation to sweat out. Jeez."

"A ghost in the tower." Nalorian chuckled. "I think I'm going to get along here. Yes, I think I'm going to like this place. It's been nice talking to you, McLaughlin."

"Uh-huh. Close the door as you leave, will you?"

7

McLaughlin's two-o'clock lecture went well enough, but when it was finished he was accosted by Mildred Mott. She reminded him of Auntie Mame's secretary, Agnes Gooch, but then a lot of female academics did. A plain, tall, gawky girl, a bluestocking who wore her dark hair in a bun, her figure under shapeless dresses, and her heart on her sleeve, Mildred tended to gush.

"Being appointed your Teaching Assistant is just the best thing that has happened to me ever! Getting to work with you, and all. Having this great experience, and an extra bit of money besides. I'd have done it for nothing, of course, for the chance to help you, and watch you interact with freshmen, and to be useful and get a taste of working with a big class. It's just marvellous! I can't thank you enough."

"Yeah, well, Mildred, I know you graduate students have got to make a buck. Lord knows there aren't enough scholarships to go around to all the Ph.D. candidates. But it was the Chairman who set it all up for you. It was the Chairman, in fact, who got me into that extra class. There'll be a lot of time involved."

"But I don't mind work. I thrive on work, Professor McLaughlin. It'll be just a super experience, I know it will."

"Call me J.T. We're going to be working together, after all."

"I hope you won't mind if I continue to call you Professor McLaughlin. Professors have always been something else to me, and I want to earn that title myself some day. Ever since I first heard you lecture when I was a freshperson, I've always admired you."

"Uh-huh. Right then, Mildred. Come along to my office

and I'll give you copies of my reading list and the essay assignment sheet for that class. It's one helluva big mob, let me tell you."

"Such a challenge. Gosh. I'm so lucky!"

It took him almost half an hour to shoo her away.

When she was finally gone, burbling about how bringing enlightenment to a few hundred surly engineers would alter the course of western civilization, there was another knock on J.T.'s door.

"Come in. Hello there, Mo. How are you?"

Mohammed Zandran Mukhar Khan was a student McLaughlin liked, or was amused by, or maybe almost conned by. Tall, handsome, rather aristocratic in his bearing but impish under his elaborately formal manners, Mohammed was a walking self-contradiction. He was determined to return to his native Afghanistan to enter politics or the civil service, but during one short year in Canada as a graduate student he had picked up the chewing-gum-snapping and hip slang of the North American student. Although he was from the northern mountain reaches of his own country, he dressed like a Florida beach boy. Mo was pretty obviously from a privileged if not wealthy family, but he was intensely infected by Marxism. He loudly proclaimed his dedication to academic study, but seemed not to work very hard, or even to be particularly bright. Not, all in all, an orthodox graduate student.

"I wish to tender my respects, Professor McLaughlin, and to present to you the compliments of my father and grandfathers, who desire for you long life and tranquillity, and command me to thank you for all that you have done to assist me during the previous year. My family is forever in your debt. You will always be welcome in the house of my father. And all that sort of jazz, right?"

McLaughlin smiled. "Mo, sometimes I wonder if you are for real."

"Please be assured that I am. And that's no hype, man."

"Back for another crack at the books, are you?"

58

"I am enrolled in the second year of the M.A. program."

"But I seem to recall that your grades last year were not all that outstanding."

"I have been permitted to reregister on a probationary basis with the understanding that I must make the minimum achievement of a B average by Christmas. That part of it is a real drag."

"I did notice you in my graduate seminar the other day. Are you sure you want to do another course with me? You may get some of the same jokes you heard last year."

"That is not important. I respect all of my esteemed Professors, but of all the lectures here which I have heard, yours are-yours are not too sickening, you know?"

"Thanks, I guess."

They talked for a while of the course content and the readings required. McLaughlin stressed the necessity to bear down and work hard; Mohammed solemnly undertook to surpass all his previous efforts.

"This year should go easier for me because I am no longer suffering from financial stringencies."

"But, Mo, I thought you'd told me that your family sent you money quite regularly."

"They do, but last year I spent rather in excess of my allowance. Purchases of necessary North American cultural goods and basic accoutrements were inescapable."

"Books?"

"Mainly hi-fi equipment. Essential when you want to bring chicks back to your pad, right?"

"I'll take your word for it."

"During the summer I managed to secure employment of a menial but remunerative nature. I worked in a large factory, which enabled me to pursue work in political education during the lunch hours. Every day at noon, you see, I seized the opportunity to lecture to my proletarian brethren on matters of dialectical materialism and Marxist economics."

"And how did the workers respond?"

"They beat me up."

* * *

Toward four-thirty, just as he was preparing to leave for the day, another student presented herself at the door. Ms. Bromley, was it? J.T. asked himself. They all expect the teachers to know their names – two or three hundred of them per year – even when they don't remember their instructors' names. The human ego is such that it forgives itself everything, and the other person almost nothing.

She wore the standard uniform of the student, jeans and a T-shirt, plus excessive dark eye make-up that made her resemble a startled raccoon. Her appearance was nonetheless remarkable. Her jeans fit her astoundingly well, and the T-shirt's frontal extension looked like a schooner billowing in full sail. She had very long and thick blonde hair which she tossed affectedly from time to time.

Ms. Bromley's face, on the other hand, was less notable. It was an open, ingenuous face, as yet unadulterated by outward signs of care or character, a blank and pancake-base-laden visage illuminated more by hope and simple good cheer than by any flicker of an idea. It was the countenance of a good-hearted child, a well-intentioned and pretty numby. Only her nose gave her face much architecture or interest. Her nose was prominent, bold, a Streisand nose. Naturally, she hated it. We all yearn for singularity, identity, yet mistrust that which differentiates us.

"Remember me?"

"Ah, yes, Ms. Bromley. I thought you told me you were dropping out to get a job?"

"There weren't all that many jobs available. Nothing fulfilling, you know? I decided to come back to university to deepen and discover myself. I'm doing your 407 class. So many bad trips have been laid on me lately, I've just got to find the inner me and get it all on, you know, get my shit together and find myself. You think you could help with that?"

"Find yourself? That should be easy enough."

"It isn't."

"Sure. Look, what you do is, you merely insert your finger under your shirt and place it on your navel. That's right, your belly button. There. Congratulations! You have now 'found' yourself. Got that?"

"You're putting me on."

"Not at all. The real question is, what are you going to *make* of yourself, what are you going to learn and create? Finding yourself is simple. What you're going to do with what you find is the real kicker. Next question."

She looked at him sceptically before continuing. "But you do know me from last year's 314 class? There were so many people in it. I always sat in the front row."

"Of course."

"I thought you'd remember, because you were always staring at my tits."

"Ms. Bromley, you must be mistaken-"

"You were. You did."

"Possibly I was just trying to read the words on the front of your T-shirt. That must have been it. Some of the slogans were so catchy and clever. I seem to recall one of your, ah, fronts that read something about baking."

" 'Sweet Cakes'? And I had one that said, 'Mount Venus University.' The one that got the most attention read, 'Be Kind to Mousies-Eat a Pussy.' "

"Undoubtedly. Your university experience has certainly taught you subtlety, at least. Now what was it you wanted to see me about, Ms. Bromley?"

"You can call me Boffy."

"Buffy?"

"Boffy. Everyone calls me that. Because I like to, you know?"

"I'm not entirely sure that I-"

"Boff. Snog. Shtup. Foop. Get it on. Like, do it."

"Yes, I see. Well. Everyone should have a hobby." He tried

manfully to keep his eyes above her neck, without notable success. "I was asking what you wanted to see me about."

"My marks. Last year my grades in your class were low, C-minus, and I've just got to get them up this time around. I'm going to work hard, honest I am. I've already started on the first essay for your course. One of your graduate students, whatsiz-face Khan–Mo–has promised to give me some pointers. And I've moved in with another grad student, Mildred Mott. Like, your Teaching Assistant? We have the niftiest little place that we share, and we're going to really help each other. See, she's helping me with economics, and I'm teaching her about clothes and styles and make up and stuff, including how to collect Professors."

"You keep losing me on those sharp curves, er, sharp turns, Ms. Bromley. Just how," and here he stared resolutely out the window, but there was no help there, "how do you go about 'collecting Professors'?"

"By getting it on with them, getting them into the sack. It's always been a great game with a lot of the girls in the sorority I belong to. Some of them have run up really high scores. One of our sisters even scored a Dean once. Sometimes it does wonders to improve a girl's marks, you know?"

"I can well imagine." In the awkward silence that followed, McLaughlin was almost surprised to hear himself ask, "How many Professors have you, ah, collected?"

"Seven. So far. Eight if you include Professor Johnson."

"But Professor Johnson is a *woman*."

"Of course. What do you think I am, some kind of bigot? Actually, Johnson sort of collected me. But it sure didn't hurt my grade-point average, let me tell you."

McLaughlin reached for his cigarette lighter, fumbled, dropped it, and groped instead for the handle of his briefcase. "Look, Boffy, Ms. Bromley, I think you might do better to enrol in a course in creative fiction. Let's forget the economics, shall we? If you'll excuse me, I really must be getting off home."

62

"I'll bet you like getting it off."

"*No*. That is, yes; but no. And I must be going. Home." Or crazy, he thought. Snapped.

"I guess you think I'm just a prize dumb doodley, don't you, Professor McLaughlin?"

"Doodley?" He knew it was a mistake to ask, but too late. It did his sense of poise and decorum no good to find himself half under the desk, scrabbling for his lighter, when he heard her laconic reply.

"Doodley. Don't you know *anything*? I mean, I shouldn't have said that, but. Here, let me help you. What do you want, a light? There. Really, you're hopeless. Doodley. Pussy. Chuffy. Muff. Slot machine. Quiff. The old twiddly-poo. Why are you looking at me like that? Do you know that you just lit your cork tip? Sometimes I wonder about you teachers, honest I do. You seem to get so upset about things. It's important to keep cool, you know? You gotta keep your yeast greased. I'll even bet you don't know what would happen if doodleys weren't lubricated. Eh? Give up?" (McLaughlin certainly gave up.) "If they weren't lubricated, women would squeak when they walked. Get it?"

He got it. But all, or almost all, he could think about was losing his job and his tenure on the lovely, lurid grounds of moral turpitude unless he regained some semblance of control over the situation. His voice box, however, seemed to have gone dry. Did his larynx need lubrication? Mygawd, no, he thought, not lubrication.

"Boffy. That is, Ms. Bromley. Will you please get the hell *out* of here?" He attempted to grapple again with his unaccountably heavy briefcase.

"Why? Aren't we having a nice little chat? I can see that I've raised more than your temperature. What's the matter, don't you like me? Probably you'd like just a little taste, admit it. Men always seem to like my boobs. I can't imagine why. Boobs are boobs, right? But if you'd like to give them the old college try, like, that's what I'm here for."

"It's out of the question, Ms. Bromley. Totally out of the question, I'm afraid. Well, no, I'm not afraid. And I'm sure you're a very sweet girl, but the thing is, this isn't my line of country, er, territory at all."

"Say, did you just make a pun there? Might be some hope for you yet."

"An ancient pun at best, and unintentional. From *Hamlet*, actually, Act Three." Instantly he hated himself for being a pedant. "Anyway, I really must be going."

"Are you trying to tell me no, or what?"

"That's what I'm trying to tell you. No."

"Gee, I don't often get a turn-down. You sure? What's there about me you don't like?" She pouted a small hopeful moue.

"Nothing. Absolutely. And it will be a pleasure to have - er - see you in my class."

"You're gonna hold this against me, I can tell."

"Not at all. It's just that I have a daughter of my own, not much younger than you. Frankly, I'd be horrified if my daughter did, that is to say, did what you do."

"I guess you would. My own father is dead."

"I'm sorry."

"Yeah. But sometimes I just can't help myself. Probably it has something to do with my nose. Overcompensating and all that psychoanalytic shit, you know?"

He looked again at her prominent proboscis. "You have a very nice nose, Boffy."

" 'You have a very nice nose!' Is that all you can say? Gee. That's what they all say. 'You have a very nice nose.' Holy jeepers."

"I didn't mean - "

"Oh, I know you didn't. It's just this thing I have about it. At least Streisand can sing, for God's sake. I remember something Salome Bey said. 'Beauty is only skin deep, but ugly is to the *bone*, man.' "

"No one ever suggested you were ugly, I'm certain."

"You're certain, are you? I'm not. When I was a kid, I thought I was all schnoz. A real Durante, you know? Ugly and undesirable. And it seemed like other kids were always taking shots. But now that I'm grown up I know that I've got this great body going for me, right? So I make the best of it. Like, put it right into overdrive and boogie, right? Can't fairly put a girl down for that. See, when I was little, my mother taught me a hymn called 'Brighten Up the Corner Where You Are.' So I do. Simple as that. If you got it, jiggle it. Why's to not?"

She paused to search for a Kleenex. McLaughlin said nothing, much as he wished he could think of something clever or soothing to reply.

"And men," she continued, "most men always seem so grateful. I mean, I hate to disappoint them. They're such big babies, really. Scratch a man and underneath you find a naughty little boy. Men are so sweet, I think; I really do. So how could I want to say no?"

"You might consider waiting for them to ask."

"Poo. Chauvinism. We're way beyond all that. And anyway, I can read it in their transparent baby faces. Like kids with their noses pressed up against the window of the body-rub shop."

"That's candy store window."

"Not with this generation, it ain't."

"Isn't. But seriously now, Boffy, I've got to be leaving. So if you'll excuse me. Maybe you could collect some other economics Professor." Bert Grimsby occurred to him, and he couldn't repress a grin.

"You're right, I could. In fact, the new guy, Professor Nalorian and I already look as though we'll hit it off."

"That's nice."

"Yeah. He's a painter and all."

"I know."

"Nice guy, he is. He seems to like you, too."

"Nalorian's certainly interesting."

"Promise you won't mention this to anybody, but he's

painting my boobs. He's so cute. Says I remind him of Renoir's Gabrielle, whoever she is."

"Do you really mean to tell me that he's–I'm not sure I believe much of this whole thing, Boffy. Are you telling me that you try this act on the whole damn faculty? First you were just trying to embarrass me, and now you're stringing me another line. Enough of the kidding, all right? Let's just forget all this and go home. You don't actually collect Professors any more than I collect teapots."

"I do. I just walk right in and offer to foop them as an even-up trade for high marks. It's a great way to break the ice."

"I can bloody well imagine. And you truly mean that it pays off in grades?"

"Last year–not in your class–I was a positive threat to win scholarships."

"Lovely leaping Jesus. Now I've heard everything. Get out of here, Boffy. I'm serious. I've got to get home. So scoot. Out."

He shepherded her to the door and closed it with a louder bang than he'd intended. McLaughlin waited a prudent interval, collecting his briefcase, some notes, his thoughts, and a few random wishful-thinkings, then put on his trench coat, locked up, and went down the staircase, letting himself out the back door.

On his way to the parking lot he passed by the University Press Bookstore. Fanning his pockets, he realized he was almost out of cigarettes. A glance at his watch revealed that it was a few minutes before five. Still a moment before closing time. When he entered the store his eye was caught by a display of new publications. There are some things an academic can't pass up, and book displays are among them. Instantly he spotted a new book that demanded his attention, a volume on Innis, which he'd long awaited, by a bright young Assistant Professor from Montreal. Now this, I've got to have.

He flipped open the cover and looked at the price with disbelief. Twenty-six dollars! Oh, well, he thought, a tank of gasoline costs about that much, or theatre tickets, or a shirt. Whatthehell. And this, he cajoled himself, is a book I really *need*. How can my lecture be given if I haven't read the last word of a fellow scholar on Innis?

Still, twenty-six bucks! From the back of his mind there trickled the recollection that among his unpaid bills was one from the bookstore which was long overdue. The bill was for one hundred and seventy-some dollars, if he remembered it rightly. Shitty-pies and damn. What to do? The need. The desire. But, the price! On the other hand, if he waited for the book to arrive in the library, how long would it be? Three months? Four? And another month to catalogue it? Too late! The urgency was desperate.

From the cashier's desk a voice announced, "Five o'clock. We're closing!"

Torn, flustered, McLaughlin made one more attempt to total up his ragged psychic score sheet. On impulse, he sidled around behind a book stack and shoved the Innis book under his trench coat and into his left arm pit. I've just become a thief, he realized. Is this how Al Capone got his start? What on God's green earth have I done? His heart pounded and the slip-knot of his emotions pulled tight at his throat. No! This is absurd. I'll put it back, he resolved.

But as he began to reach under his coat, he noticed a female student looking at him quizzically. Was she from one of his classes? He smiled wanly. If he took the book out from under his arm and tried to replace it, would she see the evidence? Or had she seen him tucking the book away? The student turned her back and walked off.

His only hope was a swift exit. Stiffening the clamp of his left arm on his grubby little secret and straightening his back, he marched past the cashier with what he hoped was a jaunty smile and went on out the door.

His arm ached. His head ached. His frayed conscience began to hurt with the sharp pang of a little boy who had for the first time skipped Sunday School and spent his collection-plate quarter on ice cream.

A muscle in his cheek began to twitch. He thought, I am a criminal. I am a moral disaster, an outlaw. Whatthefuck have I *done*? Am I losing my mind? Risking my reputation, my career, for heisting a goddam book?

But by the time he reached his car and fumbled for his keys, the thought uppermost in his increasingly numb brain was, All this, O Lord, all this, and I forgot to buy cigarettes.

* * *

When he got home and skulked through the door, Trish called, "Is that you, J.T.?"

"Were you expecting Leonard Cohen? Or Robert Redford?"

"No, but a girl can always hope. Hang your coat up, and don't leave it on the banister. You're worse than the kids. Did you have a good day? Did you think brilliant and profound academic thoughts?"

"Hunh. The day was nothing much." Boffy and larceny skipped through his mind. "Uneventful."

"Come into the kitchen, dear. I'm making chicken cacciatori. Pour us both a highball, will you?" She paused and scrutinized him. "But you look positively flushed and flustered. Is there anything wrong?"

"Nah. I'm a bit tired, is all."

"You look all on edge."

"No, I'm fine. Had a talk with the new man, Nalorian, today, and just grabbed a sandwich at my desk for lunch." He passed her a drink. "Have you got any cigarettes?"

"Yes, but don't light another one. You just put one out."

"Did I? I didn't notice."

Trish turned from the stove and confronted him. The instincts of a wife are fathomless but acute. "You seem to be a bit strung out. You sure you're feeling level? Have you been thinking too hard about that silly lecture? I'm a bit worried about you, J.T. You don't seem entirely yourself. You can't let the bastards get you down, you know? You seem a lot more twitchy than usual. Maybe you should take it easy tonight and go to bed early."

"Yeah. Maybe I should, at that. But I've got to get on with the script for that public thing on Innis. And Jossy going out with that greaser with the motorcycle doesn't entirely put my mind at ease. Daughters can be more of a worry than over-drafts. Where does she find these creeps, anyway?" he gnawed at a fingernail.

"Jocelyn is going through a rebellious phase, that's all. She'll come out of it. Let's go into the front room and sit down."

"Sure. I've been going through a bad patch, I guess, and probably I fret too much. My teaching went tolerably well to-day, though, and I–Trish, where is all the *furniture*?"

"It's nearly all there. Settle down and drink your highball. I've made a very good dinner that you'll enjoy."

"Nearly all there? Nearly! How can you talk about dinner when the furniture is all gone? What in the name of the blue-assed, buffalo-slaughtering bastards of Batoche are you tell-ing me?"

"Well, really, J.T., your language. Would you like me to top up your drink?"

"Patricia, I'm asking you. Where is the furniture?"

"Do you mean the couch, dear?"

"I mean the couch, and the green chair, and my chair. I mean, have we been burgled? Whatthehell is going on around here?"

"Well, I was talking to an upholsterer the other day, and I found the most di*vine* material for the couch, so I thought I should go ahead with it, you know?"

"But we discussed all that last month. We agreed we couldn't afford any upholstery work until after Christmas. Didn't we agree on that?"

"Afford! Really, J.T., you do go on. If we only did what we

could afford around here we'd hardly do *any*thing. I found this great material for the couch which was not at *all* expensive, and you know that the old thing was *pos*itively in *shreds*, wasn't it?"

"So the chairs have gone to the upholsterer, too? Not just the couch, not just one chair, but two chairs? I don't believe it."

"But they were so *tat*ty. Think of what we've saved on the trucking, since the man doesn't have to make two trips."

"I hope the man doesn't expect to be paid until February, either."

"Are we expecting some kind of a bonus in February? I didn't realize that."

"We are expecting to be bankrupt, and not in February, but most probably in November. Jeez, Trish, I don't know how you could have done this."

"But you *are* an economist, J.T. Economists know all about money and like that. Just a little upholstering shouldn't hurt. It'll only be a definitely *li*ttle bill, not even a thousand."

"Arrrgh. We just don't have a loose grand to spare right now, or next month either, for that matter. Don't you realize that you're going to end us up absolutely flat broke?"

"Now, now, dear, don't be melodramatic. I know you'll think of something. A few pennies more or less can't hurt. Are you ready to eat?"

* * *

While J.T. and his wife were debating the sorry state of their domestic exchequer, Boffy Bromley was engaged in quite different extra-curricular diversions. After leaving McLaughlin's office she had hurried home to keep a previous appointment. She winkled out of her tight clothing and decided she had just enough time for a quick sponge bath. While dabbing her best perfume on several cunning spots she examined herself in the bathroom mirror. Experimentation with her long mane of wheat-blonde hair decided her to leave it flowing loose. Retouching her make-up took only a moment. She stood on tiptoe, the better to admire the body in which she took an entirely pardonable delight, and inhaled and twitched her pectoral muscles as she contemplated her most prominent assets. These full, up-tilted breasts she secretly regarded as the abundant answers to her youthful prayers, and many men had shared this reverent opinion. Her large aureola were dark; she enhanced the colour of her delicate nipples with a touch of lipstick. More than satisfied, she returned to the bedroom.

The apartment, which she shared with Mildred Mott, was hers for a while. Mildred could be counted on to be in the university library most evenings until at least seven. Their rooms were standard apple-crate accommodations above a store on Spadina Avenue, just south of College Street. A small living room gave access to an even more minuscule kitchen and, down a narrow hall, was a bedroom which contained a scarred chest of drawers and a set of twin mattresses on a dusty floor. Beside one of these mattresses was propped a large mirror in an old oval frame, adjustable to reflect the gyrations of sublime combat.

On this mattress, only ten minutes later, Professor Nubar Nalorian reclined, nonchalant as a well-fed cat. She had welcomed him at the door and urged him to hurry about undressing. Now he lay on his back, unclothed, with his hands clasped behind his neck. Straddling his loins, Boffy, no less nude, rocked back and forth and up and down like a little girl cradling a rocking horse between her thighs. She was a dreamy rider, enjoying a gentle canter and producing more sweet juices than she knew she possessed.

"It's wonderful how long you can last, Nobby."

"One of the consolations of advancing years, my poppet, involves the triumph of the will over mere energy. If you'd known me as a youth, you'd have known only a simple automatic pistol, effective but too quick off the trigger. Now I am a more stalwart spear-carrier in the legions of Eros. I can remain stiff and resolute for a good long while. A minor virtue, but one in which I pride myself."

"I don't know how you can talk so much in the middle of all this, and still sound like a CBC announcer."

"BBC. But, dear girl, why shouldn't one talk while making love? It helps to prolong the bliss, and keeps all channels open. There are only three levels of communication: physical, linguistic, and intuitive. Happily, sex involves them all. What is it if not communication? Isn't sex the highest form of knowing? That's why the biblical lads called it carnal knowledge."

Boffy did a wide-swinging high-toss and twirl. "OoooOOh. I just came for the third time."

"I know. I watched your eyes dim and glaze over."

"Sometimes," said Boffy, leaning back, but without losing her elastic rhythm, "sometimes I think you are, well, watching me. Are you really there, or are you just a voyeur?"

"Both. Voyeurs are self-conscious, and so always there. The artist in me is always the appreciator. The ecstatic viewer is the aesthete. But you'll have noticed that I am still, ah, participating."

"You're so controlled. Is your mind icy? You're *studying* me," she repeated.

"Never doubt it. I'm memorizing. It doubles my pleasure. Most people don't notice things. Why not pay attention? To paraphrase Plato, the unexamined woman is not worth probing."

"Do you really care about me, Nubby?"

"Is the rain wet? Do dogs' tails wag?"

"What part of me do you like best?"

"Your nose, my sweet."

"You're kidding."

"I'm not. You nose gives you character, distinction. It is noble. It is you."

"I wish it weren't."

"Never fight the inevitable, dear girl. Rejoice in it."

Boffy tossed her hair and laughed. She then closed her eyes, began a laugh from the depths of her throat, and emitted a gurgle. "Gggghuuuhhaawh. I just had another little one."

"Splendid. Roll, Fotis, roll."

"What–who is Fotis?"

"A woman in a book by Lucius Apuleius. Never mind."

"I mind. I listen to everything you say. I think I love you, Nubar."

"Nonsense, my dear. You merely care for me, as I do for you. But love? You cannot love what you do not know, and you cannot know anyone you have not suffered with. Love is a word bandied about too loosely by the young. It should be saved for more meaningful occasions, such as anniversaries, not early and easy encounters."

"But somehow I wish you didn't *look* at me like that, not during."

"One of the things I most enjoy is the way you begin to laugh before you come, the way you chortle when the ripples hit. It's intriguing, to me, to watch faces when they are experiencing the pinnacle moments. Some gasp, some moan, some almost swoon and faint, while others like you become incandescent or chuckle with the intensity of it all. I knew a man once in Cairo, who was thrown out of Sheppard's Hotel because he insisted on firing off a pistol at the supreme instant. His neighbours complained, but he seemed to need the fireworks as blazing punctuation. Some people bite, do you see? Others merely sigh and float, but whatever they do, I particularly enjoy the unpredictable facial expressions of rapture and release. I'm thinking of doing a whole series of paintings on the subject. 'Portraits of Joy.' "

"You're off your rocker, you know that Nubby? But it's your turn now." She increased her thigh-swirling tempo. He smiled, stroked her belly and kneaded her heavy breasts, then soon subsided into jellied quietude.

"Tell me," Nalorian asked after several minutes, "have you tried your collecting routine with other of my immediate colleagues?"

Boffy lit a joint, inhaled deeply, and offered it to him, but he declined with a shake of his head. "Well, I did make a suggestion to McLaughlin not long ago – before you and I got together, of course – but he didn't connect."

"Really?"

"Nope. He liked the bait, but he didn't take the hook. He isn't a bad guy, but he's a bit nervous, you know?"

"Interesting. I like McLaughlin, but he does seem rather on edge. I sense in him a desperation that goes beyond nerves. His springs are so tightly wound, like a nine-dollar watch, that he could do something erratic at almost any time. It isn't clear to me what makes him tick, but there's one of those WASP Canadian time bombs in him somewhere that seems to have a hint of potential quirkiness in it."

"Oh, Nobby, you do exaggerate. He's just your common-garden Prof who doesn't know what to make of the real world."

"Perhaps. Anyone else?"

"Not this year. But last year I did try it on with Professor Grimsby."

"Bert? Good Lord! What happened?"

"Nothing much. I walked into his office and made my play, like I lifted my T-shirt and showed him my boobs."

"And?"

"His eyes sort of misted over. I thought he was going to, you know, cry or something. But he just stared. Then he muttered something about sexual harassment, rushed out of the room, knocking over his waste-paper basket, and leaving me just sitting there."

"I'd like to have seen that," Nalorian grinned.

She finished her joint of good Colombian spliff and got up to make coffee. "Mildred will be coming in soon. Would you like me to invite her, to make it a threesome, before we get dressed? I've been teaching her and turning her on. Imagine me as a teacher? But she's a quick learner. She might have Mo with her, though. Would you like a foursome?"

"Certainly not. Your generation seems to like sexual en-

74

counters more various and voracious than mine. Please believe, dear girl, that I'm a lover, not a swinger; a connoisseur, not a consumer. Groups hold no interest for me."

"All right, Nubby. I'm just trying to please you. Mildred has a terrible case on McLaughlin anyway. Now that she is his Teaching Assistant, he's become her big crush as though she were a twelve year old, and she talks about him all the time."

"And the university is supposed to be a place of rationality," Nubar chuckled. "If we intellectuals act as we do, small wonder that the rest of the world is off the rails of reason. Poor Mildred having a crush on McLaughlin is like a brood hen trying to hatch a hand grenade. She's overmatched. If only the world had taken David Hume seriously. We do not choose with our minds, you see? Reason is merely the servant of the emotions."

Boffy served coffee and lit another joint. Nalorian permitted himself one puff, if a deep one. "I should be moving along home," he said.

Boffy pouted and suggested another little slide down the slopes of lubricity. "Or are you too played out, Nubby? It's all right if you are."

"Never that tired, pet. But I might need some slight stimulation."

She disappeared behind a closet door and re-emerged wearing her hair piled casually on the top of her head, a chunky costume-jewellery necklace that hung down between her breasts, a gold chain belt, and high spike-heeled boots.

"Wonderful. I can see how you're teaching Mildred. Dressing for these events is even better than undressing, as any student of male psychology will tell you. We all live in worlds of fantasy, don't we? And fantasy is usually more compelling than reality."

She pranced in front of him just long enough to rivet his attention. He reached for her, but she darted out of the room. When she returned, she had a jar of grape jam which she spread over her nipples. Soon the jam was gone.

As they closed and joined, Boffy breathed, "Tell me another poem, Nubar."

"Yes. Yes:

> 'I burn my candle at both ends,
> It will not last the night.
> But oh my foes, and oh my friends,
> It gives a lovely light.' "

"I love it when you quote poems for me. What is your favourite poem of all?"

"Favourite? There is one, called 'Remembrance,' by Emily Brontë that is very special–but no. Here is something that many travellers have found solace in. Perhaps not entirely appropriate at the moment, but it goes, from our old and early friend Anonymous, I think:

> 'Western wind, when wilt thou blow,
> The small rain down can rain?
> Christ, if my love were in my arms
> And I in my bed again!' "

She sighed. "That's lovely. I like those short ones that I can understand. Anyway, why don't you just relax and stay the night?"

"No, not tonight. My domestic obligations make that impossible. But perhaps we'll find ourselves out of town one night. Another time."

8

It was one of those mornings. McLaughlin's eyes felt pinched and yellow, like pee-holes in the snow. He had to wait almost fifteen minutes for his daughter to come out of the bathroom. The toothpaste tube had split, emitting green gorp onto his thumb but not his toothbrush. He had a pimple inside his nose which distended and reddened one nostril. His uncertain hand dropped the electric razor into the wash basin and damaged the shaving head of the noisy, whirring machine, which then proceeded to tear gory chunks out of his neck as he tried to manoeuvre the snicking blades around the edges of his beard.

The paper boy had not folded the morning *Globe and Mail*, and the sports pages had blown away into the shrubbery. To find out what had happened to the Blue Jays in Yankee Stadium yesterday would require Moslem-like abasements on hands and knees under the bushes or a wet-slippered pilgrimage down the neighbour's driveway, and he figured to hell with it.

Breakfast was Instant Quaker Oats, a sad, lumpy mistake; pathetic little ersatz dehydrated flakes which, when subjected to boiling water, attained the alarming consistency of *papier mâché*. Doesn't anybody make real porridge anymore? he lamented. But Trish didn't much care much about breakfast, loudly decrying the evils of greasy frying pans when sunnyside eggs were at issue, and herself preferring plain bran muffins. The kids silently shovelled in a breakfast cereal hyped on T.V. and loaded with all the flavour and nutrition of dry hay.

His old battered briefcase sat in the front hall where he had left it last night, full of unmarked essays on the subject of "The Causes of Inflation." Krist. If he knew the solution to *that* one, he'd be rich and famous. Instead, he was impecunious and anonymous, but he'd have to invent some fancifully impressionistic comments and grades for that huge pile of hopeful freshman excrescence by Monday at the latest.

Kicking off his slippers, J.T. shoe-horned his feet into last year's (on sale) twenty-nine-dollar suede Hush Puppies so that he wouldn't have to go down the basement to shine his "real" shoes. He pulled on a ravaged grey Harris tweed jacket over his dark blue turtleneck, said a surly goodbye to his family, forgot his briefcase, and dumped himself into the car.

The Camaro's untuned motor pinged like a diesel as he drove south into Cabbagetown to pick up Cutty, whose own car was in the shop for a brake job. J.T. pulled up in front of Cutty's white-painted, carriage-lamped house and honked. His friend emerged. The two of them grunted at each other, neither liking days that started with barrages of conversation.

As they turned along Wellesley Street, heading west to the university, McLaughlin was suddenly hit by one of those inexplicable but ineluctable waves of black emotion. It was like driving into a brick wall of abject futility. What if he got to work on time? What if he didn't? What if he emptied the classroom with his plonking lecture, or received a standing ovation? What if he wrote a brilliant bit about Innis, or filled several legal-sized lined pages with surpassing nonsense, like whackadoo-whackadoo times two, what difference would it make? Thirty years from now, or three months from now, J.T. reasoned, who would remember, or care? If the whole freshman class got A grades, would nirvana be reached? If the entire class got zero, would the world stop turning? The price of oil would remain the same. Starvation in refugee camps would continue. Leg traps would still hold furry animals in agony. Newspapers would still publish Ann Landers and horoscopes, crossword puzzles and stories of the substitution of one tyranny for another in distant, improbable places. Amnesty International would submit more reports on political torture by grinning thugs. In lands where multinational corporations substituted white sliced bread for food and Nestlé's Quick for mother's milk, the ubiquitous poor would await the blessings of missionaries or Colonel Sanders or Johnny Carson or death, whichever came first. McLaughlin had a stinging urge to turn the car around and go back to bed.

At the corner of Wellesley and Yonge, he watched a small boy kick a dog in the ribs for no other apparent reason than to show the mutt who was boss. The light changed and the traffic moved forward. McLaughlin used that as an excuse not to get out of the car and cuff the boy, but he knew it was only an excuse. Yet if he belted the kid, would the little prick not simply hurry home to clout his own little sister?

At the corner of Wellesley and Bay, McLaughlin saw a pair of young blind people, a man and a woman, treading along carefully, arm-in-arm, sweeping their white canes tentatively across the sidewalk like soldiers feeling out a minefield, but all the while smiling and chatting animatedly to each other. They each carried tape recorders, and wore Chiliast U. jackets. Obviously they were making their way, slowly, toward university lectures where they would enter into cheerful but unequal competition with sullen clear-eyed louts from Rosedale and Forest Hill for degrees and for jobs that might not exist unless affluent and connected Daddies opened the doors. Somehow, the blind couple got to him.

"That bastard!" J.T. blurted. "That unspeakably unprincipled, vicious bastard!"

Cutty yawned. "Who?"

"God."

"Oh."

They covered the rest of the route in silence.

* * *

From that auspicious beginning, the day continued its downhill course. J.T.'s morning seminar degenerated into a tiresome slanging match between a surly Marxist and a shrill Reaganite conservative. At lunch he was burdened by leaden shepherd's

79

pie at the Faculty Club and a turgid disquisition on interest rates by the relentless Grimsby.

When McLaughlin straggled back to his office that afternoon after his three-o'clock lecture, he decided to get his chaotic desk cleaned up and to deal with some of the accumulated bumph. There's nothing like a well-organized office, he reflected, and obviously his was *nothing* like a well-organized office. He threw out a number of publishers' advertisements, bills, reminders of committee meetings, and an invitation to take part in a conference on Prioritizing Public Policy Objectives Through Value-Oriented Social Accounting Management. "Imbeciles," he muttered.

His eye scanned a memorandum from some Smyton Hall administrative yahoo which detailed the President's concern over escalating costs of xeroxing materials for undergraduates. Study of the problem by a high-level committee had resulted in the creation of a special task force to crack down on the situation. He made a little circle in the air with his finger and said, "Whoopee." The memo further informed him that the first act of the task force was to fight the "profligate waste" by "identifying every document copied in a particular week and making a photocopy of it."

High-level thinking is always a treat, he ruminated, and turned to a manila envelope which yielded a new report from the Ministry of Corporate and Consumer Affairs. Flipping it open, he read: "The internalization of externalities through the imposition of legal liability works toward introducing the optimal level of deterrence. Unremedied defective consumer products yield, inter alia, by way of social costs, a higher than optimal defect rate."

"Sheesh. Why do I worry about being a neurotic when there are all of these bent nincompoops running around loose?"

He went down the hall to the men's john. On the wall above the urinal was a new bit of graffito. "A degree in the Humanities teaches you to despise the money it prevents you from earning." Now that I can relate to, J.T. thought.

When he got back to his office, the phone was ringing. He

snatched it up and heard Trish's voice. "I'm glad I caught you before you left, dear. On your way home, will you stop at a grocery store and pick up a couple of cans of clams? I want to make clams with linguini, and I haven't got quite enough. And a few extra tins of dog food; we're almost out."

He protested that he had only eight dollars and change in his pocket, but she assured him that would be enough.

An hour and a half later he was in a store and doing the necessaries, but he noticed that there were no prices stamped on the items he wanted. With careful politeness born of probable insufficient funds, he asked a clerk what the prices of these particular things might be.

"Dunno," said the pimply boy.

"There don't seem to be prices marked on the shelves, either."

"Nope."

"I see. Well, do you think you could find out for me?"

"Are you kiddin'? I don't price 'em, I just stack 'em."

J.T. approached the cash desk and stood in line for several minutes with his prospective purchases. When he got to the head of the queue he inquired again what the prices for the several cans might be. The cashier snapped her gum at him and said that the prices would be shown on the screen of her processor when the machine scanned the lines on the labels.

"Um, these little lines?"

"Yup. The machine reads them and it tells you." She began to move the cans over the scanner.

"Now wait. Could you wait a minute? I'm not sure that I have the right amount, that is, I'm not sure of. . . . What I'd like to know is, what these things cost."

"How would I know till the machine does its number?" Cans and processor held their own secret dialogue as she fed in the items. He watched, impressed but not reassured, as the numbers danced on the screen. More whirring and buzzing and blipping resulted in a total being flashed up in tiny purple lights. "That'll be nine dollars and eight-two cents."

"Golly, I seem to have, that is, I may be a bit short. Could I just take the one can of dog food and give you back the other one?"

"The machine doesn't back up. It doesn't have a reverse on it, you know? Nine eighty-two." She snapped her gum once more.

"Well, the thing is, I've only got eight bucks. Let me see. And thirty-five cents. Surely you could start the tabulation over again without this one can?"

A woman in line behind him began to shuffle and mutter.

The cashier looked past him with vacant eyes and intoned that the total had already been rung up.

He groped his pockets in a desperate search for more money. A man further behind him barked, "Could you move it along, buddy? There are others waiting, you know."

"I'm terribly sorry. There seems to be a slight problem here. I wonder whether I could have a word with the manager?"

More grumbling in the line behind.

"Are you certain we couldn't just deduct one item? I really don't need that other can of dog chow, and–"

Over his shoulder the woman spoke more loudly this time. "Some people. Really. Of all the brass."

The cashier drummed her fingers. "We're closing soon, you know? Nine eighty-two."

J.T. continued to fumble through his pockets in forlorn hope of discovering additional funds. "Would you take a cheque?"

"For nine bucks? You gotta be joking. Anyway, no cheques without the manager's signature, and the manager ain't here."

"Well, this is embarrassing, but–"

"Mister, do you wanna pay your bill, or what?"

The comments from the growing line-up behind were becoming more pointed, even rude.

"No. You can stick your cans back up between your shelves. No." He glared about him and marched out of the store with as much dignity as he could muster, which wasn't much. And he was clamless. Even dogfoodless.

Around the table that evening, the silence hung heavy over the McLaughlin family. Jossy pointed out that linguini didn't go so well with macaroni and cheese. Trish sighed, and J.T. pretended he didn't hear. The dog growled, and J.T. only just resisted the temptation to kick it.

* * *

Although McLaughlin had gone home early, most of his colleagues were still at the office. Emerging from a late interview with the Chairman, at the end of the day, Nalorian bumped into Grimsby in the corridor.

"Still here, Bert? How are you?"

"So-so. You?"

"Going grand," Nobby beamed.

They talked of students and curriculum problems and government cutbacks in university funding. Grimsby spoke wistfully of taking early retirement. Nobby asked about McLaughlin's impending public lecture. Bert insisted that J.T. might lack a cutting edge of confidence, but that he was basically a good guy, and Nalorian was relieved that he could agree with the lugubrious Grimsby on something at least.

"Well now, step into my office," Nobby suggested with more cordiality than he felt, "and tell me more about this most unusual department. Do have a chair. I think I'm gradually learning the local ground rules. Our chief has just insisted that if I stay around next year he'll want me to do a course on 'The Limits of Economic Growth.' Odd man, Wright." Nobby lit a Romeo y Julieta Palmas Reales panetela.

"And what did you say?"

"I said, yes."

"But, Nubar, most of your work has been on the monetary side of growth and development. How can you agree to teach all that stuff about 'Limits' and 'Zero Growth'?"

"I merely flip the coin and read the other side. That bothers you, I see. Did you ever try to hang a painting by Kandinsky or Braque upside down? Most of the damned things work just as well. As Wright might say, 'Obversely, we reconnoitre the convenient converse.' There's a man with a nice sense of the ridiculous, our Chairman. I like him. Anyway, artful inversions may shed an unexpected light on the original intention. The grand conception is what matters, eh? Apart from that, growth, shrinkage, booms, busts–they're all one to me."

"I'd have thought that Wright's proposal for what you should teach might, um, violate your principles."

Nalorian guffawed. "Principles? I have very few of those."

"Everyone has principles," Bert persisted. "They *must*."

"Oh come off it!" Nobby could detect in the big muddy eyes of his colleague not only disappointment, which seemed ever present with the man, but also hurt, so he started again more gently. "Principles, you say? Well, maybe I do have a few kicking around somewhere. Yes. For my diversions, I have my chosen pleasures, many of which are quite extravagant. For my work I have a tight grip on professional techniques–most of which, like Keynes' multiplier, work just as well backwards as forward. In the big playground of life, Bert, I enjoy the swings."

They looked at each other amiably for a few silent moments. Nalorian tacked and jibbed, attempting to turn the conversation toward new journal articles, the irrationally mutable prices of gold, oil, and soya beans, and whether J.K. Galbraith's latest pronouncement was batty or the clear-headed observation of a sane man in a profession of numb-skulls, with Nobby upholding the latter view. Bert, however, returned in his slow, unrelenting manner to what interested him most.

"I'm still not sure why you'd accept that–eccentric teaching arrangement. Did Wright pressure you?"

"Not at all. Unless you'd call the hint of potential unemployment pressure." He chuckled. "I told Wright that I could handle *any* assignment."

Bert pondered this information for another long moment.

"I guess what I'm asking is, don't you have any, um, convictions? Do you *believe* in anything?"

"You're serious about this, I take it? Yes, I see that. Bottom lines seem to be what interest you most on the grand balance sheet, eh? Well, a full matched set of 'beliefs,' as you so charmingly call them, would only be weighty baggage which might restrict the jaunty itinerary of the brisk intellectual tourist. But I'll answer you."

Nalorian made a steeple of his fingers, and smiled at a point on the wall beyond Bert's shoulder. "I try never to be unkind. I believe in reciprocity; a large and good word, don't you think? And I believe in joy. Happiness is salubrious."

"Happiness isn't easy, of course," Bert grumbled.

"But it is! I sometimes think I should teach a course on it. No student would doze off in *that* class, and it would be a damned sight more practical than monetary theory or double-entry bookkeeping. Most of the rules are simple. Shall I try them on you?"

Bert frowned. "I might be able to make do with the notes for the short course, but I'm not sure I could stand a whole semester."

Nalorian peered closely at Grimsby. This man, he decided, would give an aspirin a headache. He has the personality of a constipated moose with terminal antler itch. "Somehow Bert, I can't visualize you as a student in my class. Most North Americans are like children, don't you think? I find them refreshing. Impatient, spoiled, soft, overindulged, loud, shallow, certain they have all the answers when their culture protects them from the big questions, totally lacking a sense of history–and therefore any perspective–barely able to read and write in a single language, never mind two or three, having spent twelve years in schools that protect them from ideas or real literature. It's all so sad. They think Homer is something that flashes on an electronic scoreboard at a baseball game."

"You said you could give a prescription for happiness."

"Did I? Well, I can. I'll lay out the rules. Seven rules."

Grimsby made a silent bet with himself that Nubar couldn't do it. He bet himself a nickel. "Give."

"Right you are!" said Nalorian. "Give. It is better to give. There's the reciprocity thing again.

"Second, find work that you like. If you don't like it, chuck it over. All work is mostly a game anyway. When you find what you like, keep at it. Happy people are busy people.

"Marry late. Never marry before thirty. You've got to grow up first, and North America inhibits growing up. My own experience with marriage has been extraordinary, but that's another story.

"Finish your formal education and travel before you marry. As Maurois said, 'To acquire culture is to prepare for love.'

"Never marry for sex. It's as easily available as popsicles, and as lasting. Marry for friendship. Passion may or may not last, probably not, but intelligence and character are forever. Never use your cock as a weathervane. The winds change constantly on everything except maturity and character."

Grimsby thought, this smug rascal sounds like Dear Abby. "I guess I'm not much interested in marriage."

"Moreover," said Nobby, ignoring the interjection, "be disciplined. Be moderate. And above all, get beyond self. 'He who would save his life must lose it,' not so? You've got to give yourself *to* something, some person, some cause beyond your own skin, or you'll become bleakly introspective and self-absorbed. Self is marvellous, but excessive self is a sinkhole.

"Never aim at mere security. Ramble along, and don't expect anything to be permanent."

Grimsby at this point came as close to smiling as he'd come in days. Nubar, without tenure and bucking for it, putting down security. Too much.

"Take risks," Nobby sailed on. "Be enthusiastic – selective, but enthusiastic. Never doubt that the diamond at the heart of your happiness is as hard, and more significant, than the lump of coal underlying your sorrow.

"Believe in joy. Believe in yourself. There has never been a 'you' before, and you're unique. As one of your baseball chaps said, probably it was Casey Stengel, 'Ninety per cent of this game is half mental.' Or, what did Shakespeare say? 'Assume a confidence if you have it not.' It works."

Bert protested, "That was 'virtue'—'assume a virtue.'"

"Same thing. Confidence is a great virtue, don't doubt it. This life is all a matter of attitude. Thinking the right thoughts is what makes all the difference in this world. March right up to life, look it in the eye, and stare it down. If you roll over, you'll get stomped; if you stand up, they'll salute. Simple as that."

Grimsby said, "That's eleven."

"What?"

"You said, seven rules. You just laid out eleven."

"Who in the name of God is counting?"

"I am. And I think, Nubar, with respect, that you may just have extruded the darndest mess of *Reader's Digest* pseudo-philosophy I've ever heard."

Nalorian grinned. "Possibly. You may be right. Eleven, do you say? There are more. But can you improve on that? Let's hear you."

"No, no. I was simply suggesting that you can't count." And, thought Bert, that you are crass.

Nalorian stopped to consider, and fixed his colleague with a piercing eye. "Don't mistake me, Grimsby. I know what I'm talking about. Students should spend less time with idiotic textbooks and more time reading Montaigne, Pascal, Santayana, La Rochfoucauld, and Confucius; the writers who tell you not what to think, but how to live."

"Now you're giving me a reading list. I ask you a serious question and all I get is a bibliography plus an excessive effusion about joy. If I had a grip on *that*, I needn't have asked."

Nobby narrowed his eyes and murmured, "Don't, I repeat, misjudge me. I'm not being facile. The horrors of life are not unknown to me. Poverty, rapacity, evil, daily torturings both natural and calculated; these are not things I've failed to notice. But in a world that is both melancholy and terrifying, I choose deliberately to accentuate pleasure–which of course includes avoiding the pain of giving pain. I'm laughing, Bert, but not at you. Humour, the collision of unexpected absurdities, is what Freud called the best of our defence mechanisms–or something like that. In his vale of shrieks and shivers, I see laughter and love as the only redemptions. And even what we call love is frequently comic. Dr. Johnson said that 'the size of a man's understanding might always be justly measured by his mirth.' No, I make no apologies for the simple advocacy of joy.''

He paused, but Grimsby only blinked, and goaded by the uncomfortable silence, Nalorian pressed on. "You asked me what I believe–not a question with which I'm confronted every afternoon. Possibly the answer should be left hidden in the diaries of adolescence. But I started to tell you. Rules apart, then, do me the courtesy of hearing me out." He lit another panetela. "Beliefs, is it? Damn it, I believe in–let me think–the amazingly resilient silly-putty of the human spirit, art for art's sake, taste, and the secret where the stocking ends. I cherish disbelief, scepticism, and I loathe fanatics. I believe that God, on the improbable chance that He exists, is, like poor Yorick, a fellow of infinite jest. Therefore, I believe in a cheerfulness. I don't see life in terms of ends or goals. The process itself, the miraculous process, is enough."

Grimsby absorbed this outburst with characteristic lack of haste. "Golly, I'm not sure how a thinking man can live with so few convictions. Just a list of platitudes about gratification, and no real beliefs."

"And I, in turn, am not sure how a man could be happy struggling along under the burden of many more. I didn't mean to get wound up about all this, Bert, truly I didn't, but since you have prodded me, I'll reiterate that a load of principles can be heavy, very heavy. Perhaps the more you discard, the faster you travel, the freer you are. Let me suggest this to you: put your beliefs in one hand, and a glass of whisky in the other, and then see which hand is fullest. Or the most pleasurable."

Bert frowned. "I'm never sure whether you're being serious with me."

"Was Mohammed an Arab? Did Wordsworth like daffodils?"

Grimsby left Nalorian's office no less gloomy and perplexed than he'd entered it, and still less than certain whether Nubar was a Rotarian con man. It worried him. But then, most things did.

9

At eight p.m. McLaughlin was slumped over the desk in his basement cubby-hole, a rough sketch of a room made of plywood and cork-board, the tiny cell he risibly called his study. He was trying to write. An hour of staring at a pristine page, however, had not revealed any new truths.

"Truths? Jeez, are there any?" he muttered. Ruefully his memory wandered back to one of the shortest, classic reviews on record: "Your manuscript is both good and original. But the part that is good is not original, and the part that is original is not good." The lines must have been Sam Johnson's. And how would any sane man dare to put pen to paper after being snapped like that?

From the kitchen door at the top of the cellar stairs, the voice of his wife cut into his vacant reverie. "J.T., what are you doing down there? Are you paying bills?"

"Just paying the sweaty dues required to join the ranks of the immortals," he answered with a limp attempt at cheeriness.

"What?"

He got up and shuffled to the foot of the stairs. "Damn it, Trish, I'm working. I'm stringing gleaming words onto a gossamer thread of economic theory."

"I didn't hear your typewriter clicking."

"I was between sentences. Thinking. You'd be surprised how little noise the brain makes when it's engaged. Even Einstein thought silently, although I'm surprised you didn't hear my mental gears clashing. Wait, I'll come up. I was trying to think of what should come next, or whether I could get away with the stilted vacuity of the previous sentence, which I grievously doubt. As long as I'm up here, I might just pour myself another thin finger of that Mortlach single malt."

"If you'd drink less, you'd think faster. And if you'd think less and write more, you'd have that lecture all done."

"Think less? The world is too much plugged with that sort of thing as it is. Eighty per cent of it is committed by journalists, and the other twenty per cent by academics who merely rechew old cuds or report computer printouts of imbecilic feed-ins. Let's not encourage *that* sort of thing."

"All right, all right. Look, I'm off to play bridge. The dog is still out and the cat is in and Davie is all bathed and in bed. Rob is doing homework and Jossy should be back about ten-thirty. Will you be all right on your own? I won't be late."

"I'll be fine, dear."

J.T. turned back to his cellar hole like a prisoner of the Inquisition being led back to the rack. "How in the hell," J.T. grumbled to himself "can a person concentrate on writing a public lecture when his private affairs and personal finances are in such turmoil?" An American Express bill of staggering dimensions had arrived that day. How would he ever push the Sisyphian rock of his credit-card obligations up the mountain of his debt? Such grubby concerns tended to distract from the eternal verities. How can one think of pure theory when the importuning bailiff is at the door? Again, as Dr. Johnson said, "A man doubtful of his dinner, or trembling at a creditor, is not much disposed to abstract meditation or remote inquiries."

Quotes sprung to hand so readily, but new thoughts were moles in the subconscious which never broke the flat surface of his mind, remaining tantalizingly underground. It had been one of those days when life seemed little more than trying to empty the Atlantic with a spatula, or exploring the Gobi Desert riding sidesaddle on an inchworm. He recalled that last year a student had timidly slid a tardy term paper on Keynes under his door. The attached note said: "I'm sorry this assignment is late. I tried to fix up the essay at the last minute, but ended up ruining it. I hope that this will be satisfactory." There it is in a nutshell.

But the lecture. He would have to get back to it. He was a

few sentences short of a full script – like twenty pages. Did he really know twenty pages' worth about Innis? Or about anything? Not bloody likely.

McLaughlin contemplated the unsullied white page in his typewriter with mounting horror. He shuffled some notes which, once intended to spark his thoughts, now seemed incomprehensible. He riffled some filing cards of dubious information left over years ago from his Ph.D. thesis, and marvelled that he'd ever obtained the degree. I'm a fraud, he thought, rising and pacing the floor. I don't know enough and have no confidence in what I do know. I always thought that after the Ph.D. thrash I'd have time to get an education, but maybe I never will. He went upstairs for a fresh pack of cigarettes, returned, lit one, and found another still burning in the ashtray. He sharpened six pencils, then fiddled with one and broke it. He prayed the telephone would ring. It didn't. On his calendar he counted the days left before the lecture. Had he misplaced some notes? Scrabbling around in a desk drawer, he found a (lapsed) life insurance policy and read through its fine print with amazement at its evasive venality, but still wished he'd kept up the payments. A slow count of the knobs and buttons on his old dictaphone revealed the number thirteen and the fact that he had no blank tapes. Walking around the basement again, he inspected the electric meters and discovered that he didn't know what the numbers meant at all. McLaughlin rubbed his forehead and cursed. He picked up his waste-paper basket, found no apparent place to empty it, and put it back. Changing the kitty litter afforded him a long perusal of an old newspaper under the cat's box. Then he realized that he'd have to go out to the garbage bin, which he did, although forgetting the overflowing waste-paper basket. He was about to sit down on the back steps to contemplate his next paragraph when it started to rain.

Back at his desk, he fumbled in his pocket for a pair of clippers and snipped at his fingernails, reasoning that short nails facilitate typing. Resolutely J.T. resisted pulling off a sock

92

and having a go at his toenails. This brave act of cosmic insurgency so stirred him that he addressed the typewriter once again. He cracked his knuckles. Under his fumbling fingers a sentence began to emerge. "The significance of the technology of the cod fisheries is not dissimilar to that of the transportation system of the fur-trading companies." A sentence! He stared at it with the kind of holy awe with which Moses must have gazed at his transcription of the First Commandment. Somehow, it had to be admitted, old Moses had the better of it, whatever his special access to divine advantage. Ripping the sheet out of the typewriter and angrily crumpling it, he looked at his self-winding watch. It had stopped. As he twisted its stem impatiently he recalled the sundial on the campus of the University of Saskatchewan, which he'd walked by almost every day during his undergraduate years in Saskatoon; the face bore the inscription:

> I am a shadow
> So art thou.
> I mark time.
> Doest thou?

McLaughlin groaned and ground his teeth. It's just possible, he thought, that I'm losing my grip. Is my brain turning into peanut butter?

Footsteps behind him.

"Hi, Dad. You didn't say good night to me."

Davie. He swept the child into his arms. "I thought you were asleep long ago."

"Nope."

"Did I remember to tell you today . . .?"

". . . that I love you!" chorused his son. It was a little family ritual. J.T. recalled with feelings of guilt that it had been many days since he'd said it to Jossy. Why is it that the older children become, the harder it is to express reality to them? Or are teenagers just increasingly like you, and there-

93

fore harder to deal with on the inner level of repressed adult childishness?

Davie grinned. "Are you playing with your typewriter, Dad? I wish I could play with it like you do. That would be neat fun."

"It isn't always neat. There are times when it gives you the galloping wowsers. Come on, I'll carry you back up to bed."

As they ascended the stairs, Davie said, "I've been thinking about what you told me about where babies come from."

"Really?"

"Yup. I liked that part about how the Dad puts the seed in the Mom and the babies start to grow. That tickled my mind."

"I'm glad."

"So I've been wondering, next time you and Mom decide to make a baby, could I watch?"

"Well, now, that's more of a grownup's thing than a kid's thing. That's more of a special and private happening, not for watching, but more just inside the family."

"Aren't I in the family?"

"Of course you are, but I meant, um–"

"So I'd just sit and watch, and I'd promise to be *very* quiet."

"Maybe I should tell you more about that when you're older, or when we go to Grampa's farm some time to see the lambs or the piglets or the little guys like that when they arrive in the spring. Some of this gets a bit complicated."

"Why, Dad?"

"I–I don't know. Probably it shouldn't, but it just does."

"Gee. It's like Mom says, sometimes you're hard to follow. You don't always make sense, you know what I mean? Fathers aren't always as clear as T.V. programs."

"You may be right. But you've got to string along with me, boy, because I'm still new at being a father and they don't teach it in school. Just like you're learning to be a kid, I'm still learning to be a Dad, and I'm not sure I've got the hang of it yet."

"But you got lots of practice with Jossy and Rob, didn't you? They're *much* older than me."

"Maybe it takes even more practice than that, Davie. Sometimes I think it must take about twenty years. And by that time the kids are all grown up."

"You're doing okay, Dad."

"Thanks, pal. I'm trying. Now pop into bed."

"And you'll read me a story? How about 'Muggins Mouse'?"

"Haven't got time for that tonight, sport. Sorry, but I'm working. Let's get you tucked in again."

"Tell me a shorter story, then, one of your own. Or make me up a poem about monsters."

"Monsters? Well, let's see now." J.T. often quoted any old poem from memory so that Davie would enjoy the rhythm and dash of the language. Once, recently, he'd recited his best partial recollection of "The Charge of the Light Brigade," realizing that his son comprehended very little of it, but did relish the stirring meter. And often he resorted to playful nonsense verse, which he made up by the lineal yard to delight the child's innocent ear. This was what he decided to try now. "Here we go then. Hang on tight around the sharp curves, and I will Ogden your Nash and twiddle your Tennyson."

"Yeah. Great. I like 'twiddle.'"

"So do I. Now listen:

> One evening the bold Snuffelluphagus
> Complained of a lack of asparagus.
> 'How can we be certain of a strong third-act curtain,
> And will the cook please get off her phisnaragus?'
> Now the Snuffelluphagus was purple,
> Also crimson from topple to turple,
> Although in his heart, no matter how smart
> He tried to be, the result would be murple."

"What's murple, Dad?"

"Sort of a gracklish colour, I think, only mixed."
"Uh-huh."
J.T. pressed on:

> "And if constables gave tickets
> To pickets lurking in thickets,
> Doesn't thou also know totally naught
> About mouses and brabdgeous awful dry rot
> Or fromageous glistening grinkets?"

"Does 'grinkets' really rhyme with 'thickets'?"
"Well enough. It'll have to do."
"Okay, but I think you lost the Snuffelluphagus."
"He does have a tendency to wander off, but wait for it.

> "Now the calorific griffle,
> Twenty per cent (minimum) piffle,
> Was divisible only by eleven . . ."

J.T. reeled off several more snappy but meaningless stanzas, and then rounded toward a coda:

> "So it is essential, as everyone knows,
> To keep strict account of one's toes,
> Making absolutely certain
> That the perologist merkin
> Yields numbers consistent with snooze.
> And that, none the worse for our woes,
> Is how we preserve our wee toes,
> And thus we admonish the cold gin and tonish
> That wankle the glip pantyhose.
> From the Snuffelluphagus.

"The end. Now go to sleep, okay?"
"Gee, Dad, that's probably the best poem for bedtime I ever heard."

"Good. It did have a certain ring to it, eh?"

"But you know what?"

"No, what, Davie?"

"Well, it seemed to be all about animals and toes and life, you know? But I wasn't sure I understood it all."

"I wasn't entirely sure myself, pal, but that's the way life is, sometimes. Good night."

10

Two days later, as McLaughlin was walking from the college to the library, Nalorian bounded up and fell into stride beside him.

"Morning, Nalorian. How are you?"

"Going grand, J.T., just grand. What a splendid autumn sun! Look at the colours in the leaves. What golden, mellow weather. Makes you rejoice to be alive."

"I guess it does. Tell me, Nobby, are you always so almighty cheerful?"

"Why not? But I'm not particularly cheerful. I'm just natural, an appreciator, an enjoyer. I didn't invent this world, McLaughlin, I merely revel in it. How could a sane man do otherwise? Look at that sky; feel that sun. I don't have a care in the world. Do you?"

"Do I? Jeez. Too right, I do. I have bills, debts, and an overload of teaching; I have a Chairman asking pointedly what I've published lately, and as for this public lecture on Innis, gawd only knows what I'm going to do about that. Slash my wrists, probably."

"Did anybody ever suggest that you fuss and fret too much? You do, for a fact. Relax. Enjoy. Do what you have to do. Do it briskly, and do your best. That's all. That's all anyone can expect. And then 'go with the flow,' as the kids say; ride with the tide and Bob's your uncle. No problem."

"No problem, eh? Fawk. It's just possible, Nobby, that you may be wrong. The old saying is, an optimist is simply a guy who doesn't understand the situation. My situation is less than easy, believe me. My nerves are shot. I'm climbing walls. And you come on all Dale Carnegie and positive thinking like some overzealous clown. I can't stand it."

"There is something to be said for thinking positively. To

paraphrase Descartes, '*As* I think, therefore I am.' Or as Kurt Vonnegut said, 'Most people mess up their lives by thinking the wrong thoughts.'"

"Aw, knock it off, Nobby."

"Merely trying to get your attention, J.T. Merely trying to stretch you a bit. In my opinion, you worry too much, and dare too little. It's a typically Canadian habit. You're always circling the wagons and buying insurance before you see an Indian, and the Indians may not be hostile. They may be bringing you flowers."

They walked a while in silence.

"Anyway, about Teitelbaum," essayed Nalorian.

"What about him?"

"I want to thank you for putting me in touch with him. He's a painter after my own heart, one I admire. When I phoned him the other night, he told me he was leaving town for the winter, to Phoenix or some such, but he lined me up with another painter friend of his named Ed 'Horn' Hopwood, who was most helpful."

"Horn," J.T. exclaimed. "Good old Horn Hopwood. I knew him in high school in Regina. Is he here? In Toronto? I didn't know that. It's been years."

"He's here, all right. Doing very well, too, I gather. Thinks Teitelbaum is Rembrant. Hopwood is selling tolerably well on his own, with a show coming up soon at Gallery Moos, but to make ends meet he's managing a bar-restaurant on Bloor Street West, and he's given me a good deal on renting a loft over the restaurant as studio space. It's a very amusing set up. Amateur strip tease contests in the bar every Wednesday night, good food, a disco in the basement, and a bit of gambling action in a back room. A jazz band sits in Saturday afternoons. Just my kind of place. I really think I'm going to enjoy living in Toronto."

"I'll be damned. I've lived here for years, and I didn't even know that Horn was around. Here you are in town only a few weeks, and you've discovered a place I didn't know existed."

"But I didn't do it. You are the one who gave me Teitelbaum's phone number, McLaughlin. You are the one with the connections. If you don't use them, so be it; somebody will. You say you know Horn?"

"Sure. In high school, he was a buddy of my friend Zinger, the Prince Albert flash, the famous western journalist. But I haven't seen Horn in twenty years."

"Lovely man, Horn. You must come over to my studio some night, and get reacquainted."

"Be glad to. Yeah."

"In fact, J.T., when we've done our chores in the library, why don't we have lunch together to pursue this, say about twelve-thirty?"

"Well, sure, Nobby. How be I meet you in the Faculty Club?"

"Not on your bloody life! The Faculty Club, he says. Have you no respect for your stomach, J.T.? Do you have no idea of food at all? You'll kill yourself, man, if you try to eat those cardboard sandwiches. I didn't work all my life, let me tell you, to become a Professor in order to abuse my gut on such vulgar indigestibles at lunch. One has standards, you must realize. So meet me in the parking lot at twelve-thirty and we'll zip over to Gaston's for a proper repast."

"After only a few weeks in Toronto, you seem to know all the right spots."

"Of course. I make it my business to know. Do you think we are going to live twice? Do you think, since there's no second chance, that we should subsist on peanut butter sandwiches? Not bloody likely. Damned if I'm willing to roll over and settle for a Coke and a hamburger when Chablis and bouillabaisse are available for the taking."

"Uh-huh. But on an academic salary, I don't normally lunch on pheasant-under-glass. Haven't been able to afford a decent Chablis in months, and I'm surprised, frankly, if you can. Just champagne and caviar all the way, with you, is it?"

"Pretty much, yes. I've never found money to be a problem."

"You haven't. Okay, Professor Rockefeller, and you also have an oil well in your back garden. How convenient."

"You misunderstand. I'll never be rich, it's just that long ago I decided not to be poor. Being poor is a mug's game. No point to it; no need for it. If I spent as much time as most teachers do in passively moaning about my financial plight, I'd be on my uppers. I'd be scraping. But that's no way to live. So I long ago decided to devote my surplus time to expanding my income rather than to bitching about the limitations of my salary. I get out and hustle. I've always picked up some consulting work, partly for business and partly for governments. They don't have enough answers. Who has? And they don't know that I don't have all the answers, that nobody does, but by the time they find that out, I've already sent them my bill for a scholarly survey of human ignorance, plus a plausible set of my own recommendations. I know more than they do, there's the point. Long after they realize that I can't provide everything they hoped to learn, I've already cashed my consulting cheque and moved on. No problem. I simply keep bobbing and weaving. And then, of course, I flog my paintings."

"Another gold mine there, I suppose."

"Surprisingly enough, there is. Modest but steady. I've never had any trouble moving a few canvases. How many Professors of Economics and recognized authorities on central banking are there who can deliver a consultant's report at nine a.m. and also offer paintings for the head office walls before noon, plus have dealers for their paintings pushing up the prices for their work in London and New York? It's all very neat. Art is very like economics, you see. It runs to impressions and fashions, and nobody knows whether the work is any good or not till some other 'expert' tells them – and none of the other 'experts' want to let the side down or blow the gaff by admitting that he's not sure either. It's all hype and con. It's merely a question of climbing onto the escalator of eager expectations among the ignorant rich, stroking and reassuring them that if the price is high it must be quality, and if the demand ever slackens, you just rig the market, double your prices, stare them down, and dare them to disagree with you. If they doubt you, hike the price again. And when your credit is low, order champagne."

"Nobby, I almost believe you."

"It would be a mistake to doubt me, J.T."

"And as you giggle your way to the bank, you also drop in at the charcuterie to pick up a few things for gastronomic delectation, is that it? Next you'll be telling me that you're a gourmet chef on the side."

"Yes. I get almost as much pleasure from my cooking as I do from my painting. But cooking is more demanding. At the stove, you've got to deliver the goods."

"It would almost be a relief to me, Nobby, to hear that you ever made a mistake when opening a can or ordering in pizza."

"Ah, well, the first principle of food preparation is never to own a can opener."

"Or a cookbook either, I suppose."

"Not at all. A good cookbook is a thing of beauty and a joy before liqueurs. The only teachers we have, after all, are experience and books. I fumbled with cooking for a long time. But everything began to come together when I discovered the *How Not to Miss the Cocktail Hour Cookbook* by some person named Lowman. A great boon."

"I do admit that Trish and I regard the cocktail hour as semi-sacred. That's when we do our best talking. There's the North American motto, I suppose: 'The family that has cocktails together, stays together.' Liquor as the cement of domesticity, and all that."

"Exactly. What better foundation for domestic civility than shared vices which ease communication? Time's short. I like to fill every hour, and with the best. Bumbling about with silences and the second-rate suits some people, but it doesn't suit Nubar Nalorian. Chances are we may not live forever."

"Well, no, not forever. It's tomorrow that I'm worried about."

"Tomorrow may be too late, J.T. It's what you do today

that matters. Learning is what you do in your teens. Experimenting is what you do in your twenties. Planning and solidifying come in your thirties. From then on out, you should wallow in it and cash it all in, break the bank. Laugh and enjoy the free lunch."

"There's no free lunch."

"But there is. You simply have to know where to find it. There's *lots* of it, in reassuring abundance, if you learn how to make the maître d' think you're doing him a favour by accepting it. Call it advertising, call it imagination, call it confidence tricking, there's no shortage of free lunch or of waiters to cater to you. Keep your standards high enough, demand the best, and a whimsical fate finally flings it into your lap, if you're cunning."

On the steps of the library, McLaughlin stopped to light a cigarette, and eyed Nalorian quizzically.

"Speaking of bonuses and perks, I gather you've met Ms. Bromley," said J.T. "She's also a student of mine. Is she doing good work for your course?"

"Work? Lord love us, Boffy doesn't know anything about work. But she has a certain primitive charm about her, and I've found her worth-cultivating."

"Or ploughing, perhaps?"

"That too. Oh, come on, J.T., you know the type. Boffy showed up in my office one day trying on one of the oldest cons in the game. 'I'd do anything for an A, Professor, *anything*.' She was giving me the tease, playing cutesy and generally being the naive and incompetent would-be temptress. So I told her to knock it off. You can't con an old con man. But she persisted. You know how she is? Quite sweet, but silly. And when she kept at it like a Barbie Doll in heat, I called her bluff. I merely grabbed her by the old filet mignon, and put her out of her misery. No big fuss. You're not squeamish about that sort of thing, surely?"

"Not really. But you ought to be careful, Nobby. Secrets are hard to keep on this campus."

"How well I know. On any campus. More's the pity. This

sort of thing has cost me jobs and tenure in more than one university in the past, I can tell you."

"Is that so? Boffy told me only that you were, um, painting her."

"I see. I'll have to caution her about that. All in the noble cause of art, you understand. She does have certain attributes which lend themselves to painterly expression, I'm sure you'll agree."

"Yeah. I'm just suggesting that you exercise some caution, that's all."

"Caution. Quite so. Never was one of my strong points. But I do get your message."

"Nalorian, the thing is, you're so goddam–excessive."

"True. It's been said of me before."

"So take it easy. That's all I'm saying."

"Wasn't it only a few minutes ago that I was suggesting the same thing to you?"

"In a different way, Nobby; in a different context."

"Yes. You may be right. Anyway, I'll see you later for lunch, agreed? At twelve-thirty?"

"Well, as I said, I'm not sure I can afford a big blow out at Gaston's."

"I'm buying."

"I'm available."

* * *

Patricia McLaughlin left the Courtyard Cafe, having enjoyed a smart and sumptuous lunch with some friends, and strolled east along Bloor Street toward Creeds. As she stopped to look into the window of Birks jewellery, she was aware that a tall man had stopped behind her. Avoiding his reflected gaze in the window, she walked on, satisfied and by no means surprised that she had attracted attention, but somewhat impatient with would-be advances from men who didn't know either how to flirt or to be decisive. Probably a businessman, she decided. Staid. Nothing worse than the crude come-on, she thought, except the faltering come-on. She increased her pace.

"Mrs. McLaughlin."

"Yes?"

"Surely you remember me. Thornton Naugle." He raised his snap-brimmed trilby just slightly.

"But, Mr. President, of course."

Thornton P. Naugle had been President of Chiliast U. for three years. A Canadian who had made good in the United States, with a reputation as a fast gun and a tough guy, he'd been brought back to Toronto after a deanship in a Massachusetts college to bring some fiscal order to Chiliast during a time of financial crunch. So far he had achieved little except the computerization of the administration at Smyton Hall and the alienation of most of the faculty. His office door remained firmly shut most days. He seldom mixed with the professoriate, seemed to know little and care much less what they were doing, ignored the Faculty Association, and bullied his Deans with a ceaseless flow of curt memoranda. A bachelor, he fascinated many of the little mongeese among faculty wives with his cobra-hooded eyes. His unkempt mat of iron grey hair contrasted oddly with a thin black moustache which marched across his frequently curled upper lip like a dark centipede. Naugle regarded himself as the Errol Flynn of academia. His six-foot-four frame was carried pencil straight in a not unsuccessful pose of power, but he had all the humour and subtlety of a refrigerator.

"I look forward to the pleasure of your company," he said with a naked leer, "when your husband delivers his public lecture. It promises to be a notable occasion."

"Oh, that. My husband carries off these little events like the Prince of Wales among the Boy Scouts," smiled Trish with more loyalty than conviction. "But I didn't suppose you'd be there, President Naugle."

"I will indeed. Couldn't miss it. I've arranged for a number of dignitaries and potential, hmm, benefactors from the alumni to be in attendance, in connection with the fund-raising drive. If all goes well, and enough money is forthcoming, we may be able to found a new college named after him."

"Really? How nice. J.T. will be most enormously pleased. 'McLaughlin College' does have a nice sound to it."

"No, no, I'm afraid you misunderstand me. Innis. Innis College is what I have in mind. But since you raise the subject, it wouldn't be out of the question to consider your husband for the position of Principal. If all goes well. You do see what I mean, Mrs. McLaughlin–may I call you Patricia? My voice carries some weight with the Board of Governors on such matters, you'll appreciate. Why don't we just pop around the corner and, hmm, have a cup of coffee together. I could explain my fund-raising plans to you and how I might be prepared to be, hmm, useful to Professor McLaughlin."

"I'm not sure that I know of a coffee shop on this immediate block, Mr. President."

"Call me Thorn. Do. And if we were to walk just a block or so to the west, we could stop in at my apartment. In addition to the presidential residence, I keep a small retreat in the Colonnade, just as a more convenient pied-à-terre for times when the burdens of office begin to press. I'm sure you'd find it, uh, relaxing. And I could elaborate my hopes for Innis College and your esteemed husband."

Patricia was no fool. She got the message, but wasn't about to play post-office or spin the bottle like a teenybopper merely for the sake of shabby institutional politics. Suppressing a desire to use Mae West's line, 'Is that a gun in your pocket, or are you just glad to see me?' she giggled and said, "Coffee would be nice, Thorn, and I certainly appreciate your interest–in my husband–but I'm afraid I have a dental appointment."

"Perhaps you'd like to have a drink later?"

"I might, except that after I get drilled I'll have to simply scamper home to make dinner."

"I must say that I envy your dentist."

"Now, Thorn, the things you *say*. You're positively wicked."

"Am I? It's easy enough, you know. Anyway, tell Professor McLaughlin that I wish him every success with his lecture. It's important to me. I'm bringing along some very important alumni for this event. I hope it will be an academic showpiece."

"I'm sure it will be. I'll tell him. J.T. is so very *cle*ver at lecturing."

"It's, hmm, a consummation devoutly to be wished, as they say. Good luck to him."

* * *

Later that afternoon, after his last class, McLaughlin encountered the mournful presence of Grimsby in the parking lot.

"Where you headed, Bert?"

"Nowhere. Home, I guess. But the damned car won't go. I think I'll walk."

"What's the trouble? Let's have a look. This your machine here? Tell me what you were doing."

Grimsby explained the symptoms. McLaughlin got the hood up and poked around uncertainly.

"I'm not really a mechanic, but we might be able to sort something out here. Turn her over again, Bert. That's it. Whoa! Wait, I smell gas. I think you've flooded it, flooded it silly. Let me get the air cleaner off – got a screwdriver? – yeah, we'll just poke the carburettor and open the butterfly. Sure. She's flooded. We'll let her sit for a moment to drain. Where you off to tonight, Grimmers? Got a date?"

"Me? Don't make jokes. I was just going back to my apartment to heat up a T.V. dinner when the damned motor wouldn't catch and I started to curse it."

"That won't help much."

"I know, J.T., I know. As Thoreau said, we all lead lives of quiet desperation, but sometimes it gets a little noisy."

"Working on your textbook most nights, I suppose?"

"No, I've almost given up on that. It doesn't seem to want to go any more than this baulky car does."

"So how do you spend your evenings, Bert?"

Grimsby popped a peppermint and stared vacantly at the motor. "I used to sit in my study, writing, or trying to write. For the last few months, truth to tell, I've just been making notes. Filling up filing cards and bits of paper, making notes for articles I'll probably never write. Laundry lists of footnotes for unfinished pages; shopping lists for the mind. Lately I've moved the T.V. into my study. Mostly I stare at T.V., often with the sound off."

"Really? What's the point of that?"

"Point? None at all. Frequently I just watch hockey games."

"You don't! Hell, Bert, you're one of the few real scholars in this department. I always think of you as scribbling away furiously at serious stuff."

"No. Hockey games. It passes the time. Numbs the mind. Sometimes I even watch hockey games involving expansion teams."

"I can't stand it."

"It's all true. Why not? Bill Hewitt seems to me increasingly tolerable. That worries me sometimes, but it may be preferable to staring at blank pages. When I find myself starting to like Harold Ballard, I'll know it's time to cut my wrists."

"Krist, Grimmers, don't talk like that. Here, try the starter again while I hold this gismo open."

"Do you really know what you're doing, J.T.?"

"Nah, but I know a little about the theory even if I'm no great hell with a wrench."

"Personally, I never knew one end of a wrench from the other, and these days I find most theory a bore."

The motor spun, sputtered, almost caught, sputtered again, stopped. Grimsby hit the starter again and again with no result. The motor declined to catch. A few more twirls and the starter slowed down, growled, and died.

"Would that be battery trouble, J.T.? Last time I heard a

noise like that they told me it was a dead battery. We'd better give up."

"Not on your life. The battery is tired, all right, but I have some booster cables in the back of my Camaro. We'll zing it with the cables."

J.T. brought his car over and put it nose to nose with Grimsby's recalcitrant machine. He opened the hood and hooked up the cables at his end, leaving his motor running.

"Now, which is the positive pole on your battery, Bert?"

"Gee, I'm never very sure about that sort of thing. I thought you said you knew what you were doing? Maybe we should just leave it and I'll call a garage."

"Never fear, buddy, never fear. I'm pretty sure this must be the negative, so we'll just snap this on here. . . . Right! Now, when I attach the other cable to the positive pole I'll shout and you punch the starter, okay?"

Grimsby nodded and slid behind the wheel.

"Go!" J.T. shouted. As Bert turned the key there was a great loud zap, a startling puff of blue flame and an impressive shower of sparks followed by an acrid burning smell.

"Was that supposed to happen, J.T.?"

"Not exactly. Jeez, what I've done, I'm afraid, is reversed the polarities, with my positive on your negative. I may have blown the circuit and melted a wire or two."

"I guess it isn't going to start then?"

"Afraid not. Shit, I'm really sorry. I was *sure* I had the cables on the right poles, but–"

"Never mind. It doesn't matter. This sort of thing happens to me all the time. Probably I'd have had to call a tow truck anyway. Could you give me a lift home and I'll call from there?"

"Sure. But damn, I really do apologize. I could have sworn that was the positive. How could I make a mistake like that?"

McLaughlin continued to express his well-intended regrets as they got into his car and rolled out of the parking lot. They drove for a while in silence.

Pulling up in front of Grimsby's apartment building, J.T.

said limply, "Well, at least I got you home to your dinner. Have a nice evening."

"Thanks a lot. You wouldn't want to come up to my place for a drink?"

"Nice of you to suggest it, but I've got to get home. Trish will be waiting. Another time."

"Uh-huh. You're lucky, you know that, J.T.? Patricia is a fine girl. What I mean is, you've got something to look forward to. To go home to. When you live alone, there's not much, uh, not much punctuation to your day."

"Aw, Bert, I'd invite you home with me, but I'm already late and we're going out tonight anyway. To the theatre. Some Pinter thing at the Tarragon."

"Pinter. Don't you get enough of that sort of vacuity every day without watching it voluntarily in the evening?"

"Well, Trish got the tickets. She seems to think that kind of stuff is profound."

"Bless her credulous little heart. Profound. Themes and variations on emptiness and solitude. To me, solitude is just a form of insulation from disappointment. But if you like that sort of thing."

"Yeah. So I'll be seeing you. Take care."

"Right. And thanks again, J.T. You must let me give you my views on Pinter sometime soon."

"You bet," said McLaughlin with a weak smile. "Absolutely."

11

McLaughlin was hard at work on Monday morning when the Chairman appeared at his door.

Greetings and affabilities were exchanged, then Wright came straight to his point. "The department, as you may know, has a guest arriving tomorrow about noon. Professor Giroux from the Sorbonne. You'll like Giroux. I'll be much obliged to have you meet him and greet him, there's a good chap, since I'm rather tied up tomorrow. Confirm his time of arrival with my secretary, won't you, and then pop out to the airport to pick him up. Can't have these dignitaries flying into town without proper attention, you know."

McLaughlin coughed. He had a class till eleven, and had arranged a boozy lunch with Cutty at the Duke of York. "Actually, Dr. Wright, I'm not sure that I can be available tomorrow."

"You do have a car, don't you? Good. I don't much enjoy driving anymore myself. And your afternoon seminar doesn't begin till four. I checked." He smiled.

"Yes, but—"

"Splendid. No problem then. Give old Giroux my regards, deposit him at the Park Plaza, and tell him I look forward to seeing him in the evening. He's a decent sort. We've booked him to stay on for the symposium. He knew our late colleague Harry Johnson, and doesn't mind the occasional nip of cognac himself. Maybe you could pour a drop into him. Just keep the receipts, and the department will pick up the tab. My pleasure."

J.T. found that he had nothing to say. He did not heave a sigh; he threw it with all his might at the retreating back of the Chairman. Still, he had to admit that the old bugger was canny.

Another man entered. "Morning, Professor." J.T. looked up. The salutation was from Mohammed Zadran Khan.

"Mo! Just the man I wanted to see. Have a chair. I'm going to let you in on an opportunity to meet the celebrated Professor Giroux of La Sorbonne. You have a car, don't you? No? Never mind, you can use mine. What I want you to do is, tomorrow just before noon. . . ." He explained the details of the task.

The student objected that he had a class with Grimsby, but J.T. told him to cut it, insisting that Mo shouldn't miss the chance to meet a scholar like Giroux, since one never knew when such a contact might prove useful. With reluctance, Mohammed agreed.

As they parted McLaughlin congratulated himself that maybe he was getting the hang of it. "I might still have a promising career after all." If he'd had a moustache he'd have twirled it.

The next day, however, did not work out quite as well as he'd hoped.

He had given Mo the keys to his Camaro at eleven-thirty and sent him off to Malton airport. Following a long, liquid lunch with Cutty, McLaughlin returned to his office just before three o'clock to find a disconsolate Mohammed sitting on the floor outside his door.

"I've been waiting for you, Professor."

"To return the keys? You could have left them in the car. But good man, Mo, and thank you. Everything went well, I trust? I hope you enjoyed meeting our visitor."

"Not exactly."

"No? Why is that?"

"The fact is, we had a bit of an accident. On the highway."

"Krist! I hope–" McLaughlin's eyes widened as comprehension began to dawn– "I hope my car wasn't involved?"

"I'm afraid it was involved all over the road. I'm sorry."

"Arr!" J.T. toppled into his chair with his head in his hands and his heart in mouth. "Sit down, Mo. Tell me the worst. Slowly. Tell me."

"Well, I got out to the airport okay, and found Professor Giroux. I fetched his baggage and everything, and when we got out to the parking lot he broke the seal on a bottle of duty-free cognac he was carrying. We each had a swig of it. He said he wanted a moment to reorient himself after the long flight. Offered me another pull on the bottle while he asked me a number of questions and reset his watch. Suddenly he demanded to know where the Chairman was, Dr. Wright. I told him I had no idea. '*Quelle indignité*,' he said, and took another slug of the cognac. It seemed impolite to let him drink alone. Hennessy Five Star, it was, and not bad stuff."

"Spare me," J.T. wailed. "Just get to the accident."

"Well, I'm all right, and Professor Giroux is all right. He's at the hotel."

"Great. Hooray. But the car. Tell me about my car."

"I'm coming to that. So everything was fine until we got to where the airport road merges with the 401. Traffic was fairly heavy. A fat guy in a Mercedes hit his brakes too hard just as we were entering the main thruway and I swerved, and maybe I was leaning harder on the horn than on the brakes, but anyway I guess I didn't slow down enough, and I smacked him a pretty good one. With the left front fender. When we both pulled over and got out of the cars, the fat guy expressed considerable disapproval of me in words I wouldn't care to repeat. His rear end was stove in a bit, on his car I mean. He took down my–your–licence number. Then when the police arrived–"

"Police? Oh my gawd!"

"They asked to see my driver's licence, which proved another bit of a problem."

"Why?"

"You didn't ask me whether I had a driver's licence."

"You mean–"

"Nope."

"Holy shit! I can't stand it."

"Then they told me I had to take a breathalyzer test."

"And you blew–"

"Right through the top."

"Sonofabitch! Enough, Mo. Tell me the rest tomorrow. Sufficient unto the day." A small moan escaped J.T.'s white lips. "Just give me the keys. Is the car in the lot?" He paused. "Say, if you popped the cork on the breathalyzer, why didn't they detain you? Why aren't you in jail for kristsake?"

"The prospect didn't much appeal to me. My family is very strict Moslem, you know, and would look with extreme disfavour on any son who used alcohol. They'd be sure to cut off my funds if they knew. So I split."

"You–?"

"Escaped. While the cops were preoccupied with the fat tub who was ranting about the damages to his precious fucking Mercedes, I jumped back into your heap and split. Made a few fancy moves through the traffic before they realized I was gone, darted out the first exit I saw, took side-streets to the hotel to dump old Giroux–he'd never budged from the front seat–and came right here."

"Sweet suffering Jesus, Mo, you're a wanted man! Don't you understand? You're a fugitive from justice!"

"No sweat. They don't know my name. It's not *my* licence number they've got." He grinned, and let the point sink in.

It sank in cold and deep. McLaughlin closed his eyes for a few writhing seconds before he said, "Out. Go. We'll talk again tomorrow, unless I'm in the slammer. Out."

When Mohammed had drifted away, J.T. rang a secretary and arranged to have his four-o'clock seminar cancelled. His hand was unsteady as he lit a cigarette. He phoned his insurance company and learned, as he'd fully expected, that apart from his liabilities relating to the crunched Mercedes he had no hope in hell of collecting for his own damages if the driver of his car had no valid licence, drunk or sober, and drunk helped not at all. His insurance agent told him, in short, lots of luck, but no claim. Zilch.

With increasing desperation, and visions of endless bills and liabilities ricocheting through his horrified mind, McLaughlin then phoned Dr. Wright's office and unburdened himself. "I need help," J.T. pleaded.

Wright listened to the long story with some sympathy and even a few suppressed chuckles. "No problem, McLaughlin," said the Chairman. "The university has a general insurance floater policy which ought to cover such distressing contingencies. But, my dear boy, wouldn't it have been better to go out to the airport yourself? You'd like Giroux. I told you he was partial to cognac. There are times when one for the road is preferable to being home and dry, isn't it? Awrumph-umph." He hung up.

McLaughlin then telephoned any number of Vice-Presidents and Assistant Provosts in the administrative offices of Smyton Hall, in increasingly frenzied quest of how to get at the university's general floater insurance. Finally, a secretary, who seemed better informed than any of the army of bureaucrats he'd yet talked to, advised him that he'd require the signature of the Dean of his division before the red tape could begin to unravel toward reimbursement.

J.T. looked up the Dean's number and dialled. Eventually a switchboard person permitted him, on the fourth attempt, to speak to the executive assistant of an Associate Dean. This snotty functionary gave him to believe that all he need do would be to fill out Standard Claim Form BSF-427-R2D2-A, stating the particulars of the university business on which his vehicle had been engaged, and further stating the number of the driver's licence of the person in charge of the vehicle, plus the driver's university staff personnel number.

"But the driver was a student of mine. He doesn't *have* a personnel number. He was merely doing a favour for me, and for the university. A student, you see?"

"In that case, we might be able to get away with his driver's licence number only, and a letter in triplicate-countersigned by your Chairman, of course-indicating the nature of his business on behalf of-"

"But I'm trying to tell you, he doesn't *have* a driver's licence!"

"Oh my. Pity, that. I'm afraid I must then suggest to you that no claim on any form is possible. I'm afraid we're wasting each other's time."

"But you can't-I mean, you've *got* to-look here, you can't leave me dangling like this!"

"You're not dangling, Professor. You have no legal thread, I fear, from which to suspend any application for compensation. Now if you'll excuse me, I have other things to do. Good day." The phone went dead.

Some cold shivers that run up spines are more icy than others. This one would have snap-frozen a blast furnace. McLaughlin faced the bleak realization that he was up a very fecal creek without a paddle.

Munching on a fingernail, and with visions of debtors' prison flitting through his tormented head, J.T. stumbled out to the parking lot to inspect the automotive remains. The Camaro looked worse than sad. The front left fender, he estimated, would cost at least four hundred to replace, and the grill and headlights krist knew how much more, before the owner of the Mercedes weighed in with his damages. The total would be enough to make an Alberta oilman blink.

In a hopeless rage, J.T. kicked at the crumpled fender. It fell off, plop, at his feet. He stared at it. Trying to repress an anguished moan, he picked it up.

With the heavy gnarled steel slung over his shoulder and his mind sagging with fatigue and despair, he marched out of the parking lot. The Dean's office was in the Arts Building, only half a block away. Shifting the disastrous fender, McLaughlin lurched down the corridor and approached the glass door behind which the Dean and the Associate Deans and their innumerable executive assistants and clerks lurked. He emitted several choice curses. Bunching his muscles, he heaved his burden of crunched metal as hard as he could at the Dean's door.

There was a sharp crash and jitter of broken glass. A filing clerk looked up in amazement, rolling his frightened eyes from the fender to what had been the door, to the sweating Professor who stood dishevelled and panting outside. McLaughlin, frazzled by emotion and physical relief, realized in a flash that it was more satisfying to be a hot gazoony with raw, outraged nerve ends, raving and tossing fenders, than to be a faceless clerk looking out of a shattered door with a slack jaw.

"I think," he assured himself as he shambled back down the hallway, "I think I just won a small one for the Gipper." He stopped and leaned on a wall. "Now when the hell am I going to win one for me?"

12

During the next two weeks the earth spun on its predictable axis while Grimsby continued to sulk, Nalorian worked out further variations on the *Kama Sutra* with Boffy, and Trish watched helplessly as J.T. drove himself to further distraction at his typewriter, cudgeling his torpid brain for something, anything, new to say in his unwanted public address.

But inevitably, the dreaded day of McLaughlin's lecture arrived. It was a warm if cloudy October afternoon. Leaves of brilliant burgundy, tangerine, and aubergine were underfoot as J.T. shuffled disconsolately toward West Hall and the appointed hour. The iridescent hues of sumptuous autumn might have seemed uplifting to some, but McLaughlin thought only that the sky looked ominous and that the dry crinkle of the spent leafage was like parchment, which was what his throat felt like.

On the previous evening, Cutty had taken McLaughlin out to tie one on, to get J.T.'s mind off his trials. The two of them had hoisted a few on the Park Plaza roof bar, and downed a few oysters as well as a quantity of Glenfiddich, before moving on to Joso's for supper. They'd rounded off the evening at one a.m. amid the noise of the Club 22, and J.T. was feeling a bit the worse for wear. To put a fine point on it, he had a mean, black, pounding hangover.

West Hall was jammed. Several formidable-looking ladies in vast hats were prominent in the front rows beside earnest Bay Street biggies from Noranda, Algoma, Argus, and the larger insurance companies, wearing three-piece pin-striped suits. A bulge of bankers nodded gravely to each other. From an aisle seat in the first row, President Thornton P. Naugle lavishly dispensed ivory smiles, handshakes, bountiful waves and murmurs of bonhomie while the cash register behind his eyes accurately rang up net worths and potential cash contributions like a Levantine rug merchant.

With five minutes to go, McLaughlin was surrounded by well-wishers. Cutty and Nalorian tried to reassure and calm him; Chairman Wright burbled inane goodwill. Boffy, Mo, and Mildred Mott reported that some students had turned out to lend support, members of his third- and fourth-year classes loyally filling the back rows, eager to beat their hands together in approbation of his every *bon mot*.

"Everything's under control," said Cutty.

"What could go wrong?" inquired Nalorian.

"It's all so exciting!" Mildred Mott trilled.

"Yeah," McLaughlin muttered. "Is there any goddam water at the lectern?"

"I'll check it out," Cutty smiled and scuttled off.

"Just look at all those frozen brontosauri in the front pews," McLaughlin observed with a shudder.

"Three minutes," cut in Nalorian. "Three minutes to glory and everything in going grand."

"Where's Trish?" J.T. asked.

"She's there beside the President," Grimsby replied. "I'm going in now to take my seat. Lots of luck."

"Thanks, Bert. How about that water? Has anyone got a glass?"

"Right here," Mildred chirped.

"Has anyone got anything stronger than water?"

"Help yourself," Nalorian grinned, proffering a silver flask of brandy.

"Good man, Nobby. Thanks. Look, what I really need is an aspirin. Bloody headache. It's all Cutty's fault from last night. I don't suppose anybody has an aspirin or a 222? If only those drums would stop beating! My head is really throbbing."

"No problem," Boffy said, rummaging in her purse and coming up with a small box of white pills. "Have one of these."

"Could I have two? I'm not sure how I'm going to get through all this. Yeah. Thanks a lot." McLaughlin extracted two tablets, and downed them with a gulp of water. "Okay. Now if you'd all just leave me to collect myself for a moment –thanks again–we'll soon get this show on the road. Go sit down. Yeah, I'm fine, Nobby, really I am. Thanks. I just need a moment to sort myself out. Everybody stop fussing, all right? In an hour I'll have all this behind me. Jeez. Is my head on straight, Cutty?"

"Just fine, buddy. I'm going out to find a chair. Take it easy. You'll do fine. Just dandy."

"Give 'em hell," Nalorian said. "Go get 'em!"

"Thanks, Nobby."

Dr. Wright strode to the platform and began his introduction. While he droned on, Mr. Zukowski emerged from the back of the hall and went down the aisle to where Cutty was sitting.

"Professor Cuttshaw, excuse me, but I think we may have a problem. Your friend McLaughlin doesn't seem to me at his ease, if you'll pardon my saying so. Do you think he's ill?"

"No, Mr. Zukowski, he's just nervous."

"I wonder, sir, whether it might not be more than that? He seems to be twitching rather unusually. Would there still be time, do you think, to halt these proceedings? I have the suspicion that something irregular is occurring here."

"Too late now, I think. Wright is finally rounding off his introduction."

"But I believe there may be something wrong, Professor Cuttshaw. I feel uneasy."

"Everybody does, Mr. Zukowski, everybody does on these occasions. Won't you have a chair?"

"No, thank you, sir, I'll just go back behind the stairs in case I may be of use later on."

"Very well, then." Cuttshaw settled back to hear what his friend had to say.

"It is abundantly clear," McLaughlin began, "that Harold

Innis was the greatest economist this country has produced. It was he who said, in connection with the boundaries and borders of our nation, which were defined by the water routes and limits of the fur trade, that Canada was created not in spite of, but because of, geography. Here is a fine nugget of truth."

There were a few more unrefined nuggets in the next few pages that he managed to stumble through, but none of the gold shone through. Few of the sentences seemed to click; McLaughlin's sandpaper throat couldn't quite scratch them off the page and launch them winging into the heavy atmosphere. He stopped for a gulp of water.

The next paragraph stared back at him from the manuscript. Somehow it seemed blurred. He blinked at it uncertainly. The turbulent river of his mind carried him close to the brink of the waterfall. He tried to cling to the rock of the lectern to prevent being swept over the Niagara into hysteric euphoria. But the lectern was not a rock. It seemed to be swooping and diving like a roller coaster.

"At this point, we must grapple with the opinion of Professor Carl Berger, one of the most perceptive commentators on the early innings, er, Innis. Berger suggests that the onions of the 1930 book. Did I say onions? That the origins of the 1930 velocipede. Why velocipede? Volume, of course, I meant to say volume. Are rooted in. In the earlier history of the CPR and the influence of Verigin. Um, Veblen. Thirsty Veblen, that is. Thorstein Veblen, you see?"

Nobody saw. But McLaughlin was beginning to see things, things he had never seen before. A warm tumescence seemed to expand his mind and push against his brain pan. Fireflies darted and frolicked in his cerebellum.

"Boffy? Which pills did you give Professor McLaughlin?" Mo asked.

"Which? I just reached into my purse and handed him some stuff."

"You sure it was aspirin? Seems to me I gave you some of

that angel dust for safekeeping the other night. Where did you put it?"

"Oh, I don't know. Probably it's at home. I think I put it – didn't I put it in the sugar bowl in the kitchen? Somewhere or other. Why?"

"I'm not sure, but I think you just dosed Professor McLaughlin. I think you slipped him a loaded whoopee pill."

"Do you really think so? I did have some genuine aspirin in my handbag here *somewhere*. Let me look again."

"You'd better. Otherwise, it may be Lucy-Innis-Sky with Diamonds any minute. But I guess it's too late now anyway. He may be winging."

He was. McLaughlin was in the swooping phase of a wild pharmaceutical loop-the-loop.

"Surely it is evident that, whichever way we worm the commotion. Worm. The contortion. Not worm. Not at all. Turn the equation. Obviously I meant – you must pardon me for reacting to the excruciating heat of this forceps – I meant to say, zwikkerhoozle. Clear as a fucking bell, of course. And thus we are confronted instantly by the force of the staples theology, er, thesis. And the insights of the banals. The canals. Not to mention the cod. Peace. Whatever."

A further swig of water did no good. As people began to wriggle in their chairs, and look at each other and at their feet, McLaughlin dimly perceived that something was going off the rails. He coughed a hopeful cough and tugged at his collar. But by now the divine fire of chemical illumination blazed through his anguished brain.

President Naugle shot searing looks at Wright, but the Chairman appeared to be hypnotized by some imperfection on the ceiling.

Confronted by the inferno behind his left eyeball, McLaughlin looked into the yawning abyss and plunged into it at a brisk gallop.

"We can therefore appreciate at one swell foop how lurching inspiration is not to be concabulated. Certainly. Not. You wear it in your head, you must realize, that to storm the later Innis, laterally if not bicamerally, requires a mind redolent, fragmented, and fragrant. With juniper. It's the berries, didn't I? And Blake knows more than Ogden Nash or Knowlton can. Can. Or malt does more, I mean to say, more than Milton cannot blindly, the prig bastard traitor. Isn't that irrefutably McLuhanesque, mechanically bridled? And his friend Donald Creighton hated biology and most biophones, but dissected frogs and became a choloric whistle, while neither H. Dumpty nor all of Eugene Forsey could transform Druids into a proper syllogism, sperm-like, into a whale. Ahab. Aye haben liebfrau mulch. Inuit be loverly? What a novel idea. But I will, with intense pleasure, meet Mr. Sartre or St. Karl for a shoot-out at the Brunswick Tavern any time you like, just as Dr. Johnson met Bishop Berkeley square-on with the toe of his hurty boot. Thus the Hudson's Bay Company, in creating our boundaries with ungentlemanly adventuring, deliberately delineated us from evil and temptation and from Tin Pan Alley, and caused Mordecai to lose his Duddy crevice moorings from Brian's diaper service, gingerly. And what if coffee is only thirty Wiebe per Dumont, would cock? You've got it, Peggy; it's all Fryed, if not mythically burnt, Norton, and up your Garp, I suggest. Respectfully. But who will plant, and who will harvest, the rampant black Mowat? Why aren't you taking notes, Robertson? Got another pebble in your mouth, eh? Never, I insist, never again are you likely to have revealed unto you where the white buffalo, whither the noble bison roam, or why the moose commonly loses one hundred sixteen pounds (or grams in ex-Celsius Deus) during rutting season, or the secret place where pumpkins go when they die. Perhaps the senate, Larry? Which seems as good a place as any to Swift the Yahoos whom I see bearing Donne upon me Wrighteously like an island, way Donne upon the Swanee River."

Wright took J.T.'s elbow and steered him off the platform. Cutty charged down the aisle and seized McLaughlin's other arm.

"Cuttshaw, for God's sake, get him out of here," Wright hissed.

"Cutty, I've been dosed," J.T. laughed. "Someone must have slipped me a doozy of a Finn, Mickey-wise. Isn't it pretty? The lights, I mean. Ravishing. If only Innis could have seen all this. So pretty. But why is your ear like that, Cutty, all neon and, you know, Camembert?"

"Take it easy, J.T., I'll get us out of here."

"But I like it here, Cutty. It's nice. If only Naugle's moustache wouldn't wink at me like that."

"I'll have your ass for this, McLaughlin," Naugle raged. "Your ass! See if I don't."

Watching all this from her seat, Boffy said, "I guess you were right, Mo. But McLaughlin is a good guy. He can take a joke."

"Yeah. But can Naugle?" asked Mo. "Can these other people? Listen to the bellowing of the gentle *haute bourgeoisie*. I've seen folks more calm and collected in the middle of the Calgary Stampede or a midnight concert by the Stones. Shit, Boffy, you've really done it."

"Professor Cuttshaw," urged Zukowski, "get him into the side hallway here. I've phoned for an ambulance."

"Damned good of you, Mr. Zukowski. Thanks." Cutty continued to shove his friend through the crowd toward the door.

"An ambulance?" inquired Chairman Wright. "Well done, Zukowski. Sort of a sic transit McLaughlin, eh? Awrrumph-umph-umph."

"I may be having a flipping *fit*," said Trish. "I may be having a terminal attack of the screaming *wow*zers. Cutty, you've got to get rid of all these goddam *peo*ple!"

"Would you like an aspirin, Mrs. McLaughlin?" Boffy asked.

"Adjourned," Wright shouted. "I declare the meeting adjourned. Refreshments will be served in the Croft Chapter House – oh, never mind."

The ambulance crew arrived. Two burly but cautious young men in white coats entered with uncertain steps from the back of the hall. They pushed in through the remnant of the departing crowd and looked around for their intended patient. Cuttshaw, by this time, had nudged J.T. into a side alcove beyond the door at the opposite end of the room. McLaughlin was sitting, docile and out of sight, removed from the resounding scene and humming tunelessly to himself with blunked out eyes like Little Orphan Annie. Nalorian was the only one with the presence of mind to take charge and intercept the ambulance men.

But as they advanced toward the lectern, the only person making any fuss or causing any uproar was the man who continued to upbraid Chairman Wright in a loud voice, the deeply incensed President Naugle. Beside himself with frustration and rage, the President stamped his feet and waved his arms and continued to bellow at Wright, emitting a stream of high-pitched invective that demonstrated surprising imagination and vigour. Wright, however, had a low threshold of tolerance when it came to being denounced in public. He tried again and again to pacify or to walk away from his loud tormentor, but the President persisted in rending the air with piercing vituperation. The ambulance men cast meaningful glances at each other and at the livid, gesticulating Naugle, and then spoke in soft tones to Nalorian.

"We were told there might be a nut case or a drug tripper that required restraint. The stretcher is right here, but we've got a strait-jacket with us if you think it might help to get the job done."

Nalorian smiled a slow smile, looked around, realized that J.T. was well out of harm's way for the moment, and decided to go for it. "Grand. The strait-jacket is the very thing. As long as you get him out quickly. Better get him before he attacks anyone or does himself an injury." He nodded significantly in Naugle's direction and from a discreet distance watched the white-coated muscle-boys bear down on their objective from behind. One caught the President by the arms while the other deftly slipped the canvas container around him.

"What?" screamed Naugle. "Take your filthy hands off me! You've got the wrong man, you cretins! Get that bearded asshole!"

"I don't see any bearded asshole, sir. Let's just go along now." The larger of the two white-coats looked to Nalorian for confirmation but that worthy had slipped away through the rear door and absented himself from the felicities. Turning to the only man at hand for reassurance, the second white-coat found himself staring into the placid face of Wright, who had begun to find the unexpected turn of events more and more satisfactory.

"Shall we get on with it, sir?" he asked the Chairman.

"By all means," said Wright. "He's decidedly intemperate. Used abusive language with me. Raving. Can't have the university embarrassed by this sort of thing, can we?"

"Right you are, sir." And they hustled Naugle out. The more he shouted, the tighter they cinched up the armless coat.

"But I'm the President, I tell you! The President!"

"Of course you are, mate. Let's just shove along quietly, shall we? Keep a firm grip on him, Pete."

Wright, like Nalorian, made himself scarce, chuckling silently behind his impassive visage.

Cutty, meanwhile, was joined by Nalorian, who wanted to know if J.T. was all right.

"Serene as a saint," said Cuttshaw, "and maybe twice as enlightened."

McLaughlin observed vaguely, "I think I had some jelly beans in my pocket, Cutty, but they seem to have melted. Gone. *Ou sont les jelly beans d'antan*?"

Nobby briefly explained that Naugle was at that moment

making his raucous and unwilling way toward Wellesley Hospital.

"Good," said Cutty, "we'll head for the General, then, shall we? Let's go for a ride, J.T. Attaboy. Off we go."

The two of them half led, half carried McLaughlin down the back stairway. J.T. offered no resistance, but repeatedly hugged and thanked his friends, muttered a few incomprehensible lines from *Winnie the Pooh*, and from time to time hummed snatches from the old Beatles' song, "Yellow Submarine." He was happier than he'd been in several weeks.

Back in West Hall, Grimsby found Trish weeping soundlessly in a corner. He nudged her out and toward the parking lot and drove her to the hospital. The attending physicians told her, however, that they had to keep her husband under restraint and in isolation. They would keep her informed by phone. Reluctantly, Trish made her way home to feed the kids and pass a miserable night.

Some of the cleaning staff insisted that, during the night, the ghost of Burke College was heard pacing restlessly in the tower. Others, of course, deny the existence of ghosts and even the efficacy of aspirin. But there are more things in this world than are dreamed of by any systems-analyst sitting at a computer.

13

J.T. slept fitfully on a narrow cot in the grip of restraining straps in the detoxification ward, surrounded by other shrieking freaks. He woke feeling like a well-trodden doormat from the lowest portals of hell, ground meat that had been stomped by a motorcycle gang, or a cadavre left over from a Mafia war. The hospital staff had worked on McLaughlin only long enough to check him out and bring him down. His head still revolved slowly and his mind remained clouded as he slunk along a stark corridor. Under the reproving eye of a head nurse, he signed himself out of Toronto General at seven a.m., and set out on foot slowly toward the campus.

He was not yet ready to face the world and still less able to face Trish. The office seemed the place to go to ease himself back into the bramble-bush of reality. Mildred Mott could be counted on to cope somehow with the engineering section of Eco. 100, and his senior seminar later in the day could be cancelled. Probably Cutty would see to all that. His head seemed to be clearing, if achey, but his body as he plodded along felt like a rusty robot with all its connections loose and its control panel jangled.

Arriving at the college, he went in the back way to avoid any early-bird colleagues and anyone else. His key didn't want to fit the lock and he kicked the door an angry smash and hurt his foot. Nothing was quite in sync yet. His office was stale and muggy. He lacked a clean shirt. In his haste to leave the hospital, he had not washed adequately. His feet and armpits gave the sensation of having come through a long night wading in a fetid swamp.

His mail was on the desk, probably put there the day before by a dutiful secretary, while he was out in the quadrangle pacing off the nervous agonies prior to the lecture.

Auggh. That. It didn't bear thinking about.

He went to the men's john, careful that there was nobody around, and splashed cold water on his still flushed face. He tried to slurp a drink of water from his cupped hands. He was desperate for a coffee. But the coffee shop presented too great a risk of human encounter. He crept back to the office. From a jacket pocket he produced a crumpled pack of cigarettes. Lit one. It tasted like dried rat shit. He grimaced and puffed again. But, *good* rat shit. He tried to smile at himself, with no real result.

That file of mail. Anything interesting? Anything distracting? He sorted out and discarded two textbook catalogues, several bills, an advertisement from a life insurance company, and an announcement of an upcoming conference on the world's food shortage, mass starvation, and global ruin. The event seemed to him less than enticing or jolly.

Wait. Here was another one of those ineluctable memoranda from the Chairman. Might be diverting, he thought.

To: All Members of the Department
From: L.T. Wright
Re: Departmental Promotions Policy

Having regard to the recent memorandum from President Naugle, together with the addendum appended by the Dean pertaining to this matter, and in response to various inquiries from junior colleagues who have expressed certain apprehensions, I feel, contingent of course on the findings of the Vice-Provost's subcommittee to be reported later, that I can safely provide absolute assurances (subject to any special clauses in individual contracts which I have not as yet checked, or previous special arrangements entered into) which all members of staff are almost certain to find satisfactory in the short run. This view, however, must remain only tentative, as I am sure you will appreciate, until I have had an opportunity to review and reassess the entire picture, budget-wise. It goes without saying that in the long run, although further analysis (and perusal of past correspondence in files which I do not have presently to hand) may prove otherwise–a possibility not lightly to be discounted in certain cases–and give one reason to hold the contrary view, unless any considerable number of members of the department have any over-riding reasons to disagree, in which case further consultations may prove desirable. Please feel free to discuss this with me at any time. I might add in all frankness that our executive secretary, Mrs. Blount, after reviewing the relevant financial projections with me, concurs completely in the foregoing opinion.

He read it again. Miraculously, it still said the same thing. McLaughlin rubbed his eyes. "Insufferable lunacy. Maybe I'm not the only one around here who's crazy. Long run, short run. In the long run we'll all be dead," he mumbled to himself.

It occurred to him to take this gem home for Trish's merriment. But no. In the gloomy context of yesterday's misfortunes, this sort of thing might be lacking in its usual piquancy. Might be too near the knuckle, in fact. Bloody hell. He shuddered.

He put his head down on his arms like a whipped dog and slumped over the desk. Almost immediately he fell zonked into a deep and mercifully dreamless sleep.

* * *

At about four o'clock he slunk out to the parking lot and managed to drive home. Trish met him at the door.

"J.T., my poor dear. Are you all right?"

"Just barely."

"Cutty told me what happened. When I left you at the General you were still hallucinating. Why didn't you phone? I was sick with worry. Where have you been? I went down to the

130

hospital again this morning but you'd gone. Do you know what it felt like when I couldn't find you? The department's secretary said you hadn't appeared, and that there was no answer on your phone."

"I was in my office. Hiding. If the phone rang, I was beyond hearing it. I think I turned down the bell."

"Why didn't you come home? Hiding from what?"

"The mean black dreads. The vultures that grin."

"Sit down. Lie down. Do you want a drink?"

"No, thanks, Trish. No. Maybe some juice. I'm still sort of strung out. Orange juice. Lots of ice. Well, maybe a smidgen of vodka in the bottom."

She fetched it.

"Do you want something to eat?"

"No. Nothing much. I feel like, maybe, a scrambled egg."

"You look like a scrambled egg. Kick your shoes off. Do you want to tell me about it? Our phone has been simply ringing off the wall. Wright called."

"I'll bet."

"He did. And Grimsby and Nalorian. Cutty says he covered for you in your afternoon seminar."

"Good old Cutty."

"Is your head clear now? What can I get you?"

"Yes. Clear. But nothing, thanks. Don't get me anything. In fact I think I'll just lie here and twitch for a while, and then go up to bed."

"Please, J.T., what's been going on? Here I've been hanging on tenterhooks all day to find out how you were, or where you were, and you just amble in and doze off. For the love of Lucifer, *tell* me about it!"

"I'm trying, Trish."

"You are. Very trying."

"Don't start. Please. Don't start."

"I won't. Really. But I can't help wondering. . . ."

They sat in silence for several minutes.

"I can't talk yet, Trish. I'm still swacked. Might be all right in the morning. It was just a bloody disaster, that's all. I'm sorry."

J.T. got to his feet and shuffled off up the stairs. His wife stared at the floor.

Their daughter Jossy appeared. "What's with Dad? I said hello to him, but he didn't even look at me. Is he all right?"

"He'll be fine, dear. Come and eat. Call your brothers."

As Trish served the early meal to the subdued children she seethed with questions and worries and doubts. She couldn't help thinking about Thornton P. Naugle.

The President. Cross as a caged cougar at J.T., and a bit of a tyrant, but still. . . . She felt there was something compelling about his raw and direct emotion. Naugle was a man who needs no prodding and asks no quarter. With J.T., now, she'd had to push and nag him to finish his Ph.D. thesis, had to encourage him constantly. "Relentless encouragement," he'd called it. He got it done, but it was a struggle. Did things always have to be such a thrash? Maybe that was inevitable, with most people.

But with Naugle, she got the feeling of an implacable force. Shifty, maybe, and devious or even cruel, but a force. Confidence. Swagger. No holds barred. He was a man of power. He gave you a feeling of, well, danger. What is it about dangerous men, challenges, Trish wondered. You can't count on them or depend upon them. Often upsetting, but arresting. There are men who seek danger on the battlefield or in the boardroom, she reflected. Some in casinos, some in athletics, or the bullring. There might be an element of shallowness, bravado, even phoniness in their aggressive posturing, but with weaker men the absence of the gut threat, the lack of the quickening tingle, can lead to dead complacency. Tough men often make danger for themselves where they find it absent, living competitively even in co-operative situations, or competing with their own stern standards if they lack other stimulating risks. Women are usually reduced to finding their challenges in sex and the exhilarating games of the heart, trying to ensnare the bold. But too much safety is cloying to the human spirit. Men like Naugle presented the irresistible risk, the go-for-broke impulse, even a whiff of captivating ruthlessness.

And J.T. What could you do about a guy like J.T.? Trish shook her head and fretted. He'd wanted to be a Professor most of his life, had even made some minor but real sacrifices to become one. Would have made more money in business, undoubtedly, but always had this thing about being an academic. Probably he was a good one, too, she admitted, modest salary and an unexpected pill or two notwithstanding. But he had so little ambition. No wish to be a Dean, much less a president. Strange. Why be in the game at all if you're not going for the big prizes? At this rate, she might be the wife of an impecunious Associate Professor forever. Lack of crisp ambition was altogether foreign to her. And there was no doubt that her endearing but unassertive husband was increasingly moody and erratic, even before the Innis fiasco. Was he strong enough to cope with adversity? Lately he seemed so tense and unsure.

Naugle, now, the ill-tempered, bad-assed President, was a different breed of cat. Good teeth, too. I like the way he bares his teeth when he's angry, she thought. A bit of menace. Used to power, and obviously loves it. Power feeds on power, and feeds the ego. Also the Id.

She sighed, and made herself more coffee. Nothing on the television. It wasn't going to be her favourite kind of night.

When Patricia finally went up to bed, later, J.T. was snoring. Looking at him, she realized that, subtly, the ground had shifted. Although he didn't yet know it, not all of J.T.'s troubles were at the office.

14

Nobby bounded out of the west doorway of the college later that week and smiled at the sunshine. Recognizing Cuttshaw some paces ahead, he barrelled down the pathway after him.

"Cutty! Wait up. I'll walk with you."

"Hi, Nalorian, how's it going?"

"Going grand. Just grand. Isn't this a lovely morning for being above ground?"

"Uh-huh. You going toward Smyton Hall?"

"That where you're headed? I'll go along. Wanted to ask you about J.T. Is he all right?"

"He'll get by."

"We'll all get by, Cutty. It's enough to be alive and kicking, even though McLaughlin may be–by George, look at that!"

"What?"

"Look at the prow on that brunette."

"Oh. Yeah. Nice looking girl."

"Isn't it wonderful, Cutty, that no two are alike."

"You mean girls? Snowflakes?"

"Tits. No two alike. It's thrilling, if you think about it. Makes my whole day. The infinite wonder of them all."

"I'd have said that *every* two were alike."

"You lack imagination, Cutty, if I may say so. You're in peril of becoming a cynic. Never take too much for granted. Life is short. He who is tired of tits is tired of life."

"That's 'who's tired of *London* is tired of life.'"

"You have it your way, or Johnson's, and I'll have it mine. Say, would you look at the jiggle on that redhead? Great hair, too, but low-slung. She's the type that should sue the city."

"Why?"

"For building the sidewalk too close to her behind. Lovely

hair, though. There's always a compensation. Marvellous."
His head swivelled.

"You'll trip over your briefcase, Nalorian, if not your eyeballs. What were you saying about J.T.?"

"Merely asking about him, Cutty, merely asking. But if I may say so, he seems more than a bit on edge. Do you think he has a grip on things?"

"Well, the disaster of the lecture bothered him a lot, understandably. He thinks the President has it in for him, and he may be right."

"No, my question goes further than that. Even before the lecture he was a bundle of jangled nerves, and chainsmoking. I think there's more to his situation than meets the eye. People can go over the edge, Cutty; I've seen it. I mean it in a friendly way, but I'm worried enough about him that I'd suggest he might go to a talk-doctor to get straightened around–even though I realize that the best of shrinks only play the Wizard of Oz and give you reassurance about what you've already got. His condition seems to me distressed, and distressing. Don't you share my concern?"

"Well, yeah, I guess I do. Certainly he's been tense since the beginning of term. I had put it down to the preparation of the lecture, which threw him a fair bit, but perhaps he's also upset and twitchy about publishing. There seems to be a problem with his teenage daughter, who's cutting up a bit. He's had more hangovers than usual, too, and there's no doubt his debts are nagging at him. Now that I think of it, he has had a lot on his mind."

"Yes, I think our friend is being got at from enough angles that he may be veering off centre, possibly in trouble, even dangerous. It surprises me, frankly, that his old friends like yourself have not been rallying around more."

Cuttshaw thought about that. "You may have a point. He does seem frazzled. But in trouble? Surely not."

"Probably I exaggerate. I often do. Anyway, why don't we arrange some little jollification to raise his spirits? It crossed my mind that we should take him out for drinks and billiards, an irresponsible evening. Just to quaff a few and stroke a few frames. Get his mind off things. What do you say? Tomorrow night might suit."

"It's not a bad thought. You and me and who else? Probably we should include Grimsby. He seems to need cheering up as much as anybody."

"Bert? Now there's a basket case. That man has problems too. He has the personality of a bookend. How could he cheer McLaughlin up? If I wanted to be amused, Grimsby would be about as welcome as a dark brown fart in a small tent."

"Oh, Bert's all right."

"I suppose. He's so full of squishing good intentions that you can't dislike him. Still, he always seems to me to be acting so damned Christlike, doing the two boards and three nails bit, all earnest and hound-dog like a martyr–with no cause. Maybe he needs a cause, not so? Or maybe he should take up boxing. He'd make a great punching bag."

"You're hard, Nobby, very hard."

"Am I? Don't mean to be. Bert is brilliant, of course. He has a fine analytic brain, but the social presence of an umbrella stand. I sometimes think he's all barnacle and no keel. Be careful of him, Cutty. He's not about to do J.T. much good."

"Yeah, yeah I know. But he's big-hearted and no trouble. J.T. likes him. I'll line them both up for tomorrow night. What shall we say, eight-thirty at the Faculty Club?"

"Done. The club's always fine for drinking, as long as we can avoid their food. And I'll see whether I can get in touch with Ed Hopwood, an old friend of McLaughlin's from Saskatchewan. Possibly we could end up in my loft for a snack and another glass or two. Say, I'll call Boffy, too, and see whether she might arrange some additional diversions. We'll make a night of it."

* * *

The next evening, McLaughlin reminded his wife that he would be out that night playing billiards, probably till late.

"You told me that before, dear. I hope you boys enjoy yourselves. You've been working too hard, J.T."

"That's the truth. Haven't had a pool cue in my hand in months."

"Alice Cuttshaw says she might drop in to see me later. She says Cutty hasn't been getting out enough either. Anyway, come and have dinner. I've made a nice tuna casserole. Call the kids."

Things were still a bit strained in the family. As they sat down to eat, J.T. said something fatuous and a little too loud about needing something warm and solid in the old belly before a big night out on the town. Weighed down by the recollection of the debacle in West Hall, he remained a bit abashed and pressed too hard, like a self-conscious drunk trying to atone for the inanities of the night before. The children stared at their plates. Patricia smiled with her mouth but looked as though she had a toothache.

The conversation jerked on fitfully, restricted mainly to "Please pass the salad" and "Keep your elbows off the table, Rob," until Trish asked, because she couldn't resist it any longer, "J.T., how did you feel, standing in front of that audience, when you knew that things had got–out of control?"

"There was no control possible. I told you all about it before. That damned Miss Bromley just slipped me a bop of bad-news blast, that's all. It was just a helluva'n unfair and debilitating practical joke."

"What does 'debilitating' mean?"

"It means, Robby, that you, er, get out of touch with yourself, surprised to the point of being dazed."

"Oh." The answer wasn't a whole lot of help to Rob, but he masticated away thoughtfully, reinforced in his boyish certainty that adults didn't always know the right names for things or much of what they were talking about.

Trish, exasperated and eager to get closer to the reality of the thing, blurted, "Look, I'm just curious to know the feelings you had, how it seemed to you in your head. You must have known that the situation–don't slouch, Jossy–the situation wasn't going to work, wasn't, well, *or*dinary."

"Ordinary it wasn't. No." J.T. lapsed momentarily into a reverie and then, forgetting the kids, put down his fork, and, staring into the middle distance, said in an uncharacteristically flat voice, "Not at all. It was, unreasonable as it may sound, it was one of those inexplicable moments of delirium or delicious euphoria or stunning wonder, the sort of–what should I say–snap or fervent flash of awareness that can happen during a great event, as when Jossy was born and I first saw her through the glass in the maternity ward. Or that can happen in the most unexpected fragment of dreary time, like while you're taking out the garbage and you suddenly see the full vanilla moon through the trees–when you least expect to feel your heart beat, never mind leap like a silver trout at a fly, and you know you've been pierced but you don't know how, you don't know why, and there you are with rainbows behind your eyes and moonlight on your face and all you want to do is fall down on your knees and cup your palms and hold that moment in your hands forever."

Without turning her head, Jossy slid her father a look of mixed amazement and pity. Was this the same parent who imposed such stern rules on her behaviour, who threatened her with every which punishment if she smoked dope?

"And then of course," J.T. added, "you notice that your hands have warts on them, and everything falls apart."

"I hate this casserole, Mom," observed Davie.

"You don't hate it at all, dear. It's very nice tuna with lovely noodles and Chinese bean sprouts and mushrooms and almonds. Eat up, or you can forget about dessert."

"Consider yourself lucky, son; with your grandmother's cooking, I used to be told, 'Eat up your cake or you'll get no meat or potatoes,'" J.T. smiled.

"I think I'd like some soya sauce on mine," Jossy said. "Davie is right. It's not too great."

"Were you listening to what your father said, Joss?"

"Yes, Mom, but he does lecture, doesn't he? He does throw around big words. No wonder Davie gets confused. Highbrow gabble like that makes me think I should drop out of school. It's all such a crock."

"Don't talk like that, please, Joss," Trish admonished.

"What's a 'crock,' Dad?" Davie inquired.

"It's anything your sister doesn't agree with or understand. When you get to be fourteen, you'll be impossible, too."

"Anyway, I think I'll chuck school and drop out." Joss now had the bit between her teeth. "I'm sick of all this wordy stuff. I'm always being preached at."

"Easy, Joss. Nobody's preaching," said her mother.

"I want to go out to a movie tonight. Dad's going out. I'll be home by eleven."

"Not on a school night, dear. Is your homework done?"

"You keep pulling me in on school nights, and you always want me to babysit with Davie, and when I do get out on a weekend, you make me hit home by twelve o'clock like a child."

"Fourteen is not exactly ancient, Joss."

"And Dad is always on about my friends and my make-up."

"You wear," J.T. remarked, "enough make-up to paint a chorus line in Las Vegas. On a girl in grade ten, it's not what I'd call cute."

"There he goes! There he goes again. I'm always being got at for something. If it isn't make-up it's my friends. And it's always school this and school that. Marks. Grades. 'What did you learn today?' I don't want to be like you guys, okay? I don't want to spend my life discussing university crap and book reviews and moonbeams. I want to be able to stay out later than midnight if I feel like it, and I want to be left alone!"

"Joss," said her father, struggling for an even tone, "you're being difficult and pushy and you're giving your mother a hard time. Back off. You'll have to be in by ten. That's the limit. And you shouldn't be going out on school nights. We've been all through this. There are rules."

"Unfair rules!"

"Now look," snapped J.T., "what we have here is a family, not a debating society. You *must* not push at the fences all the time. Stop giving your mother such back-talk. Why do you shout and go on about a curfew that we've discussed for months? Accept the rules and stop bucking. This is a family, not a revolutionary cell, and we try to co-operate. These continuous tensions are counter-productive. We don't conduct our affairs through slugging matches or adversarial relations."

"Adversarial? What's that supposed to mean, adversarial?"

"Your father means your attitude stinks, dear," Trish said.

"Well, I'm going to the movie. And I'm all set to drop out of this school mess and move out of this prison and get a job. I can't stand it."

Neither could her father. "Look, Trish, will you try to cope with this? I've got to go or I'll be late. Make her see reason, okay?"

"Sure thing, Your Highness. You just walk off and I'll man the barricades. Thanks a lot. I hope you're better with the pool cue than you are with the psychology."

"What's psychology, Mom?" Davie asked.

"Psychology," said Trish, "is what you do when you know the urges and you haven't got a clue what the results will be or what to do about them. What you use when you want the other guy to do what you want him to do. It's—I guess it's a mind game, Davie. A form of play in the mind to see who wins."

"I like games," Davie said. "Can I have dessert?"

15

The snooker balls clicked jauntily as Nalorian sank a red and started another run. After sinking a pink, a second red and a blue, he deliberately missed a shot and left a set-up for J.T. But Nobby didn't permit the rhythm of the game to slow the velocity of his talking. He was trying to keep the conversation bouncy. It wasn't easy.

"The balls are really rolling for you, Nobby," said Cutty.

"Going grand. So, anyway, the upshot of it was, my New York dealer sold the painting for a cool four thousand, and it was just a weekend's daubing."

"Nobby, you were going to tell us about your background," J.T. put in. "When did you stop being a 'starving Armenian'? I thought your passport was British."

"Right. British. I stopped starving, but I've always been Armenian, passport or not. My background is about as mixed as can be. Mother was French and I was born in Kirovakan, where my father was headmaster of a school. Since then, well, the Wandering Jew has nothing on the itinerant Armenian. Been wandering, quite happily, since I was a boy. Name a place west of Turkey, and I've been there. Hunh. So whose play is it?"

"Cutty's. But you've often threatened to tell us more about yourself," J.T. persisted.

"Nothing much to tell, really."

"Oh, come on."

"Might bore you. Tonight we should just have some sport. Come on, drink up."

Cutty said, "Okay, let's hoist a few, and up your kilt, and we'll shoot some pool, but enough of the skittering. Put J.T. out of his misery of curiosity. Personally, I don't much care if you're a former bullshit commissar from Azarbaidzshan or an agent for the PLO, but give. We all got here somehow. What was your route?"

"Hunh. If you insist. Well, when my father got the family out of Armenia in 1936, when I was seven–"

"And already spoke eighteen languages, and painted like Raphael, doubtless," Cutty rumbled.

"Not quite. Things were a bit dicey in 1936, and the only place we could get to at the time was Warsaw–out of the frying pan, you might say. In Warsaw, my father's brother had an import business. I still speak a bit of Polish. During the war, we didn't quite manage to get out ahead of the Germans. The Nazis were not kind to my family, and eventually I went to ground in the ghetto with some people who helped me. Orphans often receive more kindness from the have-nots than the haves, I've found, which is why–good shot, Cutty–one of my few moral inclinations has always been toward the underdog. But that's another story. I took a little part in the Warsaw uprising of 1943, and it was during that intense unpleasantness that I met Mrs. Nalorian. She was a leader even then as a girl in the Resistance. A year older than I, and lovely, and gallant. Probably the most beautiful woman I've ever seen. Eyes that could incinerate you, or melt hard steel. She suffered certain indignities at the hands of the Germans, but eventually we escaped together to Sweden, and, in 1944, we managed to reach England. I wanted to join the army, but I was too young, and the war was almost over. Some distant relatives of mine in London, in Bethnal Green, gave us shelter. There I was, a fifteen-year-old boy with a sixteen-year-old girlfriend, but I managed to get a toe-hold on the educational ladder. Later I married Mrs. Nalorian when I was still an undergraduate at the London School of Economics. After my B.A. we were parted while I worked for two years under contract in a mine in northern Sweden to earn some money. Subsequently I won a scholarship, and she worked as an editor and translator, since she knows more languages than I. We both kept at it while I did doctoral work at Cambridge. I had almost no seat in my trousers then, but without her I might have had no trousers at all. Any time we became impatient about scraping by on translator's fees and scholarships, we remembered Warsaw and clutched each other, and got on with it. Those were good days, yes. Grand days. And after our wanderings in more recent years, we've enjoyed North America and come to care about Canada. Is it my shot?"

Bert looked at Nalorian as though he'd never seen an Armenian before. A few thoughts occurred to him about the relative comfort of growing up in Canada, even during the Depression. He took a reflective pull on his pint.

J.T. lit a cigarette. "You know, Nobby, I get the impression that you've just told us a tiny capsule of a two-volume novel."

"Well, life is short. But history is debased these days, and nostalgia is better abbreviated. There are endless books on some squalid little fiddle like Watergate, but few enough on the Warsaw uprising or the Resistance. I've often thought of trying to write about–some of those things."

McLaughlin remained curious. "That still doesn't tell us how you ended up in North America, never mind Toronto."

"Well, that story too can be clipped. Nothing very startling. You see, when I came down from Cambridge, I needed contacts and I needed money–urgently. That would be, what, 1952. The best openings seemed to be abroad. I worked for the World Bank for two years and made a lot of connections. But the academic world always seemed more attractive. So when I got into the university circuit, I did stints in Santa Barbara, Lyons, McGill, Washington State, Melbourne, Purdue, Texas–you name it. But somehow I never lasted long in any one place, never got tenure."

"That, I suppose, would have had something to do with your inclination to get co-eds between the sheets faster than you got articles into print?"

"Too right, J.T. Women have always been a weakness of mine, I admit."

Grimsby frowned. "You mean, you've lost several jobs because of–improprieties with students?"

"And with the wives of colleagues, too often influential col-

143

leagues. But fornication, yes. I sometimes think that if I'd ever had a female student who was a mute, I'd have won tenure and settled down years ago. But they do blab. As it is, my steep slopes to unemployment have always been greased with vaginal jelly. Then they hand me back the slippery dong and send me down the road. It's all a slidey little game the fates play on us."

"What in the world does your wife say about all this? I can't imagine why she hasn't left you. She must think you're mad."

"Well, Bert, I try to spare her as much as I can, of course, but she came to terms with life and with me many years ago. We have a rather free relationship, actually. Mrs. Nalorian and I leave a few convenient spaces in our lives in the interest of domestic tranquillity. She writes poetry and translates. Very good, too. She keeps busy. And Mrs. Nalorian knows I'll be home by seven for the cocktail hour and for dinner. Every night. Only brief trips excepted. We have, you see, remained *interested* in each other, that's the ticket. It's seldom that Mrs. Nalorian has ever bored me, and only infrequently do I bore her. Exasperate, yes, but not bore. The bedrock is respect. Because we have never ceased to respect each other, we've never ceased to care."

"You make a vivid case for being an old lech and an insistent sort of pseudo-affectionate bastard," said Cutty. "But with the casual dollies, don't you get bored with the chase? Why don't you bloody well stay home?"

"Chase? Who said anything about a chase? It took me years to realize that I was the astonished recipient of such eager largess precisely *because* I didn't pursue it. Coax, wheedle, beg, and you'll get nowhere, not so? Try to ignore it, and it will follow you. Slow ovens, ten; pressure cookers, zero –that's about the size of it. Obvious need is the ultimate turnoff to sportive women, particularly Lady Luck. It's a primary rule of psychology, I believe." Nalorian couldn't help but look sharply at Grimsby, who stood staring at him spanieleyed.

"I'm no satyr," Nobby continued. "I seek little enough, and seldom turn a hand or bother sniffing around, but I'm content to fondle whatever kittens a wilful fate flings into my lap. It's just the whirl of the corpuscles, the urge of the gonads that won't be denied, that incessant itch that can never quite be scratched into quietude. People say they are motivated. They're not. They're merely compelled like these billiard balls, and hate to admit it. Show me a man who says he fully controls his own life, and I'll show you a self-deluded twit, or an insensate lump. The thing about lumps is that they are so damned humourless."

Cutty chalked his cue. "You seem to set great store in amusement, Nobby. What do you want to be when you grow up, a stand-up comedian in a burlesque show?"

Nalorian, as always, ignored the sarcasm and surged ahead while sinking a red and starting another run. "You were asking me about the reasons for my, ah, unusual professional mobility. So I told you, candidly. Nothing to hide. And the rock-bottom 'why' of it all is that I can't seem to cope with women who are too serious about sex. I always have trouble with ladies who are too solemn about the Great Game. Since it's all physically and aesthetically ludicrous, 'neither convenient nor decorous,' as Shaw said, I never could take it seriously. Hard to stop, but still harder not to smile and plunge on.

"But don't take it all too seriously, there's the thing. If you let things get too heavy, you lose all perspective on human folly and become trapped in the pincers of earnestness. Too awful. All life is a tease. We need meaning and purpose, but the Sphinx refuses to speak, no? We ache for adequate answers to the big questions, and there are none. Sex is merely the physical manifestation of the cosmic tease. I never could resist the titillation. It's too good a joke not to go along with. But it always gets you into trouble. In fact, of all the jokes that God plays on man, sex is one of the best, don't you think?"

Cutty couldn't resist taking another swipe. "Jokes, eh,

Nobby? I suppose you'd be willing to favour us with your neon-lit interpretations of other 'jokes' that the Deity likes to play?"

"You don't have to answer that," J.T. snapped, thinking that this was not the sort of banter that he'd expected over the brew and the billiard table.

"No problem," said Nobby. "I'm always ready to reply."

"Could you doubt it, J.T.?" Cutty mumbled. "Could we stop him?"

"Jokes. Yes." Nalorian was imperturbable. "God's little drolleries would include–try that brown ball, Cutty–would include pride, freckles, cancer, kangaroos, snowmobiles, communism, Islam, piles, footnotes, death. Certainly death. Or democracy; that's a real thigh-slapper. And always finding new ways for the innocent to suffer, thus creating the entire theology lark; there's a limitless guffaw if ever there was one. Oh yes, God is a great prankster. It isn't his fault if we fail to get the joke."

"Nubar, I wonder," Grimsby queried with gentle earnestness, "wouldn't it be easier if you really believed in God? Or at least in natural order and decency? Under all your glib cynicism, you seem to be an optimist who doesn't believe in–in even optimism."

"What? I'm no cynic. Garrulous, often carried away, but no cynic. A realist, and in this world there's not much of a line between realism and irony. But much of this conversation is your fault, Bert. It was you who prodded and got me off on all this."

"I didn't say anything," Grimsby protested.

Nalorian glowered. He had to blame his excesses on somebody, and Bert was a born patsy. "Wasn't it his fault, J.T.?"

"Not really. I guess we were all goading you a little. We'll all know better next time. Hey, does anybody want another beer? Cutty?"

"Don't mind. Give the bartender a shout. Floyd! I guess he's watching T.V. Black ball in the side."

146

"Good shot, Cutty. How did you lads get me into this?" Nobby beamed his high-voltage smile. "Let's drop it, shall we? I'm expecting Hopwood along soon. He'll shoot pool, if you chaps won't."

But Bert had fastened onto something with the tenacity of chewing-gum on a rubber sole. "You talk of jokes and scuffling along, Nubar, bulling it through like carefree animals. Tell me your formula for scuffling. I'd like to know."

"We'd all like a simple formula, Grimmers. *Any* one might do. But not knowing, we jog along and swap facile lies. I lean to the view that the world is a pathetic barnyard in which we should cavort and crow while we can, always trying to be as graceful and considerate in the process as the crap on our boots allows. That's all. Gather ye rosebuds, and watch where you step. In a short life, there's no surplus time for worry. Just get on with it."

Grimsby stared his wounded-sheep stare. J.T. lined up a shot carefully and scratched.

"Bad luck," said Cutty. Then he blurted, "How can we be sure this guy isn't Ann Landers in drag?"

McLaughlin muttered to him, "Put a lid on it. Do me a favour; let him run with it."

"Always brittle, eh, Cutty?" Nalorian grinned. "I reveal no secrets, merely myself. Could it be that you are afraid of what's in short supply these days, simple candour? Or of yourself?"

Cutty pulled at his pint.

J.T. almost shouted, "Let's rack 'em up again, then, Bert. Whose break?"

Nalorian, impatient and more exposed than he'd expected, kept on filling the silence, irritated more by Bert's innocent gaze than by Cuttshaw's sardonicisms. "So we make well-planned moves, and life responds to our gambits with risible counter-impertinences. We try to confront and challenge the odds. We shift and evade and try to cover up before attempting another ploy, and God merely smiles and dishes up some fresh waggish affront, some inventive absurdity or unexpected indignity. Fighting it out to a draw is probably a kind of triumph. Good losers laugh, Bert. So do good winners. The game's the thing. Hunh. Doesn't anybody here drink any more? I'm no camel, for God's sake. I have a terrible thirst on me. Where's Floyd?"

Cutty allowed he'd put the blue ball in the top left.

Nalorian bet him a buck he wouldn't. He didn't. "Flipping jinx," Cuttshaw grumbled, paying up. Floyd appeared with a tray of refills.

McLaughlin was beginning to respond to his new colleague's directness. "You do wear an unusual medallion, Nobby, most days."

"Constantly. You're observant, J.T. It was an early gift, given me by Mrs. Nalorian when we married. This one side is an image of Sassountzi David, or David of Sassoun, an Armenian liberation hero of the eighth century. The other side carries a little saying, a family motto, inscribed for me by my wife in my mother's tongue: '*Il faut vivre au delà de désespoir.*' "

"What does that mean?" Bert asked, stolid and unilingual.

"It means, 'We must live on the other side of despair.'"

Bert blinked. J.T. sipped his Lowenbrau. "Cross bank on this red sumbitch," said Cutty.

Bert said, "I can't be sure how you can claim to know about, ah, adversity, and still seem to be so buoyant. In my own case, call it Puritan upbringing or whatever, I guess I'm never sure whether I'm supposed to be happy. Trying to avoid pain may be enough. Have I any, er, right to be happy?"

"For God's sake, Grimsby! Right? Rights are what you seize for yourself against any and all odds. We all bring our own rattling skeletons to every feast, and we don't need you pulling long faces and playing the mortician. Christ, man! Try to snap around. If you can't be happy, at least be cheerful!"

A banging and bellowing announced the timely interruption of Hopwood's arrival.

"Hopwood! For kristsake, ol' Horn! How the hell are you?"

"Fine, J.T. It's been a long time. Nobby told me he'd met you. Why didn't you look me up? What is it, five years you've been in Toronto?"

"Seven years since I got back from Ottawa. But I've been chained to a desk – busy as a flea at a dog show. And I didn't know you were here. Whatthehell. You're looking great, for a stubble-jumper. Horn, hot damn! Give us the old school yell, whaddya say? Come on: 'Cha HEE, Cha HAW, Cha haw-haw-HAW! Rip 'em, smear 'em, eat 'em RAW!'"

They flung their arms around each other like a pair of tipsy delegates to a brewers' convention, laughing and back-slapping, overcompensating for the embarrassment about the gulf of years and divergent experience between them, but genuinely happy to see one other. Nobby performed the introductions to Cutty and Bert, then went in search of the bar-man. McLaughlin demanded to know what Horn was up to these days.

"Painting up a storm. I have a show coming up at Gallery Moos in January. Meanwhile, I'm finishing up the commission I got for the sculpture to plop in front of your new building here at Chiliast U."

"What building is that?" Bert asked.

"The new Social Sciences Building, Korchinsky Hall. A brutal pile of concrete, but I may be able to liven it up. More of a fountain than a statue, but I think you'll like it."

"I'll be damned," J.T. bellowed. "What sort of a geyser will it be? Is it gurgling cherubs on the laps of the Muses?"

Horn grinned. "You'll see when it's unveiled. Isn't there supposed to be some big-deal ceremony for the opening within a few weeks? I just work here, but I'm delivering it soon. It's merely another work of conspicuous genius."

Bert said, "I'm going to try this red ball in the corner, but don't anybody watch; I'm not awfully good at this." Nobody watched.

Quietly, Cutty asked why Hopwood was called Horn? McLaughlin said that his friend once played trumpet in a dance band in Regina; also that this sharp-featured five-foot-four little bastard had been known as the most horny critter that ever threatened the maidens of the Saskatchewan prairie.

"How have you managed to stay alive as an artist in this Philistine country?" J.T. asked. "I thought you'd have gone to New York or Paris."

"No," Hopwood replied, "I've been determined to make it here in Canada. It's meant some hustling, of course. I've been a waiter, a truck driver, a barn painter, you name it, but I've gotten by, and always found some time for my own work. If you want to do it badly enough, you can paint in an unheated garage. And I've done that, too."

"Damned right," Nalorian cut in. "I remember when I was a student, I did anything and everything for a shilling. Dishwasher in a restaurant, I was, and for a while I sold vacuum cleaners door to door while Mrs. Nalorian scruffled away at translations and giving French lessons. I once sold pornographic postcards in Soho. And did I ever tell you, Horn, about making up plots for a hack writer of pulp fiction?"

"Don't think you ever did," Hopwood smiled into his pint.

"Oh yes, this acquaintance of mine wrote thrillers for the cheaper magazines. He could grind it out, but had too little imagination, so I sold him plots and story lines. Gimmicks for murder mysteries and the like. One of my best outlines, for which I earned the princely fee of five quid, was for a story about a bank robbery."

Cutty winked at McLaughlin. "That's what you need, J.T., a how-to-do-it guide to quick bucks."

"In fact, the premise was a bearded man not unlike McLaughlin, who wore a trim goatee. To do the robbery he shaved himself clean and put on a simple disguise so that he could walk into his own place of banking unrecognized. He grabbed the lolly and ran out, then shed the disguise and glued on a false beard, exactly like his own previous fringe, so that he could stash the money and walk back into the bank as his own respectable self before the police arrived." Nalorian elaborated the yarn with customary length and self-congratulation, adding: "My writer friend made quite a good score with that yarn. And later I sold him rather a perky notion of a murder involving a hat-pin that–"

Bert interrupted to inquire whose shot it was.

"Oh. Mine, I think," said J.T. "But what is it you do, Horn, in this den of iniquity where you work?"

"Well, for a time I was a beer-slinger. After I worked up to be manager, I brought in belly dancers and some strippers, not to mention some amateur skin shows. The salary is no great hell, but I talked the owner into giving me free use of empty space on the third floor as a studio. Had to get more room when I started this sculpture and fountain thing, which is why I rented the place to Nalorian. Matter of fact, it's a great little spot. You must come and see it."

"I'd like to," McLaughlin nodded.

"And you run the entire shooting-match, do you?" Cutty inquired.

"You might say that. I'm the bouncer on Saturday nights. I hire the girls and book the music and manage the joint generally, as well as supervising some of the gaming tables. Sundays I balance the books. Yeah, I guess I do most everything. After closing time you should see me stick a broom up my ass and sweep out while I'm dashing around to lock up."

As the desultory talk went on, Cutty made a run of four red balls, two pinks and a blue. Grimsby, meanwhile, kept taking off his glasses, swiping at them with a dirty handkerchief, and putting them back on. Bert found that, as so often, he had little to say, nothing to contribute. No one meant to exclude him, but he remained on the periphery. At one point he offered, "I like fountains," but no one responded to that interjection, and cheers went up as Hopwood sunk a particularly artful cross-bank shot on the green ball.

Nalorian leaned nonchalantly against a wall and contemplated how maladroit people like Bert have an ingrown tendency to withdraw into nervous and pointless self-centred activity when they are unsure of themselves, how they twitch silently on the sidelines for a while and then, flustered by their inability to connect, rush in with harsh and irrelevant stabs at conversation which cut the air, even slice the cords of easy civility, and leave small but jagged holes in the fabric of calm camaraderie. Just a walking solipsism, was Grimsby.

Bert, for his part, popped a peppermint into his mouth and scratched his head about Nalorian. How had this newcomer, this vivid interloper, not only got himself so quickly accepted by cutty and J.T., but become an instigator, an arranger of billiard games and parties, a centre of attention? He was just a little too smooth, this Armenian, a little too flashy. Why did the other guys seem to like him? Grimsby had been around the Economics Department for twenty years, had known McLaughlin and Cuttshaw since they were graduate students, and this was only the second time in many months that he'd been included with them in an evening of billiards. Horn was interesting, but Nalorian remained the vital pivot. Nubar had something special going for him, all right, yet Grimsby was damned if he could tell what it was. There must be, he concluded, some trick to it.

Bert took another reflective sip at this pint. Cutty, he thought, was well liked by everyone, a great favourite of J.T.'s, and yet he seldom said much, didn't often tell jokes, just kept his head down and worked away and ran up scores as he was doing now with the blue ball. J.T., less cool and coiled more tightly, lit his four-hundredth cigarette, then returned to reminisce with Hopwood about half-remembered, half-prevaricated high-school exploits which enclosed them in some sort of nostalgic thicket through which they groped toward contemporary common ground. They seemed able to find things to laugh about. Bert wasn't sure he saw the humour in most of their thrusts, and decided that they were all playing games, games of which the rules were not apparent to him.

Nalorian insisted that after they'd determined the local

billiard championships, they should all go back to Horn's club, maybe take a brief whirl at the gambling tables, and have a bit of midnight supper in his loft.

J.T. liked the sound of this, except for the gambling. He was, as usual, short of funds. A quick check of his pockets revealed twenty-two dollars and change. Not much for a fling at the tables. Signing chits at the Faculty Club was easy enough, since the bills wouldn't arrive till next month. Still, he had in the back flap of his wallet a one-hundred-dollar bill. Away back in August he'd done a short quick-and-dirty piece of journalism on reasons for the decline of the Canadian dollar. A thousand words. The sort of thing he could sometimes toss off in an evening if he took it casually; quick throw-away writing, in contrast to the preparation of his academic essays or the Innis lecture which had been torn from his soul one phrase, one word at a time in great self-conscious agony. *The Financial Post* had paid him two hundred and fifty dollars for it. He'd given a hundred dollars to Trish, put fifty dollars toward his overdue book bill, forgotten about the bite the tax man would take, and kept aside a hundred for himself for spree money. It had already earned him a number of free lunches when he'd waved the C-note at colleagues while eating in little restaurants and been delighted when they couldn't easily make change for it. With a little luck, he could continue to bluff along and keep the hundred-dollar-bill intact.

Nalorian chalked his cue and said, "Watch this nifty cushion shot on the last red, and I will then clean the table."

Cutty bet him ten that he couldn't, but he did.

Grimsby said, "Say, guys, what would you do if you had only six months to live?"

They all stopped and stared at him. Cuttshaw banged the butt of his cue on the floor and snapped, "That's it, Bert, cheer us up!"

Nalorian frowned. "Why do you ask?"

"Well, I have this neighbour," Bert said, "who was told that his cancer of the liver was inoperable and that he wasn't likely to last half a year. I was interested to know what he'd do with the time. What would you do?"

"Not that it would bloody matter," Cutty grunted.

"I'd finish up another statue," Horn allowed, "and do one last series of paintings. Then I'd stock up on some heavy drugs to make sure that my final days were as painless a float as possible. It's a helluva question, but that's what I'd do."

"I was just interested," Bert persisted. "This guy couldn't decide what to do, and he merely went into his office every day as usual as though nothing had happened, as long as he could. He was an accountant. Just went along to the office. I thought that was interesting. But it's a good question, isn't it?"

"Oh, it's a *lovely* question," Cutty muttered.

"Maybe your accountant friend had as good an answer as anyone," Nobby observed. "We all do what we must. Now, let's think about moving on to the Blue Venus, what do you say?"

But it was the only time they'd paid much attention to him all night, so Bert pressed his topic. "What would you do, J.T.?"

"Eh? Damned if I know. I guess I might sell my car and anything else I could get my hands on, and go to the Riviera or some place like that. I'd certainly try to get some money together for a final kick at the can. But I'm not sure that Trish would think that was a possible idea. She'd want to go first class or not at all. And she's probably right. I don't know. Jeez, Bert, you sure ask some doozies, don't you?"

"Sorry," said Grimsby. "I was just wondering. I just-"

Nalorian, darting across the wasteland of Bert's upsetting field of speculation, pushed up a laugh and suggested that the whole thing reminded him of envigilating final exams for a gymnasium full of freshmen at his last teaching post. There were some four hundred students writing a three-hour exam in Accounting 1A. "They were all working away at their answers with the standard pocket calculators-most of them couldn't add or subtract without calculators – and suddenly hands started to go up. Hands started to wave in the air in distress. Ten or twelve students, you see, had the batteries run down and quit in their little electronic machines. It was a hell of a bind. Dead batteries, so everything came to a halt. Rather a pity."

"So what happened?" J.T. asked.

"I suppose they flunked," Nalorian said. "I've often thought of that as the risible symbol of modern universities. Dead technical circuitry, and nothing to fall back on."

"Kind of sad," Bert observed.

"I suppose. Anyway," Nalorian beamed, "let's move out of here and go over to Horn's club."

16

Fifteen minutes later they all trooped into the Blue Venus. Hopwood led the way. The downstairs bar-restaurant was crowded but there was no action at the moment on the tiny stage, so Horn shepherded the group through a side door and up to the second floor. There, a small group of cigar-chomping men at the back of the room were absorbed in a heavy game of poker and scarcely looked up at the new-comers. Toward the front was a blackjack table presided over by a bored dealer, who nodded at Hopwood and Nalorian while sliding cards with a casual flick to a portly man flanked by two smartly dressed young women. The only noise in the room came from the dice table where a shooter importuned Dame Fortune at the top of his voice every time he rolled the cubes.

Bert gaped around like a rustic cleric in a whorehouse. "Is all this legal, Nubar?"

"Not entirely, no."

"Do you think we should be here if it's illegal?"

Hopwood grinned and explained that one of the punters at the craps table was an alderman, so it was unlikely that the police would be paying any calls.

Cuttshaw wandered over to the blackjack table while Horn pressed a buzzer to order drinks. Within minutes, Cutty grabbed a good streak of cards including two twenty-ones in a row, and was ahead eighty dollars. "I think this evening is shaping up," he told the dealer. "Hit me."

Horn said, "Why don't you take a hand, J.T.?"

"Maybe later. I don't have much of a head for cards, really, even when I'm sober. I guess I'd better stay out of it."

"Nonsense. Everybody likes a little flutter now and again.

Here, come over to the roulette table and I'll spin a few numbers for you."

McLaughlin declined, saying he'd just as soon watch, but Nobby urged him to have a go and Hopwood took his elbow and steered him toward the wheel just as a waitress in net stockings arrived with a tray of drinks. J.T. accepted a scotch on the rocks and, propelled by his two exuberant friends, allowed himelf to be nudged into a seat at the empty table. Horn took up his station at the wheel and gave it a vigorous spin. "How much are the chips?" J.T. asked. Anything he liked, Hopwood said, or suggested that he could just lay out money. J.T. fanned his pockets and protested that he hadn't much cash with him, only to be told that the house would accept his cheque. Realizing how little good could come of such elasticized paper, McLaughlin instead fumbled with his wallet, extracted his hoarded one-hundred-dollar bill and tossed it on the table. "I don't suppose you can change a C-note?"

Nobby slapped him on the back and laughed. "Around here, a hundred *is* change."

J.T. started to reach nervously toward the bill to retract it just as Horn announced, "Seven, red. You win."

"I do?"

"Sure, your money is on red, isn't it?"

"Yeah, but–"

Horn put a pair of fifty-dollar chips on top of the bill that sat on red and spun the wheel again. McLaughlin reached to extract his winnings, but in his haste, spilled half of his drink. By the time he had the scotch set right and started to reach a second time, Nalorian stayed his hand, telling him to let it ride.

"But that's two hundred beans on the line!"

"Certainly, but these things go in runs. Trust me."

"Krist, I don't know, Nobby."

Hopwood said, "Number thirty-six, red," and added four more fifty-dollar discs to the pile.

"I told you so," Nalorian smiled. "Leave it once more."

"No, I think that's enough for now."

At this point Boffy Bromley rushed up, jogged J.T.'s uncertain arm as she embraced Nalorian, and distracted everyone except Horn.

"Guess who won the amateur strip-tease contest?" Boffy gushed.

"Undoubtedly you did, my dear," said Nalorian, twinkling.

"No. Mildred. I won the wet T-shirt prize, but Mildred really socked it to them in the strip."

J.T. stopped in mid-reach. "Mildred Mott?"

"Definitely," squealed Boffy. "Isn't that super?"

Hopwood said, "Number eight, black," and swept away McLaughlin's pile.

"Now just a damned minute," came the protest.

"Steady on, J.T. Wouldn't do to be a sore loser."

"But, Nobby, I wasn't, I mean I didn't even notice that–"

Nobby laughed and signalled Hopwood not to spin again. "We'll all go upstairs, I think, now that the girls are here. Collect Cutty, will you–where's old Bert?–and we'll just pop along up to the loft, where I've arranged a bite to eat."

McLaughlin was still blinking and gulping and looking back at the roulette table in disbelief as the group filed toward the stairway.

The third floor consisted of one large, open space with a window facing south and a small skylight. In one back corner there was a minimal kitchen behind a bar counter, with a washroom behind that, and in the other corner was a partitioned area, a sleeping alcove. A trestle table had been set up in the main room with place settings for ten. In the absence of table cloths, two white sheets had been thrown over the long trestle. Dixieland jazz by Sydney Bechet and Louis Armstrong blared from an old stereo unit set against the bedroom partition. Propped up along one wall was a row of ten or twelve paintings of various sizes which seemed to be portraits of women laughing or making faces.

Nobby beamed around the room and at his guests, who now included Boffy and Mildred and two girls of Boffy's acquaintance, who had been runners-up in the wet T-shirt contest, plus a somewhat older woman, a stripper, who danced under the *nom de guerre* of Superba van Snoob. "You can call me Joyce," she said in a whisky-cracked voice. Nalorian performed elaborate introductions and recharged the glasses. He then turned down the volume of the record player and urged everyone to tuck in to the tray of *hors d'oeuvres*.

Grimsby, gazing with fascination at the spangly costume and swooping neckline of Ms. Mott, accepted a morsel from the tray. He munched it, dropping cracker crumbs all over, and observed to Cuttshaw, "This jam tastes fishy."

Cutty broke up. "That's caviar."

"Oh." He shyly helped himself to another.

"Can you believe this guy?" Cutty whooped.

McLaughlin said, "Easy, pal."

"But Bert's just like that fellow I introduced you to years ago, from Edmonton, and we took him out to a seafood place, remember? And when they put a boiled lobster down in front of him, eyes and antennae and all, he said, 'I'm sorry, I don't eat bugs.'"

"That was a long time ago," J.T. observed. "We were all young and green once. Bert just forgot, that's all."

Hopwood, snapping his fingers, asked one of the wet shirt girls to dance, and they bopped around the room for a few manic turns.

Drinks and canapés went down well. McLaughlin kept circling the room to avoid being cornered by Mildred, who persisted in batting unreasonably long eyelashes at him and refilling his glass of scotch.

J.T. examined a few of the canvases against the wall. "Are these yours?" he asked Horn as the dancers spun by.

"Nah. They're all Nobby's. This whole shlaboo is Nalorian's since I moved out. Not bad, though. He has some raw talent."

Nobby walked over. "See anything you like, J.T.?"

"I like them all. They're very alive. Arresting faces and vivid colours, but they look as if they were seen from behind a soft veil, or through a haze of wishful thinking."

"For that, I thank you and offer you one as a gift. Yes, yes, it's my pleasure. Choose any one you like, please. This is my new orgasm series, portraits of ladies in the throes of pleasure. 'La petite mort,' as the French say. Just a few more and I'll be ready to mount a show, probably in New York. They're all merely blatant masterpieces, but I'll do more next week. I'm delighted that you like them."

"It amazes me that they contain so much energy."

"Do you think so? Energy is just what flows out when you relax. I try to get it out, not hold it in. Conservation is for trees, not people."

"Still, I'm impressed that you find time and juice enough to teach and write academic stuff and still put so much into the painting."

"Not so much, actually. I devote the bulk of my time to the main concerns of the gentleman: style and sex and self-expression. All pleasure, but with some focus."

"And personal relationships?" McLaughlin asked. "Friendship? Where do you include that? It's obvious that you've gone to some trouble for us tonight."

"Naturally I subsume personal relations under style and creativity. Life, my dear fellow, is an art form, and where would we be in life without friendship? I flatter myself that I have some natural proclivity toward it. Selectivity is the essence of creativity, and I select people with as much care as I choose my palette. As Oscar Wilde had it, 'I put my art into my life, and merely my talent into my labours.'"

Cutty rolled up and said, "I'm not sure you've got that exactly right. I think he said–"

Nalorian cut him off. "My dear Cuttshaw, not to worry. A gentleman never bothers to quote exactly, for fear people will think he had to grub away and look it up. Now come along and let's have some supper."

"But are you always so loose with your quotes?"

Nobby chuckled. "Does champagne have bubbles? Do penguins have cold tails?"

Soon they were all seated at the long table. A waiter from downstairs appeared with oysters and poured abundantly from chilled bottles of a good Chablis. Nalorian insisted that Cutty switch places so that Bert would be beside Joyce. Boffy burbled about how Mildred had walked off with first place in the amateur strip contest. "The emcee introduced her as 'Candy-pants,' because she wore those edible bikinis from Lovecraft, you know? And threw them to some bald guy at ringside."

"Splendid," bellowed Nalorian. "Capital. I congratulate you, Mildred, and implore you to share this new-found talent with us all. Yes, yes, absolutely. I know. Get up on the table; here, let me help you. Boffy told me that you were all prepared, not so? Of course. What is art if it is not shared, eh? I'll just see to your music."

He changed the record to some thumping 1960s disc of "Night Train" and Mildred, first looking steadfastly at the ceiling, and then more deliberately at McLaughlin, went into her routine. She'd toked up enough that she was very loose. Her costume was entirely black. Slowly she began to move to the music with an astonishing sinuous grace. Cutty cheered and clapped encouragement while Grimsby turned stop-light red, and, pulling the edge of the table cloth over his lap, tried hard to focus his attention on an oyster, but that inoffensive bivalve reminded him of the wrong thing. His hand shook as he picked up his wine glass. To his confusion he found that Joyce was nuzzling his ear, which didn't help.

Mildred undulated up and down the table, tossing preliminary bits of clothing aside with an increasing abandon which, in an earlier era, might have been described as "gay." A quick withdrawal of hairpins demolished her usual neat bun and released a long, shiny tumble of ebony hair. She tossed her tresses defiantly. There was no doubt that she had moved far beyond economics and shapeless bulky sweaters into new fields of knowledge.

"She looks," Horn sighed, "the way hot fudge tastes." Boffy asked McLaughlin whether he realized his Teaching Assistant had such previously concealed talents. J.T. shook his head. Nalorian leaned over to Bert and advised that most women, particularly good-looking women, possess somewhere deep inside an inclination toward exhibitionism. They are often torn, he suggested, between a desire to dress up and a desire to undress. One should therefore relax and let the lady enjoy herself. "Besides, she's quite an unexpected delight, and has a most eloquent bottom." Bert, however, continued to stare at his plate in consternation.

Mildred's nimble feet moved to the thump of the primitive music, but she kept the upper part of her body under a slow and deliberate erotic discipline. Her hands butterflied over the most tempting roundnesses of her figure, stroking and insinuating, then removed her skirt as though unwrapping a gift. Slipping a sly hand behind her back to unclasp the filmy black-lace bra, she shrugged her shoulders out of the straps with a rhythmic languor while still holding the cups closely against her. For several beats she held a statuesque pose, meeting the eyes of her rapt audience with an impudent stare before letting the bra fall. Her burgundy-tipped breasts emerged like tributes proffered to princes. She flicked her tongue and saluted each nipple with a moistened fingertip. Pausing momentarily to savour her growing sense of power, Mildred tossed her long curtain of hair again and, with an arresting allegro of swivelling hips, went into a proud, bouncing strut that rattled the dishes. Cutty roared and Nalorian's eyes brightened in appreciation. She pirouetted into her final movements of simulated paroxysm, slipped off the last impediment to boastful nudity, and flung the wisp of panty at McLaughlin.

He promptly ate it.

Bert started to lurch to his feet, apparently intent upon leaving, but had one foot tangled under his chair and was pushed back by Joyce. He grumbled something inaudible about vulgarity and how could civilized people? Really!

Boffy led the applause for Mildred, who actually blushed, but seemed more than pleased with herself as she hopped off the table and recovered some of her clothing. One of the other girls started to help Mott into her clothes, but Boffy stood up and told her to hold it. "I've been itchy ever since we got soaked in that T-shirt contest. Let's have dinner topless. Why not? It's a party."

And they did that.

A waiter brought bottles of a most acceptable St. Emillion. Nalorian rose to propose a toast to new friends and to Chiliast U. Everyone knocked back the wine with gusto. Nobby announced the imminent arrival of Veal Marengo, with sautéed mushrooms and pearl onions, plus baby carrots glazed with maple syrup. A chocolate mousse would follow.

"Bloody marvellous," said Cuttshaw.

"Certainly," rejoined Nobby with evident satisfaction. "*Omni experiri, omnique gustari*, wouldn't you say?" When Horn wrinkled his brow, Nalorian translated: "'To experience everything, to enjoy everything,' there's the thing." Heads bobbed in cordial agreement.

J.T. turned to his host and proposed a toast to Nobby. "If this is the way you entertain, I hope you'll be staying with us a long while here at Chiliast."

Nalorian acknowledged the gesture and went on to say, "Yes, I've always meant to settle down and remain in one place. Fully intended to, often, and I've made solemn vows in the past. But things keep popping up, delectable things like Boffy here, and irresistible temptations of an unsuitable nature have plagued me. And that, as they say, is when the clit hits the plan, not so? Do I want to stay? Hah. Do pigeons like statues? But life is imperfect, my friends. We shall see. Meanwhile, drink up and let's make a jolly time."

Hopwood cast an artist's eye at the nipples jiggling before

him and noted how J.T. was staring at Mildred like a cat at a goldfish. "Boys will be boys," said Horn, draining his glass, "and men will be children."

Nobby, catching his eye, muttered, "In the great carnival of life, Hopwood, shills like you and I have certain advantages."

"*D'accord.*"

Grimsby, having shoved in a fast helping of veal, made another move to rise and leave. "I really should be going."

"Not at all," Nalorian insisted. "There's dessert to come."

Boffy winked at Joyce, who moved over and sat on Grimsby's lap. Bert flushed and broke into a sweat. Joyce purred, "Maybe you don't realize it, Professor, but I'm your date for tonight. You shouldn't neglect me, you know? And I wouldn't neglect you. From where I'm sitting, it feels as though you could use a little relief. Why don't we go into the back room, just us two?"

"Well, that's awfully kind of you, but I must be getting along. I have papers to mark tomorrow and–everything." Bert dumped the woman from his lap and struggled to his feet. He made for the exit, but stopped and intoned a ritual thanks to Nalorian.

Politeness was his undoing. Nobby sighed and tipped a signal to Boffy. In a twinkling, five topless females descended on a stunned Grimsby, picked him up bodily and, amid shrieks and giggling, bore him into the sleeping alcove at the back. Sounds of girlish glee. Bert struggling. J.T. goggling around uncertainly. Hopwood smiling. Nalorian pouring more wine. Grimsby made several yelps and grumps of protest. Just before he was smothered in rollicking feminine flesh, Bert's voice was heard to squeak, "Let go of my winky!"

Hopwood helped himself to more veal. Cuttshaw leaned over to Nalorian and inquired what the hell was coming off. "I suppose you set this all up?"

"In a manner of speaking, yes, although I did not foresee a result exactly like this. I did have it in mind, though, to provide a bit of diversion for our colleague. It may do him good, don't you think?"

"I'm not sure. Bert is Bert. What exactly is happening to the poor bastard?"

"Unless I am very much mistaken, he is, as they say, getting his beans snapped." Nalorian went over to the record player and turned it up to cover the commotion behind the partition.

Cuttshaw considered for a moment, and then broke into loud laughter. "Whadaya think about that, J.T.?"

"Damned if I know. But it's too late now, isn't it?"

"Too much," commented Horn. "We'll never make a modest Canadian out of you, Nobby. You're too damned excessive."

Nalorian passed another bottle and proposed a toast to excess and to gratuitous pleasures of the unexpected. He was launching into full oratorical orbit when Bert returned, clutching at his trousers.

Grimsby stared balefully around him and cast a particularly accusative eye at Nalorian. "I've been attacked," Bert said in a flat voice. "Molested. I've been, damn it, raped."

The expression on Bert's face caused Cutty to pause for a moment, but quickly he went into convulsions of laughter.

Grimsby stood glowering around helplessly. He then adjusted his clothing and went off into a corner to suck a peppermint and feel sorry for himself.

J.T., torn between sympathy and hilarity, went over and put an arm around Bert, but was pushed away by his disconsolate colleague.

As the girls re-emerged from behind the partition and jostled each other for refills of wine, McLaughlin went over to Nobby and quietly observed, "You may have gone too far with that little caper."

Nalorian pursed his lips. "You might be right, at that. Believe me, his reaction is not what I wanted or expected. But life is full of these unlikely surprises, isn't it?" He sighed.

"Do you happen to recall the lines of a poet named Greaves? Seventeenth century, I think. Not inappropriate.

> 'Have done, have done then! I now bewail my hap,
> Repentance follows with an after-clap.
> Ay me, my joys are murdered with a frown,
> And sorrow pulls untimely pleasure down.' "

J.T. looked around, then peered back into Nalorian's face. "You do revel in your arcane erudition, don't you?"

"Believe it or not," said Nobby, "there are times when I don't."

17

Embarrassment always takes a heavy toll. During the next week, the billiard players tended to avoid one another. Degradation, however inadvertent, makes everyone uneasy. McLaughlin found himself ducking his colleagues in general, and Bert in particular. Even Nalorian was not high on the list of those he wanted to chat with after the Blue Venus debacle.

But Trish had expressed an interest in getting to know the lively Nalorian. She'd heard enough to realize that he was a vivid and unusual man. Wouldn't he and his wife come to dinner on Friday night? J.T. said that he'd invite them, and on a Thursday morning he set off down the hall in search of Nobby.

McLaughlin was waylaid, however, by Grimsby. "How about a coffee, J.T.?"

"Not right now, sorry. I'm looking for Nalorian to ask him about something."

"Oh, well how about lunch when you're free?"

"I'm awfully busy at the moment, Bert. Catch you later, okay, pal?"

"Well, say, at least let me tell you this joke I heard. It's good. Let me just remember how it goes. You'll like this one. It seems there is this young monk. In the monastery. And he requests an interview with the head of the monastery. You with me so far?"

"Yeah, but–"

"So the young monk says, 'Father Abbott, I've come to be forgiven for my sins, but I have to confess that after my leave I came back with a dose of syphilis.' And the abbott says, 'Thank God, my son, I was becoming awfully bored with that Beaujolais.' "

"Bert, look, the way it should go is, the monk says he's got a *case* of syphilis, and the abbott–you see? Wine comes by the case."

"Had you heard it before?"

"Yes. That is, no, but I figured it out, and–anyway, have you seen Nobby?"

"I think he's in his office. But you'd heard it before, had you? So how be we have lunch together later on?"

"Not today, I'm afraid. Thursday is my heaviest bit of teaching. Maybe tomorrow."

McLaughlin gently detached himself from Grimsby and went on down the hall. He found Nalorian tacking a note to his office door. The note said, "Back in ten minutes."

"You just leaving, Nobby? Something I wanted to ask you. Got time to go for a coffee?"

"I was just on my way. The fact is I'm dodging off for a tiny bit. Got to do something, with little time to spare."

"I see. Back in ten minutes, though, eh? Where are you off to?"

"Bermuda."

It took McLaughlin a second to get this together. "*Bermuda*. Sweet krist in a hammock! I don't suppose I'll be seeing Boffy in my Friday seminar?"

Nalorian smiled. "Chances are you won't, no. I just had this urge for a bit of an outing."

"Uh-huh."

"I'm on my–our way to the airport. Cancelled only the one Friday class, and my Teaching Assistant is going to administer a test to my Monday-morning group. With any luck, I'll be on deck for lectures Tuesday. No big thing. A little jaunt."

"Nobby, I'm not being critical or anything, it's just–do you think that note of 'Back in ten minutes' is an adequate, you know, cover?"

"I see what you mean." Nalorian took the note off the door, turned it over, and solemnly printed "Called away to urgent meeting." After a further second's thought he added, "with a publisher." "That should keep one from perishing," he chortled. "So, what was it you wanted to ask me?"

J.T. shook his head and turned away. "Never mind," he said. "Never mind."

"See you later, then," Nalorian cried, bounding away with long loping strides. "Don't work too hard."

McLaughlin was so distracted as he returned down the hall that when he re-encountered the inevitable Grimsby he impulsively invited Bert for dinner Friday. Bert accepted with alacrity and was effusive in his thanks.

J.T. realized that Trish would regret the substitution. He wondered to himself, now whythehell did I do that? But at least he might be able to get back on a more even keel with Grimmers, and assuage the nagging feelings of guilt about neglecting a forlorn friend.

* * *

On Friday, when J.T. reminded Trish that he was bringing Bert Grimsby home for dinner that night, she was much less than overjoyed. Bert, she thought, is such a good, simple, lovable person–and such a drag. Talking to him, for all his intellectual ability, is like talking to a Bartlett pear. Hoping to make the best of what promised to be a heavy evening, she decided to prepare in advance and leave in the oven for automatic switch-on a pot of plain but tasty Chicken Garrison. She'd decide whether to serve it over broad noodles or rice when the time came. And off she went downtown to plunder and pillage the ladies' wear sections of Holt's and Creeds on Bloor Street.

Later in the day, however, driving home and more than slightly dreading the evening, Bert occupied her mind. Where *does* J.T. find these people? Bert was capable of listening (which is half the battle), of sentiment and sweet-tempered kindness, but not of lightness, not playfulness. What ruined his social and sexual chances was a ponderousness, a remorseless conversational weight. He'd use the same flat, relentless tone of voice if he told you that interest rates were being adjusted downwards, or that the world would end tomorrow, or that he loved you. No variation; neither twinkle nor zip. Trish did not envy her husband the company he kept.

Nor was J.T. feeling very frisky or enviable. At five-thirty he was driving home with Grimsby in Bert's car, struggling to make conversation about Argonaut football scores and Maple Leaf hockey prospects, but making heavy weather of it with the morose and monosyllabic responses of his colleague.

As they rolled up Glen Road toward North Rosedale, they passed two overprivileged little scions of the *haute bourgeoisie* on the sidewalk. One of these gleaming urchins, full of childish rage against his overindulged and mindlessly coddled circumstances, flung a rock at Grimsby's car. Crack. The stone shattered the glass of the driver's side window. Shards of glass hit Bert's cheek and drew a trace of blood. J.T. emitted a yelp of surprise and outrage, but Bert drove on, not even blinking or changing his expression, never taking his foot off the accelerator.

"Bert, for kristsake, stop!"

"Why?"

"Let's chase those little bastards and catch them! Stop! Are you cut? Let's go after those nasty wee shits and bang their heads together!"

"No point to it. We'd never catch them. Really. You're so excitable, J.T. Don't distress yourself. I try to ignore such things. Windows can be replaced. Life is full of these inconveniences."

"But are you bleeding?"

"No, not much. Why bother about it?

"Because–damn it, because you can't let them get away with that sort of crap. This fucking world is bad enough, without letting baby hoodlums stomp all over you. You just got *shoved*, man! You've gotta shove back, make the little farts *pay*!"

"I don't let these things bother me, J.T. If I did, my whole life would be an uproar. It's tiresome, but I wouldn't want to sweat it. Anyway, we're almost to your place. Do I turn here?"

"Yes. Jeez, Bert. You amaze me, sometimes."

Once they arrived, the talk over cocktails was slow. Trish tried hard to leaven the conversational lump with upbeat tales of her shopping expedition that afternoon and the doings of the kids, but got little more than solemn grunts and wan smiles out of Grimsby while J.T. socked back one or two drinks too many and chewed apprehensively on a fingernail. Dinner went well enough, with Jossy not at home that night, and Rob on his best behaviour; Davie had already been fed. Grimsby became almost animated in his expressions of appreciation for the modest meal set before him. "Excellent chicken," he muttered several times.

"I suppose you eat out a lot," Trish commented, "and use the smart restaurants? Do you have dinner often at Fentons? Or the Courtyard? You bachelors have more time and money for dining out than we do. I wish we could go out more."

J.T. studied his wine glass.

Bert said, "Out? Not really, It's a treat for me to sit down in a home to a properly cooked meal and a tablecloth. I'd eat out more, I guess, except that I hate to eat alone in public places. Vaguely embarrasses me. Better a baloney sandwich in front of the T.V. than a crowded restaurant with couples and large parties staring at you while you pretend to be waiting for a friend who hasn't shown up yet. It's so-disappointing. Undignified."

"Maybe you should get married, Grimmers," J.T. grinned. Patricia pushed at a cuticle.

"I was married once, J.T. Didn't you know?"

"No kidding? Were you? You've never mentioned it that I can recall." As he thought about it, he realized he had once heard some departmental rumour to that effect, but it was then, as now, rather difficult to imagine. "What happened?"

"Nothing much. This was years ago, of course. She was a

librarian. We had coffee together for about eight weeks, and I guess we were both a bit lonely, so we got married. Nice girl named Paula. Big brown eyes, she had, and she seemed to think Professors were, you know, quite interesting. On the honeymoon, we went to Niagara Falls – which I thought was the right thing to do – but on the honeymoon she laughed at me. Laughed. Almost got hysterical, once. Said something about me treating her like a seminar and not like a woman. How are women supposed to be treated? Different from other people, I guess. I don't know. She said I was too fumbly. Anyway, she up and quit me in about six weeks. After she left, the sorrow spread through me, as quiet as cancer, and as sharp. Didn't I ever tell you this? No? Well, one night she just wasn't there. She left me a note, saying she thought I might be better off on my own and something about having a conversation with an encyclopaedia being no less agreeable. She wished me luck, which was nice of her. I never did know what became of her. Strange. As far as I know, she never divorced me. So I guess I'm still a married man, come to think of it. I'm not sure."

This unlikely outburst left even Trish without much to say, while her husband stared at his guest in pity and bewilderment. She started to clear the dishes. The men straggled off to the front room with the promise of coffee to follow.

"We don't seem to have any cognac," J.T. apologized, "just raw Spanish cooking brandy. Would you like a snort of scotch? Teacher's, it is. Let's have a scotch, okay?"

"Very nice," said Grimsby.

They sat on opposite sides of the small fireplace, and McLaughlin rearranged the logs to produce a small blaze, even though the autumn weather was still warmish.

"Very nice," Grimsby repeated. There ensued a long minute's silence, like Remembrance Day.

"So how's your work going, Bert? I'm always interested in your work."

"Well, I wanted to ask you about that. I'm having a bit of

trouble with chapter nineteen of my textbook. The chapter on International Trade Theory. The problem seems to be-"

Trish returned from the kitchen at that moment. Hearing Grimsby's drone, she had no compunctions about interrupting. "I'll be going upstairs now, if you'll excuse me, to read pamphlets on some hospital volunteer work I may get involved in. I'll let you boys have a good talk. See you later." Trish shot J.T. one of her looks that said "I'm sorry but I can't hang in." "Don't sit up too late" was the further message she conveyed by tapping a finger on her wristwatch beyond Grimsby's view as she said good night.

When she had withdrawn, Bert launched himself again. "About this trade theory chapter, J.T. Maybe you'd read it for me and make some suggestions. The thing about it is-"

Davie suddenly roared down the stairs and threw himself onto his father's knee. "Are you going to read to me tonight, Dad?"

"Not tonight, son. We have company. Off to bed you go. Your mother will tuck you in."

"But you didn't say it!"

"Say what, Davie?"

"Did I remember to tell you today. . . ."

J.T. believed family rituals were best practised in private. He whispered, ". . . that I love you."

Davie beamed. "Me, too."

"Say good night," said his father.

"Good night, Mr. Bert."

"Good night, David," Grimsby replied. "But before you go, tell me what you like best."

"Our dog Max!" Davie shouted. "And sometimes I like my brother Rob, but other times I don't. And ice cream. My Dad and I like cream, don't we, Dad? Or doughnuts. I *love* chocolate doughnuts. And sugar doughnuts. But my Mom says they're not good for me, and Dad says they don't grow on trees."

Bert considered this in his unhurried way. "Doughnuts

probably do grow on trees, or so our friend Nubar would argue. It bears thinking about."

"Who's Nubar?" Davie asked.

"Just one of the guys we work with," said his father.

"Oh. I'd like to meet a man who understood about doughnuts. They go good with lunches."

"Well," J.T. insisted, "they go *well* with lunches."

"Yeah. You got it," chirped the boy.

Davie finally allowed himself to be shooed upstairs and J.T. waved the bottle of scotch around in a tentative manner, managing to press only another half-inch on his guest. Pouring himself another too generous shot seemed merely a just and prudent compensation.

"You don't know how lucky you are to have a boy like Davie."

"Sure I do. He's a good kid. Where were we, Bert?"

"Just relaxing. Very nice, too. But the thing is, J.T., I was hoping I could get you to read my section on International Trade Theory–"

"Any time, sure." McLaughlin lit a cigarette and made noises about the price of gold, but somehow he never got back to the necessitous chapter. Bert sighed.

"There are days when I wish I could sort all of this through and get it right," Grimsby scowled into his glass. "I wish I could get it down on paper just so. It's difficult. I guess I try too hard. Maybe I'm just depressed."

"Are you really, Bert? That's a helluva thing." He helped himself to scotch and more ice from the sidetable. "How long have you been depressed?"

"About ten years."

"What? You're kidding."

"No."

"Oh. Jeez. I'd never, you know, realized. Seriously. Things are pretty good, though, aren't they? I mean, your writing is moving along. Fairly well. Slowly. But moving. What's so depressing? Krist. Your work is always good stuff. And you're a bachelor, not poor, and free as a seagull in a windstorm.

174

What in the hell is wrong with that? Your ass is pretty well hunkered down deep in the academic butter-tub, I'd say. What's to be down about?"

"Nothing. I don't know. Everything. I sort of wish I could chuck it."

"No problem. Why don't you take a year off. A sabbatical. Go home for a while, or maybe to Europe. Regroup."

"Home? Have I ever told you about home, J.T.?"

J.T. fought back a sense of alarm. "Not sure that you have, much. No. I remember you came from New Brunswick, and got your Ph.D. at Yale, but–"

"My father was a fireman in Fredericton. He must have read a lot while sitting around the firehall, because he gave me books, encouraged me to read. But he never said much. Taciturn man. My mother read the Good Book, was active in the Baptist Church, seemed to endure her narrow life with resignation. Any time my father got a few dollars together, he plunged on penny stocks. A quiet rainbow man, I guess, always hoping against hope for a pot of gold. Silver mines in the Yukon, uranium in Labrador, dry-hole oil wells in Manitoba. But he never got a nickel back from any of them. When he died, we found drawers full of stock certificates, boxes full. All worthless, you see, and after lawyers' fees we realized about six hundred dollars on the lot. He died in '73. It turned out that he had even borrowed against his life insurance to buy speculative stocks, so Mom didn't have much after he went. My Mom wasn't far behind him. She just gave up, I think. Maybe I will have another touch of that scotch, if you don't mind."

"Uh? Certainly. Help yourself." There must be some question to ask at this point. "That's rough. But did you have happy times? I mean, as a kid?"

"Well, I suppose I did. What can you say about growing up, except that you grew up? I worked hard at school. 'Swotty,' they called me, because I swotted away at the books. Education seemed to me a way of escape, so I was glad to work at it.

"One thing I wanted in earlier days was a dog. I begged for a dog! From about the time I was in kindergarten, I guess. Finally my father brought home a mongrel pup, given him by one of the boys at the firehall. Happy? I was beside myself! That dog had the most velvety big floppy ears, and a tail like a frenzied metronome. I remember we chased each other. He'd jump and bark and want his belly scratched. The thing was, though, I got sick. Asthmatic sort of thing, and a rash. Turned out I was allergic to dogs, so my mother got rid of him. My parents meant well, though, and we took in a stray cat as a sort of consolation prize. Orange cat. Tough, with ragged ears. It didn't much like to be petted. Used to zap me with his claws, I remember, if I got too familiar. I wanted to fondle it, but he spat and slashed and took big chunks out of my hide every time I tried to pick him up. The brute got on well enough with my sister, though."

"I didn't know you had a sister."

"Mavis? Sure. She's still back home in the Maritimes. Mavis always loved animals, maybe because she got on so well with that ornery cat. She studied to be a veterinarian."

"Do you see much of her?"

"Not a lot. She dropped out of the vet college because of an unhappy love affair with an Italian bricklayer in Moncton, and took a job with the Humane Society, just to work with animals. Her job turned out to be disappointing. She operated the gas chamber. Putting unwanted animals 'to sleep,' as they called it. I think it bent her mind. She told me that she was obliged to kill as many as fifty superfluous dogs and cats per week with the lethal vapours. Couldn't stand it, of course, so she quit."

"What does Mavis do now?"

"She has a job in public relations for a meat-packing plant."

J.T. took another deep gulp of scotch. It was clear that the conversation needed a different turn. "But your family wasn't poor, Bert, was it? You didn't grow up deprived. I mean, my parents were never rich either, and on the prairies in the thirties, when I was born, we didn't exactly wallow in luxury. My own father went bankrupt once in a trucking company. And Cutty's parents lost their farm during the Depression near Wetaskawin before oil was discovered under the homestead they had to abandon. But you didn't suffer much like that, I suppose, if your Dad had a steady job in the Fire Department?"

"We were never poor, exactly, no. But we never had much. Things always seemed more–well–temporary and disjointed than poor, if you know what I mean." Bert stared into the fireplace before continuing. "Strangely enough, my parents didn't own a house. We moved every two or three years from rented house to apartment to rented house, while waiting for those dreamland investments in penny stocks to soar. Oh, my father bought a bungalow years later at my mother's insistence, long after I'd left home, but when Dad died the mortgage still wasn't paid off. Still, we did have the summer cottage."

"A cottage? There you are, now. You should go and rest and recreate yourself at that cottage. Where is it?"

"Was. It was on the Saint John River. Mother got the land, on good frontage, from a relative. During the war, in 1943. Wartime conditions meant that you couldn't buy nails or even lumber, even if you had money. Dad managed to buy a section-foreman's shack from the railroad. What it was, I remember, was a boxcar with two little windows, plus rough panelling and some insulation. He had it moved onto the lot and stuck a big old woodstove into it. We built a long verandah and sleeping-porch on the front. All rough amateur carpentry, but it made a nice enough cottage. And a two-hole outhouse in the back. From the open door of the outhouse, which was up the slope, we had a fine view of the river. I always liked the river. Moving slowly, you know? Restful."

"Sounds like a great place."

"It was. Beautiful country around there. In the autumn, the leaves blazed in colours you wouldn't believe. Ecstatic, rich colours of the autumn burst out every October before the bare-branched winter death. Oh, God, I loved the place. That cottage was the centre of my universe, a refuge. No matter how often we moved around in Fredericton, the box-car cabin was always there, always my ready and certain retreat when the ice broke up and spring released us from snow and school and the embarrassment of narrow rented walls. It was the one thing I could count on, or belong to, you see? Well, I don't mean to become maudlin about it. You know what I mean.''

"Sure. So, I was asking you before, why don't you go back and spend some time there?''

"Can't. Sold. It's all gone now. When my father became ill he sold it. It was the one thing the family had, the one thing I cared about, and I always said, 'Don't ever part with the cottage.' But my Mom said, 'Herbert is away in Toronto now. He doesn't come home much.' And my Dad said, 'Yes, the boy is ungrateful. Neglectful.' Golly, I was just busy. So when Dad became so ill that last summer of his stunted, well-intentioned life, and a fellow walked up to the back door one day and offered to buy the place, he sold. Ten thousand dollars. Cash. Maybe just a forlorn impulse of acquisitiveness and despair, maybe a quick escape, but he took it. I'd have given him ten, or twenty, or more if he'd asked, but he never did. Ten grand! The land alone was worth probably twenty. Still, it's not the money that bothered me then or bothers me now, you understand; it's that he gave away my place, my permanency. I can't tell you how I felt. Have you ever come home and found your dog has been given away? You might get another dog, I guess. I never did. But you'll never get another home. And when you can't go home, where do you turn? The bottom has fallen out. You've been diminished.''

Bert grimaced and popped a mint into his mouth.

"You never told me that before," J.T. said in a low voice.

"Didn't I? Suppose not. I don't much like to think about it.''

The silence that followed was as heavy as an anchor. A wet log in the fireplace rolled away from the sputtering flame.

"Hey, you wanted to talk about that chapter of your textbook," McLaughlin exclaimed with spurious tangential enthusiasm.

"That's right. But maybe not just right now."

"Oh?" Wrong again, thought J.T. Out of whack. Nonwhackadoo. "Well. Yeah. Let's have another scotch, shall we? Why not! There we go. No, no, go ahead–there's lots more ice, really. I'll get some. And while I'm at it, I'll just go upstairs and take a leak. Gotta splash the old boots, eh, Grimmers?" He tried to coax a laugh from his own throat, but failed. "Be right back."

"Jeez," McLaughlin mumbled to himself as he went up the stairs. He looked in on Trish, and found her already in bed. She merely whispered an insistent avowal that she had no flipping intention of coming back downstairs. She rolled her eyes and snapped off the bedside light, clutching at the covers and turning over with pointed emphasis, a soundless but eloquent comment on what she thought of the evening's enjoyment. He couldn't blame her.

After doing the necessaries, he paused in the bathroom to snip an errant hair out of his nostril, and combed his hair twice to delay the trudge back downstairs. When he returned to the living room he found Grimsby rubbing his hands, peeling little balls of dirt and dead skin from his left palm with his right thumb. Rub, rub, a nervous affliction of vacuous intensity. Lady Macbeth's sleepwalking was a kittenish romp compared to this guy's scraping at his fat, fleshy hands.

Before J.T. could attempt any new bright conversational gambit, Bert said, without looking up from the arduous process of scouring his grubby palm, "Does any of us ever really grow up? We scuffle along through school and through the larger college of hard knocks. We acquire 'experience,' and brittle shells, like clams. The trouble with acquiring experience is that it makes you 'grown-up.' And the trouble with being grown-up is that it makes you old. Not inside, necessarily, but certainly outside. Here I am, forty-eight, and still admitting to the feelings of a baby. If only it were possible to live a long time without growing stale. The India-rubber bounce of youth becomes the dead weight of the bowling ball. Grown-up? Damn it. I guess none of us ever ceases being the little boy from the particular place where he first experienced river currents or wild raspberry bushes. Probably our hearts always remain where we first sniffed the careless native flowers." Grimsby subsided and the dying fire hissed.

J.T. sipped his scotch. He cleared his throat and tried to rouse himself like a deaf man attempting to rejoin an unheard conversation. "Did you ever try writing short stories, Bert? Or poetry? Sometimes you get off some pretty fair phrases. 'Careless' was almost the right word for flowers, you know?"

"Did I say that? Oh. Sorry. I didn't mean to –"

"Don't for kristsake apologize. You really had it by the tail there for a minute on a good downhill pull. Might be the booze, but you seem to get the words rolling out. You don't often talk like that."

"I guess not, no. Don't often get the chance."

The following oppressive conversational lull impelled McLaughlin to try another ploy. "Look, Grimmers, what you need is a change. A shift of gears, or maybe a year off. A sabbatical, there's the thing. Why don't you apply for a research grant and trot off to Europe on a leave of absence? I don't remember you taking a sabbatical recently."

"No. Not really. Can't say as I'd like it, or trust myself to try it."

"Why the hell not?"

"On the one hand, I might have too much idle time, too little to do, and bog down further, or hate myself for doing nothing. On the other hand, I might like it. Might like the irresponsible leisure so much that, well, I'd be afraid I'd never be able to pull myself together to do a stroke of work again."

"I'm not sure I follow."

"The question is, *what* to do? What's worth while? If I spent four or six years writing a big book, I doubt whether a handful of people would notice, or care. Not sure I want to be bothered. No, my problem is, given limited time, how do you decide what's worth doing? Maybe nothing is, maybe nothing matters."

"Now wait, you surely have some–goals, Bert, some ambitions?"

"Used to have. I think the trouble was I got what I wanted too early and too easily, then couldn't really decide where to go from there. I wanted to get out of the Maritimes and to travel, see Europe, and I did that in youth hostels while I was still a student. I hoped for a professorial position at a decent university, and here I've been for twenty-three years at Chiliast U., a very good institution. All of this fell into my lap while I was in my mid-twenties. And I hoped I could publish, see my name in print, and send off-prints home to my parents and my friends in Fredericton. So I did that. It wasn't hard. But most of it, frankly, proved disappointing. Not much fun." He paused to pop another mint.

"I know what you mean. Still, there's always travel. Jeez, I envy you that footloose thing. Spain, Crete, Rome, the Riviera–gawd! That seems to me like dying and going to heaven."

"No, J.T., that's not my sort of thing. And what am I going to do, trade sitting alone in a Toronto restaurant for sitting alone in a Paris bistro? I can watch other people having fun without crossing the ocean."

Just one more track to try, J.T. thought. Somehow Bert always caused him to grope desperately for any positive straw and almost forget his own troubles, even though trying to get the big lug to loosen up was like trying to teach a giraffe to slink under a limbo bar. "There's your thing, now. Friends! Women or marriage apart, you've got friends, Bert. Everybody, well, likes you. You don't have an enemy in the world."

"Or many friends, it seems. No, I haven't been lucky in that. Oh, good guys like yourself, but most are preoccupied with their wives and families. Not free to travel with a bachelor like me. Might be easier if I were homosexual, but I don't seem to fit there either. My oldest buddy from high-school days never left Fredericton; he seldom answers my letters, and when I go back to visit him, he appears to regard me as a pretentious big-city fop who's too darn grand to relax with – much as I envy him and, you know, miss him. Friends? I value them, believe me. But they're few. Do you know the greatest social disease of our time? Not the clap, not poverty, not drugs or pollution. It's loneliness. No one wants to know about it. Isolation. And do you know who my best friend is?"

J.T. paused. Now that he thought about it, he couldn't give a quick name to that doubtlessly burdened unfortunate. "No, who?"

"You."

"Aw, Grimmers. Jeez. But – I'm flattered, yeah, I really am – it's nice of you to say – but."

J.T. wondered what Trish would say that would be evasive and polite? She could skitter out of a tight corner faster than a puppy fleeing from a threatened bath and still come up smiling. His own smile froze and cracked under Grimsby's soft stare. What to do now? Trish would have a slam-dunk response, but what? Offer him another scotch? Or a Twinkie, or a slit-veined exchange of blood-brotherhood, or maybe a mention in my will? Now wait. How can anybody be hard on the guy? He means so well. He's laying it all out, and can't be rejected. Poor bastard. But what to say?

Finally, after an awkward hiatus and some hyper-friendly facial contortions, J.T. could think of nothing other than, "I'll just go and check whether Davie's asleep, okay? Only be a minute."

Getting out of the room was like fleeing from a leper, and he couldn't remain too long upstairs without giving offence.

McLaughlin lingered outside Davie's room as many minutes as he dared, then retraced his steps, but he was no more than halfway down the stairs again when Bert's unrelenting voice ploughed into the next dry furrow.

"There you are. Everything all right? Weren't you going to give me a few pointers on how to spice up my chapter on international trade?"

"Well, it's getting sort of late for that. Another time, eh? Let's just have a last splash of the distilled waters and then I think we should pack it in. I'm a bit tired."

"Of course. You bet. Another drop and I'll be off. Honest, I do regret. . . . Say, let me tell you a joke! It's a good one. Let me see now, it goes: What's the difference between a stick-up and a hold-up? Give up? Twenty years. Get it? The first time I heard it, I thought it was about some point of criminal law, but actually it's about aging." Bert continued to chortle at his own limp jibe for several dragging seconds, apparently trying to convince himself that he'd just surpassed Woody Allen. Then with an abrupt twist he asked, "Do you believe in anything, J.T.?"

"I guess I do. Doesn't everybody? Why do you ask?"

"I don't know. I guess I'm looking for something. I put the question to Nubar once. It isn't clear that he believes in much. Anyway, tell me what you believe in."

"I'm not sure I could, hell, reel off a list, just like that."

"Try. I'd be interested. Such as where you stand on purpose, ends."

"Purpose? Good krist!"

"And truth–and maybe integrity. I've always worried about things like that. Although recently, I must say, truth seems like something I misplaced in an old pile of lecture notes, and integrity a parcel that I lost on a number seventy-nine bus.

"It's for sure I don't have any world-shaking views on truth. Jeez. Maybe we should go back to international trade theory at that. No? Well, I mean, I believe in–lots of things. My emotions are more like ping-pong than straight lines, but we all have the special private things that we care about, don't we?"

"I'm not sure that I do."

"Uh-huh. Well, damn it, I believe in–where to begin–in Babe Ruth, Arthur Koestler, Lili St. Cyr, F. Scott Fitzgerald and Bertrand Russell." J.T. reached for the bottle of scotch. "I believe in Albert Camus and Salvador Allende."

"Those are just people, not beliefs," Grimsby objected. "Not principles."

"I don't much care about principles. They let you down, and seldom fit. It's people I believe in, specifics."

"But–"

"Don't interrupt. You started this." J.T. hiccupped. "I believe in Gabriel Dumont, Flann O'Brien, Nye Bevan, and Fred Exley. I believe in myths, Studebaker Avantis, Bransom anchovie-stuffed olives in Beefeater martinis, the urgency of assisting the underdog, manners, decency, solar eclipses, and the sanctity of the printed word on the page. I'm very keen about oysters, Buck Clayton, Kay Kendall, Sam Johnson, naps on Sunday afternoons–after brunch, after not going to church–and the Round Tables of King Arthur and the Algonquin Hotel."

Grimsby opened and closed his mouth like a goldfish, but McLaughlin, warming to his subject, waved him off. Lavishing another generous quantity of the old infuriator into his glass, J.T. plunged on between gulps.

"I believe in single malt scotch, H.L. Mencken, and Gray's *Elegy*. I'm convinced that Marx was a bigger bore than even Hegel or Wagner, if that's possible. My instinctive faith goes out to the Loch Ness monster, whooping cranes, chinooks, libraries, and nasturtiums. Certainly I do not believe in sherry, Vice-Presidents (administrative), Margaret Trudeau, life after death, Saint Thomas Aquinas, or processed cheese.

184

"I believe in the indestructibility of Model A roadsters, the university, friendship, the Saskatchewan Roughriders, John Newlove's poetic liver, the human spirit and its itch to create. Porch swings excite my attention, as do mermaids, Jon Vickers, conscientious objectors, peons, peonies, Black Holes, and Tallulah Bankhead. Crocuses are nice. I have faith in spurts of imagination and the willingness to take risks and welcome surprises. I believe in Paul Robeson, Satchel Paige, whales, Robbie Burns, the Parthenon, and that stupidity is everywhere and invincible – particularly when public opinion is being measured by loonies with slide-rules. Implacable is my opposition to the Liberal Party, T.V. dinners, Oral Roberts, pantyhose, crab grass, racism, bigotry, and the Hun. Count me as a resolute foe of Miss America, bus tours, psychology, condoms, disc jockeys, and jogging. Foursquare I'll always stand for the abolition of the Canadian Senate and pay toilets, plus the removal of all taxes on wine, books, pogo sticks, teddy bears, and crotchless panties.

J.T. paused to burp and to drink, but he was not to be stopped.

"I believe there is but one God, and Louis Armstrong was his prophet. Never would I doubt the words of Yeats, the keening truth of highland bagpipes, the pitch of Bix Beiderbeck, or the imminence of the second coming of Woodie Guthrie. I believe in beauty, fun, Guinness stout, lobsters, Mozart, Thurber, bell towers, schooners in full sail, and hot corn meal muffins. And I sort of like turtle-neck sweaters."

Bert blinked at him uncertainly. "You never mentioned your book on Innis, or economics. The whole discipline of economics."

"To hell with Innis." He hiccupped again. "Screw economics."

"Hmmm. That's a handy little arsenal of preferences. I suppose it's a fairly adequate provisioning for a Mother Hubbard's cupboard of prejudices, but I don't see how you manage to avoid the basics – rules to live by. It sure wouldn't much help a person to decide what to live for."

"Live for!" J.T. whooped. "That's like what Satchmo said when he was asked to define jazz. 'If you have to ask, you'll never know.' "

Grimsby's large, muddy eyes were sad. "You may be right. But here am I drowning in a sea of disbelief and you toss out, not a life-preserver, but a roll of Lifesavers."

"You don't think that's enough, huh? Well, pencil me in as an enthusiastic immoderate. Maybe confused, even superficial. But bouncing. Trying! Shit, I never said I had any truth by the tail. The question was yours, and my answers will have to do for me, if for nobody else. Put me down on the big scoreboard as 'undecided.' A cheerful agnostic, if not too sober. Life? Yes. Beliefs? Principles? A definite 'maybe.'" He paused, and avoided Bert's solemn gaze. "Anyway, I think we should call it a night."

"Oh. I suppose, yes. It's been a very nice evening. I do thank you."

After finding Bert's coat and easing him out into the night, McLaughlin sank back into the closest chair, exhausted and drained. He puffed a last cigarette and wondered whether trying to carry the leaden weight of Bert's gloom was worth the amount of nervous energy expended. "Best friends. Holy whistling krist." There were times when J.T. thought he just couldn't stand it.

* * *

The next morning, mercifully a Saturday, McLaughlin awoke to a headache, a singed flannel tongue, and Davie shouting into his ear. "Mr. Bert is downstairs! Why aren't you up, Dad? He says he's going to show me about doughnuts."

J.T. lurched to the bathroom and drank at least two oceans of water with a Bromo Seltzer chaser. He pulled on trousers, and, moving his feet with deliberate care not to jostle his head or his rebellious insides, ventured slowly downstairs with Davie prancing ahead of him. Trish's greeting was cool, and sure enough, there in the kitchen was Grimsby, beaming with cordiality, a mug of coffee in his fist.

"Orange juice," McLaughlin croaked. "Orange juice."

Trish handed him a glassful, while looking the other way.

"Come on, Dad, Mr. Bert says we're going outside."

"Outside. Yeah. Right. Why are we going outside, Bert?"

"To see a little something I arranged earlier this morning, for David. Come on."

Grimsby led the way out the back door into the garden. "Look there," he announced with a small smile of shy pride. "A doughnut tree." The spectacle was unlikely but wonderful to behold, at least to the delighted eye of a bemused child. Bert had made an early visit to a Country Style Donut shop on Yonge Street and had bought a load of mixed sinkers. These he had festooned by threads from the branches of a diminutive crab-apple tree in McLaughlin's back garden, each round confection dangling and turning in the breeze as a sweet invitation to clutch and snap. Plus ju-jubes, cheerful, gaily-coloured little rabbit-turd confections he had encased in plastic bags and hung by bits of string from the lower branches.

But the doughnuts were the thing. They dripped from the tree like gooey sugar-plum fairies that were overweight and distended, winking with airy centres. These insouciant sweeties were of startling variation, maple doughnuts and lemon doughnuts, doughnuts stuffed with jelly, and blueberries, and cinnamon. There were apple 'n' spice doughnuts. There were honey-glazed doughnuts. There were doughnuts resplendent in chocolate icing, strawberry frosting and toasted coconut coating, plus a few orange crullers. No plain doughnut dared show its hole to the glorious assemblage of mad-dumpling splendour. The innumerable munchables were the superbly sticky, the chuckly results of some wild-eyed pastry cook's deranged imagination. Where recently there had been crab-apples there now hung an exuberant riot of vivid pastry yummies, a veritable three-ringed circus of mad delectable happy-cake goodies.

Davie stood rapt, his eyes as wide as platters. Then he leaped. He snatched a chocolate-chip hoop from a lower twig, and fell laughing to the ground, stuffing the sugary squish of gorpy treasure into his avid mouth.

Trish turned and gave Grimsby a hug.

That worthy said, "Have a jelly-belly, J.T. I like the black ones, myself. They're very nice."

J.T., shaking his head slowly, said, "Aww, Bert. Good old Bert. You're all right, you know that, Grimmers? You're all right."

And then they all had breakfast.

18

On Tuesday morning, Professor Nubar Nalorian kept an appointment with a physician at the University's Health Services Centre. Nobby had applied to buy a package of life insurance, and his initial medical report had not been all positive. The forms for the life policy had been filled out in triplicate, with his wife as beneficiary, but the doctor had summoned him back for some further tests.

The doctor told Nalorian that he wanted him to drop into his lab for an electro-cardiogram the following Thursday. "No time for that at the moment," Nobby insisted, promising to show up for all that nonsense at some future date, when he could spare the time, maybe in three weeks.

"Let me level with you," said the M.D. "You might have a suggestion of a heart murmur. The tests are only to check this out. Your blood pressure is a bit elevated. You're not overweight, which is good, but I strongly urge you to cut down on the cigars, and maybe slow down a bit. Your body needs a rest. Look, your lungs are abused, and your heart is protesting. You give me the impression of a harried man who needs more sleep. It's more than possible that, at the pace you seem to live, you're killing yourself."

"Everything is possible," Nalorian agreed evenly. "But the strenuous life may be preferable to the long life, not true? If you try too hard to postpone death, you merely slow down existence. I prefer life to be brisk and intense."

When the doctor shook his head sagely, Nobby pressed on. "It may be that my mother was reading Omar Khyam before I was born, but in this daily extravaganza that I call life and you want to call middle age and high blood pressure, I'm still getting on with it, and swinging my axe, and let the chips fall where they may. My mother, God rest her soul, had an expression, *'Il n'importe qu'on vive, mais comment.'* That means–"

"My dear sir, you needn't translate. 'It matters not that we live, but how.' And fair enough, I suppose. Nevertheless, my opinion as a medical man is that an electro-cardiogram is indicated and that further tests are desirable."

"Tests bore me."

"Still, they may be revealing. I just want you to take care of yourself. I'm not trying to squelch you, Professor Nalorian. Prudence, that's all I recommend. If you want to trade quotes, I'll go along with you. Who said, 'Live–live all you can. It's a mistake not to.' "

"Grand. That's good thinking. Dylan Thomas?"

"Henry James, in *The Ambassadors*."

"Never would have guessed. Somehow it inspires confidence in a patient to have a sawbones who can quote James, bloodless old bore that he was. Always chewed more than he could bite off, didn't he? Myself, I'd rather bite off too big a mouthful. By God, my teeth are still sharp and I'm still chomping away at the rare prime rib of life, and I'm not much fussed about a trifling touch of heartburn or heart murmur or whatever. We must feast, you'd agree? The bowels and the other offended organs just have to cope with tonight's fortunate overload, and let the dim morning take care of itself."

"I believe," said the doctor, "that at some early medieval feasts they used to place a skeleton at the banquet table to remind themselves of mortality."

"Yes, but the bony wasted presence was never depressing to the true reveller. The skeleton at the feast merely added an extra dimension of awareness, a certain piquancy, not so?"

The physician shrugged and smiled. "You may be right. Shall I look forward to seeing you at the same time in three weeks?"

"Call it four weeks," Nalorian said. "I'll be able to find the time by then. Why not?"

As he left the doctor's office, Nalorian lit a cigarillo, and wondered what Boffy was doing that afternoon.

* * *

That same Tuesday morning McLaughlin, having left the car with Trish, emerged from the subway station and found himself walking beside Chairman Wright. They exchanged greetings and non-committal pleasantries, realizing it was impossible to avoid one another's company for the stroll south from Bloor Street.

They both cast about in some desperation for a neutral topic of conversation, chatting about the weather and the problems of parking, until they drew abreast of the new Social Sciences Building. This mass of slabbed concrete now stood revealed in all its surpassing barbarity because of the recent removal of the high-fence construction hoardings.

"So there," said McLaughlin, "is the building you'll be opening at the ceremony tomorrow."

"Quite so. We certainly need the space," Wright observed, "and what with the unhappy cutbacks on university expenditures, we are fortunate to have–Good God!" Wright stopped short. He stared and gestured with his umbrella at the new structure. "Is that–I'd never really looked at it before–is *that* our new building? Bloody awful looking pile." He scratched his ear with thoughtful dismay. "Isn't it a pity that the so-called modern buildings on the west campus are such abominations? The old campus is so pleasing, so comfortable, but the new buildings are unfortunate. I wonder who designs them?"

"Chowder-heads, obviously," said J.T. "Probably an idiot relative of some twit on the Board of Governors who specializes in pseudo-Russian Stalin-Alley gigantism. These crushingly impersonal cement-block buildings give you only one message: that you are an insect, a grubby little thing of total gibbering insignificance, and that power and the system are everything. It's a shame to see this sort of inhuman architectural crap anywhere, but on a university campus it's unforgivable. The President must be either asleep, or a Philistine, or both."

"Committee decision, undoubtedly," Wright sighed. "You mustn't be too hard on the President. The institutional structure of the university imposes on him certain, ah, straitjackets, as it were. Awrumph-umph! We all work within regrettable constraints. But I didn't know you took these matters so seriously, McLaughlin. Hmmm. I don't suppose that, if I were stricken by a sudden illness and was unable to attend the ceremony, that you'd like another–shall we say–redemptive bash at public speaking this week?"

McLaughlin shuddered. "Not really."

"No. Might not do. I suppose, as Chairman, the puck stops here. If you can't stand the heat, get out of the ice-house, isn't that what they say? I must admit I'd be just as happy to stay home and watch the ceremony on television. T.V. is the scapegoat of reality, I think. Awrumph-umph. And the opening jollities are all arranged. Should be a good show, with the Premier and the Lieutenant-Governor in attendance. Yes, a splendid occasion." He twirled his umbrella and gave the building another hard look. "So I'm supposed to officiate and speak at the opening of such a thing, am I? We'll see about that. The tongue is a two-edged sword, eh? Frightful prospect, though, I must say."

They walked along another few paces in mute if troubled affability.

"And by the way, McLaughlin, my secretary will be asking you and Cuttshaw and probably Nalorian to be attendants at the opening. We do have some quite special guests arriving for the Harry Johnson Memorial Symposium this week to mark the great occasion. There'll be Wolfe from Edinburgh, Jones from UCLA, Van Rinjdroop from Capetown, and other heavyweights."

J.T. said he'd be glad to help.

"Good. Well, I must leave you here. Plenty of administrative chores to do, and that blessed speech to write, which may require an hour or two. I hope to make my address memorable – and appropriate. Uneasy lies the head that wears the Chair, eh?" Wright veered off and sauntered on his way.

* * *

If McLaughlin was fretful about his university problems, he'd have been even less delighted with the world had he known what his wife was doing. That same afternoon Trish met President Naugle for lunch.

The President was not much for subtle, but he was hell for persistent. In recent days he had telephoned Patricia several times, pressing pointed and tenacious requests for a quiet rendezvous. At first she had tended to laugh at him. Naugle, however, after his brief but inconvenient encounter with the ambulance men, included in his invitations to Trish jagged reminders of his power to retaliate and harm her husband's career or to assist it if he chose. Not for nothing was Naugle known as the meanest sonofabitch on the campus. He was used to having his own way, and opponents or people who delayed him in the fulfilment of his desire tended to be trampled. She was sensitive to the potency of his naked threats, and it was not the sort of issue on which Trish could ask J.T.'s advice. She was somewhat confused.

Moreover, she was no little intrigued. Lots and lots of men came on to her, but few with the force of Naugle. Flirtation was one thing, but pile-driving demands were something else. His blandishments, if not gentle, were calculated for maximum impact. He pressed her with the confident vigour of a feudal baron, and included just enough admiration and candied words to stroke her neck or almost turn her head. His messages had a quality of hot-stallion assertiveness that resembled obscene phone calls by a semi-civilized fanatic.

Imitation, she considered, is probably not the sincerest form of flattery. A lot of very bored women would prefer honeyed words and a frank stiff prick. When it comes to getting a lady's attention, insistent raw lust and the urgent flaunting of a tumescent male member will often prove difficult to ignore. That, plus a sense of adventure to add a hint of danger and excitement, could lift matters beyond the mundane. In a world of pasty sliced-bread relationships, forbidden fruit has a special tang.

President Naugle was a most uncomfortable and discomfitting man. A swashbuckling risk-taker, a grinning pirate, he eventually won Patricia's agreement to have lunch with him at La Scala, a pricey restaurant not much frequented by Associate Professors.

She arrived dressed to kill, or at least to slash and wound. He was solicitous, charming. They circled for position over martinis. During the lobster bisque they probed and fenced. When the piccata of veal was served, with a good white Soave Folonari, they took the buttons off their foils and began to cut and thrust toward a palpable hit.

Naugle asked, "What do you want, Patricia? There's very little I couldn't provide. My resources, you understand, are not inconsiderable, and you'll always find me generous–particularly under conditions of, ah, reciprocity."

"What I want is for J.T. to get what he wants. Promotion. Salary increments. Recognition."

"All of that must go across my desk, you understand."

"I suppose it must."

"Absolutely. I'm in a position to rescue him from the depths of his last performance. I can be forgiving, my dear, and useful–if I get what I want. What I need."

"And that is?"

"You."

Trish toyed with her salad. "Are you always as blunt as this, Thornton?"

"I hate to waste time. When you know that someone is going to say yes, must say yes, I find it's effective to press them to blurt it out. Shortcuts are economical. Dawdling always bores me."

"I haven't said yes."

"Yet. You will." He swirled his wine and rivetted her with an arrogant stare. His mouth smiled, but his eyes didn't.

Trish could play that game too. "Why don't you write a brisk presidential memorandum on The Role of the Mailed Fist in Foreplay?"

"You'd find my foreplay more than interesting, and my endgame exhilarating, I promise you."

"No doubt you have your own preferences and–fetishes, Thornton? Let me see. Probably you're into S and M. With me as the M, and you as the thrilling S. It's all too predictable."

"On the contrary, when we get to the bondage, you will tie the ropes. Or the silken threads. Would you like that?"

"Maybe. Not much. I'm not sure. But beating you might have something to be said for it, at that."

"You're so sweetly old-fashioned, my dear. But with me, your inhibitions will vanish. You will become a witch, a bitch, a voluptuary. You will become a priestess of evil. In my apartment I keep a full stock of costumes. I will dress you. I will undress you, very slowly, like a *geisha*."

"Thorny, do you by any chance write for *Cosmopolitan* in your spare time?"

"I have no spare time. And when we close, when you say yes, our every moment together will be intense, fulfilling. I will fill–all your empty spaces, parts of you that you didn't realize were empty."

"You sound like a salesman for fibreglass home-heating insulation." Patricia waved at a waiter for coffee.

"Keep in mind," the President purred, "that I could do so much for you. And for your husband. As I've said, I can make him. Or break him." Naugle flashed his teeth again. "He could be Principal of a college, or a Dean. Or he could languish at the bottom of the Associate Professor rank. Forever."

She suppressed a shiver and feigned an artful yawn. "Or be invited to Harvard. Or go into the civil service for about double his present salary."

"Unlikely. I have connections. Don't ever doubt that I have clout in places beyond this university. People in my position provide references, don't forget. And sometimes blackballs." The teeth gleamed. "So why not yield to superior force, my pet? Why not admit that you want–what I want. It's inevitable. You wouldn't have come to lunch if you weren't interested. I will have you, you know. All we need do now is settle on the time and the place. It's so simple, and so mutually advantageous. You'll be thrilled, I guarantee it; thrilled and rewarded."

Trish paused. She looked at her watch. "Oh, look at the time. I really must be going."

"But you'll say yes."

"I'll think about it."

"There's nothing to think about. There's everything to do. Shall we say next Thursday at three?"

"I said I'd think about it."

"But what more is there to consider?"

"Thornton," she said, "I admit you're not uninteresting. There is a certain up-front candour about your proposition. No one could call you shy, and there's a refreshing quality to your directness. I don't mind flattery and the unabashed brandishing of sheer power." She lit a cigarette and eyed him with a hard twinkle.

"Then, we understand each other. Ah, my beauty, my dazzling golden-haired lovely, I will make you happy beyond–"

"But there is one other thing, Thorny."

"Tell me."

"You tend to be–"

"Yes?"

196

"When we get right down to it, you're such a *bore*."

He scowled.

Trish laughed. She rose from the table, gathered in her purse, and stalked out of the restaurant, twitching her hips just a little more than was necessary, leaving him to reflect on himself, his strategy, his hopes, and the bill. To Naugle, the price of lunch was trifling, but he had no wish to pay the heavy price of failure, or be embarrassed. Like all players in the big games of power, he could suffer almost anything but a bruised ego.

19

That evening, Bert Grimsby sat down at his desk to make one more attempt at rewriting the concluding chapter of his textbook. The project had seemed to him interminable, but he was now determined to wrap it up. As he worked in a desultory way, his mind wandered. If the bloody book ever was finished to his satisfaction, which seemed a harsh unlikelihood, it would probably prove unpublishable. If by some bizarre stroke of fortune it did get published there'd be no money in it anyway. With the author's royalty at ten per cent, this would provide him with a wage rate of maybe two dollars an hour, before taxes, and before expenses. And textbooks, of course, did not count as "scholarly" publications for salary increments or academic brownie points. So why continue? Why bother? The prospect depressed him.

By eleven p.m. he'd done what he could to complete the last chapter, reducing its length in this fourth draft. He reread it and remained dissatisfied, but stacked the manuscript on the corner of his desk and wandered into the kitchen to pour himself a drink.

His apartment was small. It was furnished in a simple and austere manner. The rather dingy off-white walls and the mushroom-coloured carpeting were unrelieved by any splashes of colour, except for one cheap van Gogh print over the dull-brown sofa. The only living thing in the minimal space Grimsby called home was a forlorn rubber plant by the window, which faced north. As he stared out at the lights of the city, it began to rain. He dropped some ice into his weak scotch and returned to his desk.

Taking out a fresh pad of paper, he jotted a heading, "Is There Anything To Discuss?," took a slow sip of his drink, and began again to write:

Most academic life consists of discursive analysis of abstract topics. We argue and debate, but I sometimes wonder whether there is anything really worth talking about.

Economics, science, history, and even politics are not suitable subjects for discussion except by experts. Laymen are in the bothersome position of requiring more information before their opinions can be interesting. It is, of course, possible, with the expenditure of great quantities of sweat and time, to become expert in a subject, say, economics. But the result then is that (a) we cannot abide the ill-informed maunderings of amateurs and (b) we become so "professional" that all we do is exchange exceedingly narrow views of techniques and technicalities with other experts, so that our discussions become more and more tedious, if not irrelevant to the sweep of public issues.

However, if we do not specialize and become sophisticated technicians, who will seek our opinions or take them seriously? And so we are obliged to travel the predictable route of the agoffo bird, spinning brilliantly in the ever-diminishing circles of arid professional journals until we disappear up our own anuses, from which privileged vantage point we shriek defiance at our enemies–although the expert sphincter is a less than ideal perspective from which to survey the universe.

Experts might, it is true, enter the popular forum and engage in politics. There are certain attractions to the public life. And yet, as in Gresham's Law (where bad money drives out good), bad politicians tend to drive out good ones. Demagogues drive out potential statesmen, reducing most issues to a lowest common denominator and debasing all issues to mere "personality." Television democracy facilitates the rise of the superficial and the vulgar, and makes chumps of us all. The simple fact is that electronic technology makes it impossible for philosophers to be taken seriously. No, most important policy questions cannot be dealt with in the public forum, and probably not even in ordinary conversation.

And what of other urgent questions? Here we are faced by (a) questions of science and (b) questions of values.

Scientific matters are scarcely discussable. The answers are merely accurate or inaccurate. How much does a bulldozer weigh? How fast does light travel? We experiment, we measure, and the quantified response is verifiably right or wrong. There is little that is interesting here, and still less to be discussed.

Values, on the other hand, being non-quantifiable and impossible to measure, might present possibilities for serious dispute. However, most interchange of opinion as to good or bad, just or unjust, beautiful or ugly, merely leads to comparison of biases or crude notation of various experiences and subjective responses. "I enjoy sonatas." "I do not." "I believe abortion/euthanasia/killing baby seals to be good." "To me they seem bad." There is no proof, no agreed standard of objective judgement, and therefore no agreement, as bickering philosophers have demonstrated for more than two thousand years. It becomes so tiresome. We cannot really discuss whether one work of art is "better" than another; we merely compare our private reactions to creative works and the feelings they elicit in us. Why bother discussing values if they are based on simple bias or taste?

In the face of such sad futility, it's arguable that we should withdraw from disputation to cultivate our personal pleasures. But the range of those pleasures seems to me limited.

To some extent I have enjoyed pursuing knowledge, but I can't say it has made me happy. Truth, if there is such a thing, has sparked little enough joy in my heart. Economics has never answered any important questions for me, questions about how to live or how to endure. I remember my mother, when I got the Ph.D., pointing to Ecclesiastes (i,18): "He that increaseth knowledge increaseth sorrow, and in much wisdom is much grief."

J.T. tells me that I should find a woman and try marriage again. Nubar always insists that with every new love there is a new beginning, a new birth. Perhaps. But in my limited experience, with every new love there is a new disillusion, a new death. Once the first sweaty enthusiasm wears off, she discovers that you are just another ordinary guy who would rather watch T.V. than go dancing, and you begin to notice that her urgent emotion is just a temporary escape from the shallow banality of her own life and her own loneliness. You each end up more bruised and disappointed and alone than before. Anyway, I think that we do not choose love; love chooses us. But it does not choose me.

Maybe I would find my life more agreeable if I believed, really believed, in something. Anything. Believers seem to be able to get outside of themselves – saving themselves, in effect, by losing themselves in something beyond self. But belief now seems so quaint and so fleeting. Does anyone believe in anything anymore? Most social "causes" seem to me simplistic if not empty, and a public belief like liberalism or conservatism is usually disemboweled on the Black Mass altar of personality-cult, exalting some ineffectual dink like Trudeau or some embarrassing oaf like Bonzo's less intelligent sidekick in the White House. I was not cut out for this sort of thing. In any case, most "true believers" become narrow fanatics, and quite intolerable.

No, I lack belief and the psychology of the believer. God speaks, but distressingly, and he says different things to different people. To me, God is mute, and although I do not resent his silence, I regret it. Worship of a sphinx is pointless. Life seems to be an enigmatic bottle cast adrift on the cosmic ocean by some lost astronaut, and when I pull the stopper on the bottle, there is no message inside.

So what is it all about? I am ready to leave this life, voluntarily, not knowing what it might have been all in aid of, and still I wonder. Life may have been about the chance commencement of the brief eternal, the way we thought it might have been, but wasn't. The shape of this terrible shapelessness maybe very definite, very circular, with a hollow centre that needs filling and is usually stuffed only with some sort of delusion, with twisted beliefs or numb acceptance. In the absence of real conviction, life is a peg with a slippery knob on which you can't firmly hang your previous joys or your indistinct memories, and your hopes slide off to fall onto a dusty floor.

Meaning? Purpose? Meaning is a cuddly innocent kitten that grows up to devour birds, or a sleek, smart cat that is hit by a car. Purpose is what the hot stars say through curved space to blind astronomers on cold and cloudy nights. Happiness is only that which precedes cancer, and every day the unbearable is sullenly reborn. The aching pressure of slapstick reality remains, even when the pre-dawn nightmare recedes. Laughter and love may be the only pillows. But I find it pains too much to laugh, no one shares my pillow, and I have no love left, even for myself.

Faced with evil and boredom if not despair, with nothing consequential to discuss, with a dull absence of belief, and with little hope of escaping from my squalid solitude, I conclude that life is not clearly preferable to death. Life is to me disappointing and unacceptable. I am inclined to grant to death the benefit of the doubt. Possibly I could be more reconciled to continued attempts at living if I thought I had any real self-determination, but we do not choose the time of our birth, our heredity, our colour, our physical capacities, or our emotional elasticities. We are like random bubbles idly blown from the soap-bubble pipe of some distracted child-god, drifting where the winds impell us, and bursting if pricked by any thorn.

Scientists tell us that in the universe, life is a rare thing. In our immediate solar system none of the other planets appears to support life.

Maybe it is just as well.

Compared to the infinity of eternal cosmic space, human beings seem to me not much more important or interesting than microbes. We live on a dreary and contemptible speck of dust spinning aimlessly around a walnut-sized blip of solar light, and still we probe for "significance" in our lives. But if you think too searchingly about the purpose of our brief and unlikely existence, you risk going mad.

Thus, in drawing my own existence to a close I am not making any angry gesture of protest or rejection. I am merely demonstrating my inability to be reconciled to life, and my indifference to it. My interest in the whole business has dwindled. I decline to go on with what seems an unsatisfactory charade. Since life is the cause of unhappiness, death may be the only cure.

Bert Grimsby put down his pen and pushed himself back from the desk. His face was a mask of resignation, drained of all hope or anticipation of pleasure, ready to stare at meaninglessness with a baleful but steady eye.

He walked to the kitchen and poured the remnant of his drink down the drain. He took an extra moment to tidy up the kitchen counter. Returning to the living room, Bert lay down on the floor to test out a method that had been in his mind for months. From where he lay, the manuscript of his textbook caught his eye and he got up, placed the pile of typescript in a large manila envelope, and wrote on it the name of

J.T. McLaughlin, plus that of his lawyer, Legg. Deliberately, he sat at the desk again and scrawled a semblance of a will, leaving his books and papers to McLaughlin and all his other worldly assets to his sister. On a wayward notion he took the time to water his rubber tree. He glanced around the room with the expression of a weary, collarless dog backed into a corner and facing the dog-catcher.

Grimsby fished in his pocket for a mint and sucked it for a thoughtful moment, then spat it out. He lay down on the floor again. With untrembling hands he pulled a plastic bag over his head, tied a cord securely around it at his neck, and tried to relax. When an impulse came over him to clutch at the bag, he pushed his hands deep into his pockets. He closed his eyes and waited patiently for his share of this world's oxygen to be used up.

20

Patricia had promised J.T. she'd attend the opening of the new building on Wednesday afternoon. The problem was, she'd have to confront Naugle. Had she said too much? Or too little? Had she shown more interest than she cared to admit? Had she led him on? Surely not. But neither had she withdrawn far enough or fast enough, and she had no wish to play sillybuggers, even though his threats regarding her husband's career were enough to give a woman pause to reflect on the harsh realities involved and the, yes, undeniable temptations of playing in the fast lane. Certainly she had no wish to be committed to anything. As she'd known, or almost known all along, the answer was going to be no. Flirtation is one thing, and quite harmless, but a definite action was another, and something she'd not entirely intended. But now there were disquieting threats. It was a puzzlement.

She did not want to have a run-in with the President, not at all, and not in a public setting. She might phone his office. But what if he were not there? She could scarcely leave a message. "Just say that Mrs. McLaughlin declines to get laid." No. It wouldn't do.

Trish looked at the clock on the stove. It was after ten a.m. She decided to scribble a short note to Naugle, a note that would head him off and perhaps defuse the situation before it went any further.

Taking a note-pad and a ballpoint pen, Trish twisted a stray lock of hair for a moment and then wrote: "Dear Thornton . . ." No. Let's keep some distance, she decided.

Dear Mr. President,
I'm really very sorry if you lack confidence in my hus-

band. I know he is good. He can make it on his own. Although he may be an unorthodox person and rather disorganized, I could not bring myself to cause him trouble or betray him merely . . .

Better let Thornton's ego down lightly, she thought, because he may in fact have the whip hand.

. . . merely for a few afternoon joys and kicks. You are a marvellous man, but we were scarcely destined to be thrown together, and I'm sure you will have no difficulty in finding other diversions and sexual partners.

I must also add that if in the future I find any evidence that you have attempted to stand in the way of my husband's professional progress, I will certainly be loud and emphatic in any court of law, testifying that you tried to make an unfortunate trade-off in an attempt to seduce me.

It was a good try, and even fascinating, but power in the end is no substitute for real stability and love and commitment. I'm sorry if I misled you, but there's no future in it.

She read this over twice. It didn't seem quite right. Trish attempted another draft of what she intended to be only a casual note, but liked the second version even less, and decided to go along with the initial squib.

Just a flippy bit of nonsense, this whole thing, she thought as she folded the paper. I'll slip it into his hand or into his pocket during the thrash of the opening this afternoon, and the whole dumb situation will be over and done with.

Trish then addressed herself to the more important question of what she'd wear to the opening ceremony, and decided on basic black, which was always easy and acceptable for these functions. "Still, that new red dress with the deep neckline and the wide belt would go well with my new shoes and my fall coat. I wonder—why not? Show them no mercy and take no prisoners." The red dress it would be.

Writing the note had taken her four minutes. Deciding what to wear took her half an hour. As she painstakingly put on her make-up, she hummed happily to herself, confident that she'd extracted herself from a raw situation, gotten off the hook, and could now look forward to an amusing day.

* * *

The afternoon yielded one of those gorgeous Indian Summer intervals when the sun is bright and the air soft and sweet. It was a day of pure velvet. Winter still seemed a distant threat and the blood ran warm in the gentle recollection of summer. A few tenacious leaves on the maples bore amber and crimson witness to the mellow lengthening of autumn's golden glow. The crowd gathering for the opening of the new Social Sciences Building was as frisky as a small boy who'd just been told that he didn't have to wear his galoshes.

Several of the faculty, including Cuttshaw, McLaughlin, and Nalorian, were posted for duty as special attendants and ushers at the opening ceremony. Chairs had been set out on the apron or square in front of the new building, facing the speakers' podium beside the fountain-statue by Ed Hopwood, which lurked under a pinnacle of canvas. The first three rows of chairs were roped off as reserved seats for dignitaries including the Chancellor, President, Provost, Principal Davidson of Burke College, and innumerable Vice-Presidents of the university, plus the Lieutenant-Governor, the Premier, the Minister of Colleges and Education, and the Mayor. Behind these worthies were seated members of the Board of Governors, the flower of the Toronto establishment, a few shrewd and flinty-eyed self-made men, but more soft and dolorous gentlemen of inherited means, whose abdominal measurements (in inches) and bank balances (in rotund millions) far exceeded their I.Q.'s. Their names read like an invitation list prepared by the Great Gatsby or a rostrum of robber barons from the *Canadian Who's Who*: the Callwood-Trents, the Edgerton-Blairs, the Clarke-Chamberlains, the Eastons, the Burstons, the Slinger-Smythes, the Dobbs-Martins, the Goodman-Enrights. That many of these eminent personages had immediate ancestors named Smith and Finklestein or Glotz and Clancy did not escape the jaundiced memory of the newspaper gossip columnists who meandered about, double-checking the spellings and the apparel of the assembled glitterati. ("Mrs. Algernon Simpson-Hurst, daughter of the late Col. Cyril Jamieson MacAulay, and wife of the prominent stable-owner and financier, chose a vermilion walking suit of pleated tarpaulin studded with rhinestone accents accessorized by a puce scarf, the entire disastrous ensemble topped by a Carmen Miranda hat of stupefying vulgarity and a gallon of trendy Bulgarian perfume that would have stunned a nasally congested buzzard at fifty paces.") It was a very smart society outing.

In the next echelon were seated a gaggle of preening Deans and their frumpish wives, delighted by the elevated social tone of the occasion, flanked by a handful of sullen faculty members who had been dragooned from their quiet library carrels. At the rear was a sprinkling of earnest and upwardly mobile graduate students, chatting amiably to the handful of artists in blue jeans and zippered jackets who had shown up to lend their moral support to Hopwood in hopes of free grog after the unveiling.

"We're about ready to go," McLaughlin said. "Where's Wright?"

"He's inside somewhere, polishing his speech and burnishing his *non sequiturs*," Cuttshaw said. "He'll appear on time after the Premier and the other poohbahs have had their innings. Not to worry. But where's Grimsby? I thought Bert was supposed to be with us in herding the gilt-edged bourgeoisie into their seats."

"Bert? Damned if I know. Haven't noticed him since yesterday. But have you ever seen such a conglomeration of gorgonzolas?"

"Don't knock it, J.T.," Nalorian murmured. "In these times, the poor, limping university needs all the friends it can get, particularly those with money and clout. Beauty and truth may be what it's all about, but it requires more than a little financial underpinning. It's easy to scoff, but we need these people–unless you like the idea of being an impoverished scholar-monk with a begging bowl? Look at Naugle out there glad-handing. He's pressing the flesh and osculating asses like a used-car salesman behind on his mortgage payments."

McLaughlin looked around and saw President Naugle moving through the crowd, the metallic beam of his toothy smile glinting off one person after another. There he was, dazzling the Heyworths and the Cobb-Campeaus with his practised and incinerating charm. And now he was embracing Patricia with altogether more warmth than was necessary. J.T. thought he saw Trish slip Naugle a piece of paper. Just what in hell, he wondered, is going down here?

Cutty gave him a nudge. "Come on, J.T., let's go find the Chairman and drag him out here. We're the escort, you know."

The two of them trotted off in search of Wright, their formal academic robes flapping behind them. Nalorian, watching them go, smiled and shook his head, thinking it was a good thing they were wearing doctoral robes and hoods which hid their cheap and baggy-kneed suits. Nobby shot his monogrammed cuffs. He wore a rakish Borsalino hat over a trimly cut dark-blue three-piece suit, a French trench coat draped casually over his shoulders. He carried pigskin gloves, which he was slapping with his right hand into the open palm of his left, when Hopwood careened into view.

Horn had imbibed a snort or three. His benign countenance was suffused in smiles and alcoholic vapours. Nalorian pounded him on the back and inquired what ineffable artistic delights might be concealed under the canvas hood, but Hopwood only grinned. "It'll be a surprise," he allowed. "It's a fucking A piece of art, but it'll be a surprise." Nobby didn't doubt it. Clearly Horn was well fortified with the enflaming waters and prepared to enjoy himself.

McLaughlin and Cuttshaw returned, flanking the Chairman, who strode briskly forward. The three men took their seats in a small semicircle of chairs behind the podium and beside Hopwood's draped creation. Wright riffled a sheaf of notes, sighed, thrust his papers deep into an inside pocket, and nodded to the President.

Naugle approached the speaker's podium and delivered himself of some otiose words of welcome. He introduced the Lieutenant-Governor, who responded with some inoffensive generalities, and then the Premier, who droned on at unconscionable length about the place of economics in the constellation of the seven lively arts.

"Or is it the eight lively arts? Or were there nine Muses? Who am I, a mere statesman, to remind this learned gathering of scholars and dignitaries of the essences of the higher arts? My friends, I make no pretence of being a scholar. I am merely a poor servant of the electorate which, in its wisdom, has set me before you to lead this grrreat province on to greater heights of affluence and accomplishment and, er, affluence for the greater good of all under our vigorous administration. An administration which has always emphasized careful forward planning for our grrreat academic establishment." Here Dr. Wright was heard to emit a derisory snort. "An administration which has served you well since even before my predecessor in the office of Premier was, er, in the office of Premier. And a grrreat man he was. One who loved learning and the arts, as I do. One who knew that the eleven Muses included, as you and I know, music! Where would we be, my friends, without music to set to, er, to music the words of the poets, of the delightful Muse of Poetry so that we might enjoy the benefits of, er, poems. Then too I think of the sublime Muses of, er, of the other arts. Among which we might include

Accounting. Yes. And let us not forget or neglect, in our list of–my notes are not entirely clear here, but you, my friends, know the list full well–our list must perforce include the Muse of Landscape Architecture, and of Political Science. And who could neglect the revered arts of Business Administration? Why just the other day a student of Business Administration gave the lie to the vile calumny that students of the commercial arts were not, indeed, sophisticated and educated persons when he wrote to *The Globe and Mail* newspaper, a grrreat and respected purveyor of culture, and opined that if students of Business Administration had not read *Anna Karenina* it was undoubtedly perhaps because they did not care for the works of Dickens. And who is to blame them? If these fine young people are getting on with the job of attending to the Muses, and pure, yes, let me say, pure econometrics, not to mention our outstanding Faculty of Educational Theory without which we might lack or even find ourselves bereft of, er, any theory of education which. . . ."

Dr. Wright, squirming in his chair, turned to McLaughlin and whispered, "Have you by any chance been feeding pills to this oaf?"

"No. He's winging it on his own."

"The man's an imbecile. But look here, who are those people marching toward us with those placards?"

J.T., who had been brooding about Trish, roused himself from his torpor. "Where? Oh, those. They will be the R.C.M.P. The student newspaper mentioned that they might stage a demonstration today."

"Mounties?" said the Chairman. "Funny, they don't look it."

"No, the initials stand for the Regional Congress of Marxist Parties. There are sixteen of these red groups on campus, and they sometimes get together for–occasions like this."

"Unprepossessing bunch of louts. They look like superannuated Hippies. I thought we were rid of that lot at the end of the sixties?"

"Well, some of them have hung around for a decade as

perennial graduate students. Others work on or around the campus in the library or in cafeterias. Many of them seem to be secretaries or directors of student groups. They lurk about, waiting for the revolution or a well-paid administrative job, whichever comes first. Meanwhile, they spend a lot of their time in marches and protests."

"Everyone should have a hobby," said Wright. "And if they can bring a halt to the verbal excrescences of the Premier, they'll be doing us all a service. Still, I don't much like the look of them. What are they against this time?"

"It's the naming of the building that's got them riled, or so the paper said."

"Korchinsky? What could they have against poor old Korchinsky? Fine chap, he was, if a bit thick. A splendid benefactor of the university. It was his estate that put up the money for this building, after all."

"But these Marxists seem to believe that the Social Sciences Building ought not to be named after a bourgeois, that is, a commercial gentleman."

"Nonsense. You didn't notice the government putting up the money, did you? Even though the Premier sounds as though he will keep talking until the national debt is eradicated. Swinish brute."

"I think he may be ending his remarks now, sir."

"About time."

Although he would never confess it, McLaughlin felt a certain sneaking sympathy with some of the things that the campus radicals had in mind, even while deploring most of their crude tactics and lamentable modes of expression. He cast a jaundiced eye over their placards. Some of these read: "Bugger the Bourgeoisie." "We Dread Honest Ted." "Boycott Honest Ted's School of Brainwashing." The sign that seemed the most jauntily inclusive in its message was a big square of cardboard on the end of a two-by-four being waved by a diminutive coed in overalls, whom McLaughlin recognized as the daughter of a prominent stockbroker: "Destroy Society."

That, he had to admit, had an ambitious generality to it. The trouble with revolution, he reflected, was that few if any of the mock revolutionaries had ever done any harder work in their lives than turning the dials on their Mommys' automatic dishwashers. Furthermore, revolutions had an inconvenient propensity to substitute one form of mindless tyranny for another. If any real social uprising broke out, most of these placard-bearers would be found quavering under the beds of some publicly subsidized student residence, emerging only infrequently to complain about the quality of the meals in the dining hall. Marxist faculty members (nearly all tenured) could most often be discovered in the offices of their publishers, raising hell about why their revolutionary textbooks were yielding such unsatisfactory royalties.

J.T. was roused from his reverie by the applause which greeted the conclusion of the Premier's address, an applause which registered more relief than approbation. President Naugle then introduced Wright, declaiming that the Chairman of the Economics Department would be the final speaker. "Dr. Wright will, on behalf of the university, formally accept this magnificent building from the Korchinsky Foundation and unveil the fountain which will grace the approaches to this stately structure. Dr. Wright."

Cutty poked McLaughlin and noted that the R.C.M.P. had taken up standing positions behind the seated guests and were ringing the ceremonial placements. J.T. nodded and thought little of it.

Dr. Wright heaved himself to his feet and advanced to the podium with measured tread. He doffed his mortar-board to Naugle and to the other dignitaries in turn, then drew a sheaf of notes from his inside breast pocket. After acknowledging "the esteemed presence of the notables here assembled," Wright cleared his throat forcefully, looked around with a somewhat sour countenance, crumpled his notes into a tight ball, dropped them at his feet, kicked them aside, and began to rumble and ramble.

"Before I declare open this imposing new building, Korchinsky Hall, I wish to deliver myself of a few objective observations. It is not often that I am afforded an opportunity in circumstances such as these to speak my mind. As I cast my eyes over this towering and, ah, ineluctable edifice into which we will be obliged, that is to say, privileged to move next week, my mind goes back to the days of Mavor and Innis and Brady. The days when this department was housed in a creaking mausoleum on Bloor Street, without what are now regarded as elementary amenities. But still we produced work of some consequence. What shall we say about the influence of architecture on life and thought? Is it possible that there exists an inverse relationship between the sheer physical size of the institutional habitation and the quality of the intellectual output?

"No. On this happy occasion we would not do well to dwell upon such thoughts. This grand new pile, ah, architectural composition, is the symbol of a new era. If there is any subject on which I decline to speak with levity, it is the splendid past of this institution. And here we are today inaugurating something fresh, something different. Korchinsky Hall. But we must cleave to tradition," intoned Wright. "For all intensive purposes, the idea of the university consists of values. Abiding values.

"Truth, trust, acceptance, restraint, obligations; these are among the virtues to which we must rededicate ourselves. There is a real and growing danger that the university may indeed produce idiot savants, or ignorant technicians such as the Premier–" and here Naugle's head snapped up "–awrrhummph, such as the Premier has mentioned. Against this sort of narrow incivility we must be ever on our guard.

"But I am in danger of speaking at too great a length." Cries of "Yes!" and "Right on!" from the Marxists. "However, before I unveil the statue committed by Mr. Hopwood, it is my duty to say a few words in praise of this ineffable building.

"Here is verily a remarkable example of what is called modern. A tribute to the implacable future. Here is contemporary architecture of a distinctly non-traditional nature.

"We must, as laymen, thank God for artists. This building, in its massive solidity, will outlast us all. If persistence is a virtue, this edifice will be an invincible monument to perseverance. Some authorities have it that greatness lasts. Art is long and life is short – or, as we might say in the academic context, *chaise longue, vita brevis.* Institutions persist. But here we are confounded, ah, confronted not merely by art but also more inexorably by planning. When we ask, with the accustomed preoccupations of the civilized scholar, 'Is it good? Is it beautiful?,' the modern inquiry must also be extended to include the concern, 'Has it been planned?' Indubitably, it has. This building is nothing if not deliberate.

"I have heard the serious contention that in planning may lie our salvation. Although some of us may be the weeist bit reluctant to be saved, we must acknowledge that all human institutions are, after all, imperfect. As the philosopher Santayana has written, 'The working of great institutions is mainly the result of a vast mass of routine, petty malice, self-interest, carelessness, and sheer mistake. Only a residual fraction is thought.' It is in this context that we must express our gratitude to the architectural planners who made this building possible.

"Korchinsky Hall is vast – or possibly I exaggerate – not one whit less than half-vast. Certainly it is not petty, nor is it careless. And incontrovertibly it is residual in all its glory. It's residue will redound through the annals of posterity as long as posterior residues are cherished."

Cutty said, "Do you believe this, J.T.? Am I hearing right, or has the old geezer flipped his brain pan?"

"Ssssh. I think the Premier provoked him. Wright is in rare form."

Hopwood wore a mile-wide grin, and Nalorian was laughing silently behind his flapping gloves, but most of the benumbed audience merely gaped at the Chairman in blank incomprehension. Wright was careful not to meet the President's fierce eye as he swept on in his discourse.

"Who could say enough about this, ah, intriguing building, this incredible boon which has been bestowed upon us? For the planners have demonstrated that it is always mistaken unwittingly to traduce the underlying ethos of a culture, whether it be represented by basilisk or by monolith, whether designed by mandarins or Sanhedrin or by triumphant participatory committee perhaps. And who can deny that the staggering result here before us is a building that is a tribute to the obliquitous mind of the planner, a building that is overwhelming in its formidable, ah, consistency. Pre-eminently, here we must contemplate resolute consistency.

"As we behold with reverential eye this great work and survey its monumental fastness, we note that its top is strikingly, yes, palindromically consistent with its bottom. Its front is a faithful correlative of its back. The dauntless order extends to its many remarkable parts. Its sides are not irreconcilable with each other. The northern façade is in awesome compatibility with the southern, and we may ratify with exclamations of approval and delight how the eastern aspect of the configuration is an emphatic corroboration of the western. All of the parts bear an obvious, one might say remorseless, resemblance to each other. Remark, if you will, how the astonished eye is drawn along the lines of sameness until we are led to perceive the essence of the implacable continuum. Witness also how every individual component implies the conjunction of the whole, and each partakes of the same cool and consistent informing concept until the vast functional oneness comes together in a resounding crash of transcendent unity so that truly and unhesitatingly we may say, 'Here *is* a building!' Here are such serendipitous elements as are of harmony begot. In the phrase of the poet, here indeed is a fearsome symmetry."

Wright paused and favoured his slack-jawed audience with

a smile of beatific radiance. It registered on him that Naugle did not smile back. Nobby was hard pressed to avoid anything more unseemly than snickering into his gloves, the Premier asked the Minister of Education what "serendipitous" might mean (and drew a blank), while from the back one bold member of the R.C.M.P. shouted, "Too Long! Enough of the self-congratulatory bourgeois bullshit!"

Wright blew his nose and began again.

"Before I pull the statutory rope to reveal Mr. Hopwood's singular font, I wish to say a word about the late Mr. Theodore Korchinsky. He was a graduate of our department and of our university. He rose from modest origins to become a man of recumbent standing in the business world, a pillow of the community. His was a life of hard work. He was, like Arnold Bennett, 'a simple man, perfectly satisfied with the best of everything.' Honour and forthrightness were his watchwords, which he watched from a discreet distance, always fully cognizant of on which side of the fence his bread was buttered. Government contracts afforded him some amusement, but his real forte was the joy of the market, arbitrage, or grinding the feces of the poor bankers to make a thousand flowers bloom. In all his dealings, his handsome face remained as impassive as a plasterboard wall, and he wore his inscrutability on his sleeve like an open book. There we perceive the secret of his immense success."

"Booo!" offered a placard carrier, not entirely sure what had been said, but confident that he was against it.

Cutty said to J.T., "Better keep an eye on the R.C.M.P.; they're looking more and more restless. Do you think they'll start something?"

Nalorian leaned over and said, "Not to worry. Horn and I have something in mind." J.T. looked at Nobby quizzically, but Nalorian went back to the pretence of hanging on the Chairman's every word.

"It was my pleasure," Wright continued, "to know Theodore Korchinsky as a neighbour on the shores of

Georgian Bay where his summer home was not far from my own cottage. I will miss the merry roar of his motor cruiser along the shore where it is my habit quietly to canoe. Compared to his, my poor tiny craft was inconsequential – but as I always say, beggars can't be cruisers.

"Permit me to add that it is a source of gratification to us all to note that Mrs. Angela Korchinsky has been gracious enough to permit her name to be added to the number of our university Board of Governors. To this position, Mrs. Korchinsky, a lady of innumerable positions, will lend her unique qualities of grace and charm. She is a lady who will bring warmth and lubricity to the deliberations of the board."

Several Women's Libbers began to stir uneasily at this point. "Sexist pig!" shouted a female Marxist in dungarees.

"In addition to her beguiling girlish style and motherly understanding, I can testify, as a lakeside neighbour, that Mrs. Korchinsky does full justice to a bikini."

"Oink, oink!" came the combined chorus of Marxist and Lib voices.

Wright paused in apparent perplexity. "Still, it is necessary to think of Mrs. Korchinsky without her bikini. . . ."

This was enough to trigger the fury of the feminists and the placard-bearing comrades alike. They began to form into groups and to advance toward the podium. The Chairman, in some consternation, began to talk rapidly of the Hopwood creation and gave the signal for the rope to be pulled which would lift the canvas from the statue. As the R.C.M.P. surged forward, chanting slogans like "Power to the People" and "Chauvinists Out," Wright turned to see what the unveiling revealed. His eyes popped and bulged. What he and the assembled company saw was a giant screw, nineteen feet high, with a small spurt of water spraying from its top, and its pointed bottom inserted between the buttocks of a gormless figure, spread-eagled and face forward over a rock set in a central pool. The raised head of the little man on the rock faced the crowd with open mouth and staring eyes. It was the figure of the taxpayer, the student, the ordinary mug, or Everyman, forcefully depicted as the unhappy recipient of a large and royal screwing.

Horn beamed. The Marxists, no less than the seated dignitaries, stopped to gape. Wright sputtered and awrrhummphed. McLaughlin looked from the statue to Hopwood with disbelief. Cutty chortled and said, "You're a genius, Horn, a raving loony genius." Nalorian tilted back his Borsalino with a broad smile and asked, "Why, Horn? Why that?"

"Oh, I don't know," Hopwood replied. "It just felt right, particularly after I looked at the goddam building. Such a dreary slab of academic masonry can't be taken seriously, right? So I decided to send it up. The looks on the faces of these creeps are worth it. Isn't it fine? I was going to create a huge prick, a giant phallus that would tower in the air and squirt soapsuds or blow bubbles, but that seemed too obvious and simplistic. Then I thought of a rowboat, with Karl Marx and Adam Smith seated back to back and rowing in opposite directions with a cascade of water gushing up between them as the financial boat sank into the pool, but I reckoned that most of these clots would fail to recognize the faces and be slow to grasp the symbolism. So I went with the big screw. Sort of effective, don't you think? To me it conveys the essence of today's economy."

Nalorian slapped him on the back. "I love it."

Cutty said, "Heads up, you guys. The Marxists are massing for action. I'd guess they don't like to see a statue that outdoes them. They're looking more and more mean."

"Fuck them," Horn sneered. "What I need is more pressure. There isn't enough water coming out of the top of the screw."

"What should we do?" Cutty asked.

"Adjust," said Nalorian. "When in doubt, adjust. J.T., nip inside and see if there's any way you can turn up the water from the mains."

"Never mind that," Horn cried. "I never did trust this

plumbing from the beginning. There's an auxiliary intake valve here on the side. What you do, J.T., is get a firehose from the lobby and we'll smack her into the side valve."

"I'll see what I can do," McLaughlin nodded and raced to the lobby.

Meanwhile, four burly R.C.M.P. honchos nipped into the front row, seized Mrs. Korchinsky, carried her forward and bore her toward the pool.

"Oh-oh," Nobby exclaimed, "I think these louts are about to fling a ceremonial blonde into the fountain, and a mature bleached blonde at that. We'll have to take some counter-measures."

President Naugle, to his credit, led a red-faced charge to the relief of the struggling Angela Korchinsky. But too late. Her captors plopped her into the pond. She came up blowing and screeching like a banshee.

Wright, who had been peering around like an apprehensive turkey at Thanksgiving, seized the microphone and cried, "I declare this–thing unveiled, whatever it is."

The Provost was the next one to be deposited into the pool, from which he emerged bellowing and spouting in loud imitation of a beached whale. "Do something!" he implored. "Do something! Stop these ruffians!"

Cutty ran to accept the business end of the firehose from McLaughlin, but it was drizzling only a tiny flow of water. "More pressure!" Cuttshaw commanded. J.T. darted back into the building.

As Cutty attempted to attach the hose to the auxiliary valve of the fountain, a burly Marxist lunged at him and tried to seize the nozzle. Cutty cocked a fist and decked the intruder with a roundhouse right hook. Another R.C.M.P. bruiser sprang forward to dispute possession of the hose, but Cutt-shaw bounced the heavy metal nozzle off his skull and rendered him equally *hors de combat* just as J.T., inside the building, twisted the main valve with a vengeance. Under this sudden and heavy pressure, the firehose leaped out of Cutty's hands. The hard rush of intense water made the hose rear and thrash like an angry boa constrictor fighting for a meal. Cuttshaw lost control of it; in fact, it sent him sprawling. He regained his feet in time to see Horn and Nalorian grab the rampaging tube and train it on an advancing phalanx of insurgent placard bearers. The cold cascade smacked into them, bowled them over, and spread them soggy and gasping against the nearest wall of Korchinsky Hall.

Counter-attack was inevitable. While Horn was on his knees trying to open the intake valve of the fountain and calling for increased squirt, totally determined that his huge screw would gush the way he'd intended it to gush, a resurgent wave of R.C.M.P. stalwarts shoved him aside and gained control over the twisting hose. Everything was awash, everything was chaos. Nalorian, drenched and stunned, rescued his hat and looked up in time to see the force of the rushing water increased still further as two large Marxist boyos struggled to hold it and wondered where to point it. Their momentary indecision was resolved when President Naugle began to emit anguished cries, and the front row of dignitaries, confused but on their feet, began to break for the escape routes and the open spaces. Too late. With superior numbers and more dogged resolution, the leftists controlled the hose and levelled a streaming assault against their retreating adversaries.

A ton of water hit the Minister of Colleges and Universities on his ample belly and knocked him kicking. The Chancellor met a smashing liquid wave and came out a horizontal second best. Splat went the Premier. A surging spurt sent two VicePresidents coccyx over clavicle into a howling heap. Gasping and spluttering, the Dean of Engineering emulated a punctured rubber ducky trying to keep afloat on a tempestuous sea, without success. The Mayor tried to hunker down behind the inadequate shelter of a chair while his gargantuan wife performed a most astonishing aqueous somersault in mid-air and fetched up thirty feet away flaunting her sopping knickers in the breeze, overturned like a giant turtle waving its indignant legs at the moist sky. The Dobbs-Martins did a startling imitation of chubby eels surprised by unfavourable currents, while the Burstons floundered about in an affecting parody of gaffed sturgeons on a slick dock. Irresistible crests of flash fluid poured into the establishment mêlée, turning portly matrons into soggy tumbleweeds pushed along the concrete like salmon in a sluiceway. Dr. Wright tipped his mortarboard courteously to the half-drowned Mrs. Algernon Fitz-Perkins, when she slithered by on her substantial belly, just before he himself was blasted by a nasty rip-tide.

As the R.C.M.P. moved their thunderous watery aim along the line, President Naugle was less than noticeably delighted. He brayed a mouthful of lurid imprecations at the wallowing world and was rewarded by a tumultuous wave that hit him square amidships and barrelled him buns over brisket toward the nearest drain. Soon not one dignitary, and not one dignity, was left unsopped or perpendicular.

J.T., emerging belatedly from his tap duty inside the building, pulled Cutty to his feet and shouted, "Whatthehell is happening? What's the score?"

Cuttshaw said, "Score? It seems to be Marxists ten, Establishment zero, and the odds are six to one that the Lieutenant-Governor, who lately floated by, will not get out of here undrowned unless his aide-de-camp is an accomplished surfboarder. It's the flood, pal, it's the deluge, and we'd better haul ass away from here before we all need gills. It's every man for himself and Neptune take the hindmost."

As they beat a hasty departure, they noticed Horn sloshing around and laughing fit to burst. He called after them, "Hey, I think we've just invented a new sport, fellas – underwater bowling, with poohbahs as ten-pins. Glorious! I just *love* it!"

Later, the newspaper gossip columnists reported that Korchinsky Hall had been "opened with a geyser of goodwill and a veritable flood of civic emotion." It was a very swell social event.

* * *

At three a.m. McLaughlin was kicking and flailing in the grip of a desperate dream. As he wrestled with his pillow, his subconscious mind flashed across the lurid technicolour screen of his cortex terrifying pictures of doom and disaster. His wife was sliding a note to some sleek hustler with a moustache. J.T. saw his own face on a black eight ball near the side pocket of a pool table. President Naugle grinned sardonically as he lined up his shot and smashed the black ball down the hole to oblivion. With frantic thrashing McLaughlin tried to clutch at something, but he was falling, spinning downward, and an eight ball has no hands.

"No! Don't! It wasn't my fault. *No!*"

He clawed at the bedpost with one hand and wrenched the blankets with the other.

"Wake up. J.T., wake *up*! You're having a nightmare."

He jerked up in the bed and looked around with wild, staring eyes. Trish snapped on a light. He shielded his face with a forearm over his brow and shuddered. His wife reached for him but he remained rigid, the collar of his pyjama top doused in sweat.

"Are you all right? It was just a dream. Get hold of yourself."

"Hold. That's it. I think I'm all right now. But I've got to hang onto that job, Trish. Got to. I was dreaming that Naugle was out to get me because of the public lecture, jeez, and now he will probably blame me for turning on the firehose. But it wasn't–I didn't–it was way beyond my control, you know that."

She looked at him for a moment in silent remorse and blinking sympathy. "Of course. Everything will work out."

"Yeah. Work out." He clambered from the bed and began to pace the floor, then reached for a pack of cigarettes on the top of the dresser. "But what if Naugle and the university give me the kick in the head with a frozen boot and the one that's out is me?"

"Don't light that, J.T. Please. Do you want me to go downstairs and make some tea, or some hot milk?"

"Unh? No. Thanks, I'll be levelled out in a minute. There were just some jaws that were snapping at me, that's all. I'm

223

fine now, really." He slid back into bed, but lay rigid as an iron gate-post. "Don't you ever get a case of the fears and dreads, Trish? Am I the only one who drives himself 'round the twist?"

"Everyone has night beasts occasionally."

"Uh-huh. What worries you? Are you all right?"

"Well, I suppose every woman thinks sometimes about getting old and losing her looks."

"No, I mean more specific than that. Is there something you could tell me?"

"I – don't know. But you mustn't fuss about the university business. The recent upsets will pass, and you have tenure, when it comes down to that."

"I guess you're right." He turned it over in his mind, but still came up apprehensive and balancing precariously on edge. "Do you know what my deepest fear is?" She merely murmured and turned out the light. "My most awful dread is being . . . found out."

"You're being silly."

"No. Being totally exposed, discovered for the ordinary, inadequate mug that I am. I always had this trick memory and the knack of passing exams. Often when I wasn't even sure what the question meant I could bluff through with a glib answer. But when it comes down to it, I'm not as bright as Bert, I admit that. And I wish I had half of Nalorian's confidence. Maybe I should never have left the civil service and come back to the university at all. Maybe I'm just not good enough."

Patricia yawned. "You're talking nonsense, dear."

"Am I? I don't know." He fought off the temptation to get up again and find a cigarette. "Do you think, Trish, that if I get the heave at the University, that your Dad would lend us some money to, uh, consolidate our debts and move? Enough of a stake to make a new start somewhere else?"

"What? Well, no, it's never a good idea to borrow, particularly not within the family. But there's no *need*, dear.

You're wringing yourself out about nothing." She yawned again. "Now won't you settle down and go back to sleep?"

"You're right. I'll try to relax. I guess it's just the prospect of failure that has me unstrung." Thoughts of being driven out of the department trickled through his mind. Even with the quasi-protection of tenure there are innumerable ways for the administration to nail a guy. He shivered. "Maybe they shouldn't have kept telling me that I had such 'promise.' In my undergrad days, and all through graduate school, they kept praising my promise and shoving scholarships at me to go further. Shit. Those whom the gods wish to drive mad they first label promising. Maybe I'll never be able to deliver. And when they screw down the pressure, I seem to get these bloody-minded impulses, these bizarre notions of throwing my briefcase into the machinery and stopping the wheels or busting out, telling them to shove it." He paused and rubbed a sweaty hand over his eyes. "Trish, listen—do you know that I, a couple of weeks ago—I stole a book? I may be losing my grip. Trish? What do you think?"

But she had dozed off, and didn't hear him.

21

The sleepless night had done nothing to help J.T.'s ragged nerves. He had to struggle to compose himself and face the morning.

When his office phone rang at nine-thirty, McLaughlin was thinking through his day's teaching and trying to gear himself up for the party at the President's house that evening. The Harry Johnson Memorial Symposium had been going well and yesterday's opening of Korchinsky Hall had proved more than diverting. He was not prepared for the stranger's voice on the telephone, or for its message.

The man said that his name was Legg. He had a package of manuscript by Herbert Grimsby with McLaughlin's name on it, and would like to stop by and deliver it in about half an hour. "Why doesn't Bert deliver it himself?" The voice on the phone gulped and stalled. Hadn't McLaughlin heard? "Heard what, for kristsake?"

"That Professor Grimsby–I'm sorry to be the one to tell you this; I mean, I assumed you knew–Professor Grimsby is dead."

Dead?

Bert? Dead? J.T.'s stomach lurched.

Legg explained that he was Grimsby's lawyer. The police had informed him of the demise of his client. Apparently Bert's caretaker had gone into the apartment to make some minor repair, had found the tenant expired on the floor, and informed the police. "Haven't the police been in touch?"

"No. My gawd. No."

McLaughlin still had his head in his hands when Legg appeared at his office door some thirty minutes later. "How could Bert be dead?"

The lawyer slowly explained the circumstances. He told

everything he knew, which wasn't enough, yet far too much. He said that the sister had been contacted, being the next of kin, and that he merely wanted to deliver the bundle of textbook manuscript to J.T. as the legatee of all Grimsby's books and papers. McLaughlin heard him out and got rid of him, then sat staring at the pile of typescript before him. Grimsby is dead. Tuesday night. He died Tuesday night. Committed – it doesn't bear thinking about.

J.T. wondered whether he had, that evening of their dinner together, said something? Should have said something? Done something? Little razor blades nicked at his conscience. There is no end to the number of warm and affectionate things that occur to a person to say – after it's too late.

He scrunched his knuckles into his eyes, looked at the manuscript again, and stumbled down the hall in search of Cutty.

J.T. spilled the story. Cutty listened with dry eyes. They looked at each other with a fearful, tense incredulity. Cuttshaw muttered, "Damn. I'm sorry. Really." McLaughlin asked, "Is that all you've got to say?" Cutty closed his eyes and replied, "What have *you* got to say?" McLaughlin's thick tongue could form no reply. After a silence, Cuttshaw said, "We never know, do we? And much as we may regret it, there are no words for it. I hate death. I don't want to know. I keep thinking of Dostoievsky's painfully accurate observation on witnessing a fatal accident: *'It wasn't me!'* Why him? But thank God it wasn't me."

Cutty suggested that J.T. should inform the Chairman. When his friend left, Cuttshaw locked his door.

Wright listened to McLaughlin's unhappy news with an impassive face. Administrative arrangements would be made. A pity. Terrible thing. But because his secretary was away ill that day, Wright wondered whether McLaughlin would go down to Smyton Hall and look after the necessary paper work.

Numb, J.T. shuffled off to do as he was told, half resentful of being an errand boy, half glad of some excuse for activity.

When he got back to his own office, he looked at the sheaf

of forms he'd been given by the Personnel Department.

Instructions:
When reporting the termination of employment or requesting any disbursement from insurance or pension funds, include Social Security Number, University Personnel Number, and certification of medical status (disability, death, other). According to regulations, deceased personnel must be proven to be inactive and beneficiaries must be verifiably non-posthumous in relation to the insuree. Form SX-B-106 must be transmitted in duplicate to change or correct data for persons not previously inactive or shown to be terminated on the PER-AN Accounts. If death was erroneous, transmit Form SS9-17B, but if the person is not certified deceased, do not transmit SX-8 correction. Note: Payroll cannot at any time reinstate or resurrect an ineligible or non-authorized person (see Section 48, Codicile D). Resurrection of a non-authorized person constitutes an irregular systems infraction and may be subject to appeal only before the Grievance Committee pursuant to Section 68-G-009.

McLaughlin ground his teeth and paced the floor. Even in death, he thought. Even in death the crap is piled on. We are born wailing, live confused, die despairing, and are buried under avalanches of bumph. Life is what happens while you're waiting for your forms to be processed. The saddest part was that Bert never seemed to have much, well, fun. Maybe only childlike people know how to handle the immediate *now*. For most of us, the present is what you ignore because you're lamenting the past and fretting about the future.

Poor Grimmers. He had been caught by the galloping discrepancies, wrung by the awkward variances, trampled by qualms and fatally niggled by the pressing disagreeables.

There was a sharp rap at the office door and Nalorian burst in. He said nothing, but gave J.T. a rough male hug. They sat down and scrutinized each other.

McLaughlin said, "So you heard?" Nalorian nodded. "The big, sad lug did himself in," J.T. mumbled. "The stupid, lovable sonofabitch did it. With a plastic bag. Jesus! Why? How can we account for that? For any of it?"

"Every person is a mystery, J.T. There's no use trying to unlock the riddle of human motivations. How can you or I hope to understand people who don't understand themselves? The point is that Bert wasn't what you have to be–comfortable with himself."

"Who is?"

"I am. You should be."

"Should be. Krist, Nobby, stow the sermonizing. It all seems so pointless. Poor Grimmers didn't really have much of a run. He was only forty-eight, did you know that? Shit. When you came in I was just thinking that life is what passes you by while you work and worry."

"No. It passes you by only if you work too slowly and worry too much. But none of us ever knows when we might get cut short, like an annoying slip of the scalpel in a bungled circumcision. Personally, I don't think of mortality often. I intend to live forever or until the scalpel slips, whichever comes first. And I'll go out without any major regrets. Most people are worrying and scurrying ants, but I've always identified with the grasshopper."

"May you live forever, then, Nobby. But I've never known anyone who did."

"Who would want to? If you crowd enough in with sufficient verve, the limited allotment is grand and sufficient."

McLaughlin was only half listening. "The thing is, I feel so goddam guilty about Bert. Maybe I let him down, you know what I mean? I guess I didn't do enough. Just last Saturday morning the poor bastard was over at my house, bringing doughnuts for kristsake, and I don't remember whether I even thanked him."

"You've no reason to feel guilty. And it wouldn't do him much good if you did. Guilt is one of the most useless negatives. Avoid it."

"Sure, avoid having feelings! Talk sense, Nobby, or leave me be. I'm not feeling too swift at the moment. This is not the time for your cheery damned homilies."

"I am talking sense. You mustn't get down on yourself. North Americans tend to be too hung up about death, don't you agree? They try to keep it out of their consciousness, sweep it under the rug. But life is merely a temporary art form, and all good art must have a composition, an end as well as a beginning. The end is often the hardest, and he made his quick and clean. What more can be said? And maybe Grimsby's ending was right–for him. '*Le coeur a ses raisons que la raison ne connaît point.*' It was his decision, after all; probably we shouldn't dispute it. Maybe he just wanted out. As for me, I often go for a stroll in Mount Pleasant Cemetery. It's a quiet place to walk, and sometimes helps me to keep a bright perspective. I think about life, you see, not death, but a cemetery is a good place to reflect on antecedents, roots, flows. And there's nothing much to be lamented about death. It's as peaceful as it is inevitable. The only thing we should grieve for is wasted time."

But Nalorian realized that McLaughlin was no longer listening. When Nobby left, he closed the door softly. This afternoon I think I'll paint, he decided. Yes, I think I'll paint.

22

J.T. was morose as he munched his dinner that evening. Didn't Trish think that they should give the President's party a miss? After all, Bert had just . . . . But Trish, in spite of feeling sorry about Grimsby, insisted that they were going. She had phoned the President's office to check whether the party was still on, and had been assured that the commitments to the international guests in town for the Harry Johnson Memorial Symposium made it imperative that the function go ahead.

"Am I wrong, Trish, or aren't you becoming a bit too familiar with Naugle? You called his office? I do wonder about you sometimes."

"Now, J.T., this is to be the party of the year. All those important economists! It will be good for your career to hob-nob with them. And we can't let the President think that you are being–withdrawn. So anyway I talked to the President's secretary, and she said that everything is definitely on. I wouldn't *dream* of missing this party."

"Uh-huh." J.T. picked up a pork chop bone and gnawed it. "I sort of dream of staying home."

"Don't be silly, dear. It's a must. This will be a big smash. We're going. Put on the dark-blue suit, with the new tie I bought you. I talked to Alice, and she and Cutty will be there. It will be fun. It will take your mind off things."

"Oh, very likely. And I suppose our kindly President is using this event to show off the international stars and to promote the fund-raising drive. He never misses a trick, does he? Even with Bert not yet decently laid away. It's enough to make me want to puke."

"Don't be difficult. Please, dear. I know how you feel about your friend, but it can't help him now. And your Chairman will expect his staff to pitch in and make the party a success. Maybe you'll make some new connections, J.T., who will invite you to conferences in Rome or London or wherever. Try to be on your best behaviour. You can be so charming when you want to be. We can leave early if you insist, but we must go along and do the necessaries. Whatever you do, don't start to be surly. We'll have a good evening, you'll see."

While he showered and changed, McLaughlin found himself adding up the number of times he'd had lunch with Bert since the term began. Try as he might, he couldn't get the number to rise above two. When he counted the times he had begged off and avoided lunch, he reached a much higher total. But hell, you can't save a guy's life by having lunch with him, he thought–then hated himself for such a rationalization. Now he was the embarrassed possessor of the textbook. If he had pitched in and taken an interest in that manuscript, would it have helped? Would Grimmers be alive now?

Maybe, he thought. And when the poor bugger came to dinner last week, obviously in a bad way and floundering, did I cheer him up? Did I throw him a life raft? No, I did not. I turned my back. I'm a selfish and insensitive bastard, a nasty curd in the sour milk of human unkindness. As he struggled with his tie he tried to recall anything positive he'd done for Bert, but all he could think of was blowing all the fuses in the hapless man's car. I think, reflected J.T., that I am a prize turd, and that my mind is turning into silly-putty. I keep saying that I love humanity, yet with the chips down I've rejected a friend. I can't take all this. And what I can least accept is myself. I am a sorry excuse for a human being.

Trish called. "Are you ready, J.T.? It's time to go." In a guttural voice he croaked back, "Be with you in a minute." He sat down on the edge of the bed with his eyes brimming. Bert. Gone. Poor old Grimmers.

* * *

Twenty minutes later McLaughlin found himself blundering

up the steps of the President's house on the Rosedale ravine. It was a vast and imposing dwelling provided by Chiliast University. As they entered the foyer and found a place to stow their coats, J.T. peered around and registered that almost every undrowned member of the Board of Governors was in attendance, as well as all of the Department of Economics, most of the invited performers at the Johnson Symposium, many of the Senior Professors from the Faculty of Arts and Sciences, plus several of the graduate students who had been helping out with the week's special events. Mildred Mott, who was standing with Professor Giroux, tipped a wink at McLaughlin, who smiled wanly. Naugle, glad-handing near the door, nodded curtly to J.T. and greeted Patricia in his customary glass-smooth manner. The President led Trish away, flashing his teeth around the room like a lighthouse beacon. McLaughlin, with a furrowed brow, watched them go, then plodded to the nearest of two bars, where he spied Cuttshaw.

"So I guess there's nothing for it but to get into the sauce," Cutty said. "I can't say I feel right about this, but Alice dragged me. Have a belt, and may it do us some good. The grog is flowing real well. We might as well tie one on. Here's to Bert."

"You've been reading my mind."

"I've been talking to Wolfe, and he invited me to Edinburgh. Very interesting guy. Why not buddy up to some of these imported stars, J.T., and you might winkle a trip or two out of it. Get trotting along on the international circuit."

"Jeez, I feel like promoting like I feel like begging for a free case of cerebral palsy. This whole thrash gives me the creeps. It makes–it makes old Bert's departure seem so trivial, you know? I don't know what the hell we're doing here."

Cutty signalled the barman to give his friend a double. McLaughlin pulled at the scotch absent-mindedly. Nalorian nudged through the press of people and joined them at the bar.

"How's it going, Nobby?"

"Going grand. Just grand. This has the makings of a very satisfactory little wing-ding. I was just speaking with Patricia, J.T. She's looking wonderful."

"Is your wife here tonight, Nobby? We haven't met."

"No, I'm sorry to say she isn't. Her health is somewhat delicate lately, and she didn't feel up to it tonight."

"Who did?" McLaughlin scowled.

"Come on, now, let me introduce you to Splumpt from Yale. And have you met Shoyama? He's a lovely man." Nobby tugged at J.T.'s elbow.

McLaughlin shook him off. "Look, if it's all the same to you guys, I think I'll just drift around for a while and get the lie of the land." He had his drink spiked and wandered away.

Nalorian suggested to Cutty that he should keep an eye on their disconsolate colleague, and moved off into the crowd.

* * *

The noise seemed to McLaughlin oppressive as he inched through gabbling groups. Over his shoulder, a not very young man wearing a toupee was leaning into the ear of a curvaceous woman in an orange dress cut down to the Tropic of Capricorn. "How about coming over to my place afterwards? Just a few friends. We're going to slosh around in my new hot tub together, maybe toke up a bit and, you know, bob for navels." "But I don't have a bathing suit." "Of course. No one does. You get to know more people that way."

* * *

An economist from Australia told McLaughlin that he was very interested in the book on Innis he'd read last year. "Are you the author?" "Yup." "I suppose you're still very alarmed about the penetration of American capital into your country?" "What? Oh, yeah. But sometimes when I back off and think about it, I thank God for the U.S. Without the

234

Yanks beside us, we might have ended up like Australia." "Well, you could do worse. Australia is a great continent." "Continent?" J.T. said, "I thought your country was just millions of acres of kitty litter." The Aussie looked at him with narrow-eyed amusement. "Do you know the book, *How to Win Friends and Influence People?* Yes? Well, do me a favour. Reread the first three chapters, and then shove it up your keester – sideways." McLaughlin permitted himself a half-smile. "Sorry. I guess I'm not at my best tonight." "Too right you're not."

* * *

Two members of the Board of Governors, men of some abdominal dignity, were deep in conversation when McLaughlin tried to slide around them. One was obviously a banker, and was holding forth on interest rates. The other said, "Hal, I've been thinking of throwing a little business your way. My regular bank has had a change of staff, and some ignorant new Vice-President kept me waiting for almost ten minutes the other day. And the young pup had the effrontery to suggest that he wanted to check my credit rating! I don't think he knows who I am. I'd just stopped by for a minute, my car was double-parked, and this twit kept me late for my next appointment. All I wanted was a lousy six million in bridge financing for ninety days. Imagine!" Involuntarily, J.T. interjected, "Six million?" "Yes, only six. Say, aren't you the young ruffian who takes dope? I'm surprised you're still on the university staff, never mind at a party like this." He turned his back and continued, "Anyway, Hal, can you imagine asking *me* for credit ratings for a mere six mil? Hell, there are days when I spill more than that." "It's preposterous, George. If you feel like it, drop by my shop tomorrow morning and I'll advance it to you. No problem." "Very decent of you, Hal." "Think nothing of it." McLaughlin, sidling away, thought about it quite fiercely.

* * *

J.T. made another hit on the bar. He decided he'd switch from scotch and have a Beefeater martini on the rocks, no garnish. As the bartender obliged, Nalorian elbowed up to him. "Martinis? At this time of night?" "Yeah, whatthehell, Nobby." "Maybe I'll have one myself. But you should take it easy, J.T." "Probably I should, but I'm drinking Bert's share tonight." The bartender fixed the drink and added a twist of lemon peel. McLaughlin looked at it, then reached over and seized the barman by the lapels. "Look, you clutz," he snarled, "if I want a lemonade, I'll *ask* for it!"

* * *

On the other side of the room, Mildred Mott, who was tricked out in a clinging dress borrowed from Boffy, and dripping mascara down her not inconsiderable cleavage, was backed into a corner by the Chairman of the Physics Department. The ardent scientist was pressing on her an invitation to lunch. "But," Mildred protested, "I'm sure I'd never understand the higher physics and all that relativity stuff." "Simple, my dear," breathed the physicist. "There's a verse about that sort of thing that will set you on the right road." He swirled his scotch and intoned:

> "There was a young lady named Bright
> Whose speed was much faster than light.
> She went off one day
> In a relative way,
> And returned on the previous night."

"Amazing," said Mott. "What are you drinking?"

* * *

As he insinuated himself through gaps in the crush toward the bar for his fourth refill, J.T. was accosted by an imposing member of the alumni with a bristling moustache, a Chiliast tie, a diamond on his pinky, a mauve shirt, and a loud, im-

236

perious voice. Did he teach Eco. 100 to commerce students? J.T. admitted it. "Then I want to ask you about the exam my son flunked last week. My boy showed me the test. Those were pretty much the same questions that were on the exam when I took that course thirty years ago. The same questions! You call that progress?" "The questions may be the same, I'll grant you, but these days the answers are all different." "By God, I can't believe this! Different answers? You guys don't teach truth, you teach fashion. Damned inadequate, I must say." "Now don't misunderstand," McLaughlin replied, "it's true that we economists are mere scoopers behind the elephants in the circus of capitalism. But in general we don't teach answers. We teach questions, and how to analyze them. But all answers in human affairs may be relative, tentative. It's the quality of the reasoning process that counts." "Fuddle-duddle. Just playing with words, aren't you? Damned imper-tinence. Look here, what I want to know is, why did my son flunk?" "Oh, I'm not sure," said McLaughlin evenly, tipping back his glass. "It might be environment, but in this case it's most probably due to heredity. Now if you'll excuse me?"

* * *

Mildred Mott interposed herself between J.T. and the bar. "How you doin', Mildred?" "Just fine, but I've been watch-ing you. Don't you think you should ease off? On the booze, I mean." "I'm perfectly okay. As George Jean Nathan said, 'I drink only to make other people seem more interesting.' Can I get you a shot?" "No, thanks, but I was wondering if you'd like to come back to our apartment later and maybe snort a line of coke?" "Good Lord, Mildred, you've come a long way in a short time." "It's nothing much, Professor McLaughlin, but Mo has been picking up a few bucks dealing, you know? And he has some very decent stuff. Boffy says we could go back to our apartment after midnight. Ever since I became your Teaching Assistant," she sent loaded semaphore signals with her heavy black eyelashes, "and ever since that wonderful party in Professor Nalorian's loft, I've been hoping that we might be able to spend more time together. I mean, with our shared class and all, we have so much to discuss. There's nothing I wouldn't do for you, Professor McLaughlin–to help with your class, that is. Nothing. I'm still so thrilled to be your assistant that I just thought we should–become closer?" "I see. Yes. Well that's very thoughtful of you, Mildred, and perhaps some other time. But tonight I hope to be able to get myself, and my wife, home early." "Oh. Of course. Still, I do hope that we'll be able to spend more time together soon and, maybe, merge some of our interests?" "Uh-huh. One of these days, sure. But not tonight."

* * *

Moving back into the flow of the party from the bar with his recharged glass, this time filled again with dark-brown scotch, McLaughlin heard two graduate students from the Economics Department speaking of Bert. His ears perked up. "No," said a tall, sallow boy with thick glasses, "he wasn't much good in graduate seminars. He knew his stuff, but he was nothing special." The gawky, greasy-haired girl he was talking to shifted her made-in-Taiwan Aztec shawl around her bony shoulders and replied, "I hear he was no hell in undergrad lectures either." "Really." "For sure." J.T. bit his tongue and moved away.

* * *

The Chairman put the arm on him. "Ah, McLaughlin, I want you to meet one of our distinguished visitors. This is Van Rinjdroop from Capetown. He was just telling me some fascinating things about his country's circumstances." Pleasantries were exchanged. J.T. tried hard not to appear distracted, and not to spill his replete glass. "Yes, I was explaining to your Chairman," smiled Van Rinjdroop, "that our country seems to get a bad press, but really we are most generous to our blacks. They are, after all, scarcely out of the jungle, and they

238

are like children. Monkeys, actually. But we do our best for them." "I'm sure you do," said Wright. "I hear the food in your jails is quite palatable." Van Rinjdroop turned to J.T. and inquired, "What do you think we should do about these black bush-babies?" McLaughlin tilted back his glass just as Trish joined them, smiling. "I think," he said, crunching an ice cube between his teeth, "that you are a fucking ignorant bigot." Patricia dug her nails into his arm, pierced him with a hot glance, and whispered, "That's *no* way to talk. You *must* apologize!" McLaughlin considered this for a moment, scrutinized the remaining ice in his glass, and then said, "My wife is right. I'm sorry. I should have said, 'You're a fucking ignorant bigot, *sir.*' " He grinned, a bit lopsidedly, and set off for the bar in as direct a line as he could manage.

* * *

I'm not sure how much more of this shit I can take in one night, thought McLaughlin as he carried another heavy drink down a side hallway in search of a washroom. "Gotta drain the radiator," he smiled to himself as a lurching wall hit his shoulder. Oops. Steady now. Here's a likely looking entry.

He pushed against the first door on his left, and found himself in a large and sparsely furnished room dominated by an oak desk approximately the size of Malton airport. Huh. If anything was clear (and nothing much was) this would be the private study of the President. The smarmy bastard. Look at these curtains. Velvet. The urgent pressure of his bladder reminded him of what he'd been searching for. Wherever. He unzipped and took a hot, happy piss on the curtains.

Readjusting himself, J.T. tried to get his bearings. "So this is the inner sanctum of our glorious leader," he said to himself. Interesting little barn of a place he works in here. I wonder whether he has anything on his desk worth peeking at? No. One mustn't poke about, mustn't pry. Wouldn't do. Still, what was this strangely familiar handwriting on this paper, half protruding from a copy of a book on organizational theory? It looks like –

"Just what," inquired a cold voice, "are you doing in my study?"

"Nothing, actually. I was just in here to take a – I mean, I came in here to, heh heh, to sharpen my skates, and when I found out this wasn't the washroom I was merely looking at your books. Quite an impressive library you have here, Dr. Naugle."

"But you were pawing over my desk. I'd be grateful if you'd explain yourself."

"Well, you see, the thing is, I'm doing a study of executive power. Pure research. The work habits and procedures of chief executives from the point of view of an economist. Um, patterns of decision-making and all that. So I thought, since I found myself in here by accident, I might just look at – your desk, you see? Purely as a bit of evidence to the social scientist as to how power is, that is to say, how decision-making is conducted and –"

"You were rifling my desk and my private papers. Admit it!"

"Oh, certainly not."

"McLaughlin, you've been a thistle under my butt for some time. We're going to miss you around here."

"Miss me?"

"Right. I'm going to see that you are dispensed with around this university at an early date, tenure or not. There are ways to deal with people like you. You're some little petunia, aren't you? First you freak out in an important public lecture, embarrassing, no, mortifying me in front of the alumni and the board. Then you get yourself involved in criminal charges involving automobile accidents and destroy university property by throwing things through the door of a Dean's office."

"But I can explain –"

"And furthermore I have reason to believe that you were behind the horrendous scene at the opening of Korchinsky

Hall, directly assisting a group of commies in causing mayhem and accute distress to the Premier and half the cabinet, not to mention other guests of the university. Do you think you're likely to keep a job here? I'll have your ass, McLaughlin, see if I don't. One way or another, I'll get you. And when I do, it will give me the greatest of pleasure to see your tail straggling down the road to rejection from the profession and to unemployment. Believe me, you're finished. Absolutely finished! I'll blackball you from one end of this country to the other. Now get out of my study."

"Something tells me you're being less than friendly, Naugle."

"Get out!"

"And you're the sonofabitch who wouldn't cancel his hoity-toity party even to mark the death of one of our best scholars. My friend Grimsby isn't even in his grave, and you're happy enough to entertain your Bay Street bonzos and your society friends, never mind making wild accusations against me."

"I notice that you've used the occasion to pour in more than your share of liquor. How long have you had this compulsion about alcohol?"

"No compulsion. I'm a volunteer."

"And a more than somewhat drunken one, at that."

"Oh, belt up, Naugle. Stick it in your ear."

"I'm warning you, McLaughlin. Shove off."

Even through the dim haze of his inebriation, J.T. perceived that he was faced by someone who did not entirely cherish his company. In fact, this man, this intemperate if not shrill President chap, seemed to desire his departure. Well, screw him, he thought. Now where was his glass of scotch? It might prove useful for throwing into the face of this distinctly ungentlemanly administrative creep, or it might even be a good thing to pour down the inside of his throat to douse the fires of his indignation. Bloody hell. Unemployment might prove inconvenient. And that tumbler of scotch was—

When he looked down, he once again noticed the handwriting on the paper stuck in Naugle's book. Lovely leaping Jesus! The hand, unmistakably, was Patricia's. His mind reeled.

"Just a fucking minute, Naugle. This letter is my wife's. What's it doing here? Whatthehell is going on in this asylum?"

"You're hallucinating. There's nothing. . . . Anyway, I want you out of here."

"Hold on now, you fast-talking shithead! I know my wife's writing when I see it. The one who has some explaining to do is *you*." McLaughlin picked up the sheet of notepaper and advanced around the desk toward Naugle, keeping one eye on him and scanning the paper with the other. Naugle began to circle away. J.T. flicked his gaze from the letter to his retreating adversary and back again, and his eye picked up a few phrases, phrases which caused his gorge to rise and a scarlet film of rage to cloud his already uncertain vision.

Nasty little fragments and devastating words floated up at him: ". . . *lack confidence in my husband . . . He can make it on his own . . . afternoon joys . . . You are a marvellous man . . . destined to be thrown together. . . .*"

It was as though he had been hit by an avalanche. His bowels felt like Jello, his mind turned to peanut butter. For a moment he could not speak. He felt all of this was impossible. Patricia? With Naugle? Preposterous.

And yet, he held the evidence in his hand.

With his eyes glazed and his heart banging under his ribs, he pushed the note into an inside pocket of his jacket – where he was not to find it again until two days later.

He advanced on Naugle.

The President moved to keep the desk between them, bawling, "That's theft. You've just stolen a paper of mine, a perfectly innocent little note. You'd better put it back on my desk at once, or–"

"*Innocent!*" bellowed McLaughlin. "You've got brass,

Thorny baby, I'll give you that. Amazing brass. And now I will also give you a thumping you will never forget. I will knock your ugly block off and ram your pearly teeth down your throat." He made a rush at Naugle, but the man was too fast for him. "Stand still and take what's coming to you, you scurvy bugger, and I'll tear you limb from fucking limb!"

Naugle, continuing to take evasive action, pulled out a pair of glasses, and slid them over his nose. "You wouldn't strike your President. You wouldn't hit a man wearing glasses!"

McLaughlin emitted a mirthless laugh as he kept up his pursuit. "Wouldn't I, Naugy-poo? If he messed with my wife I'd kick the living shit out of a man with a halo and nail-holes in his hands."

With a rasp-throated roar, J.T. jumped up on the desk with an agility that surprised even himself. He leaped at the retreating President and managed to clip him with one round-house right hook on the ear in mid-air. McLaughlin hit the floor and came up charging, but Naugle was quicker. The President made a headlong rush for the door and dodged through it just as J.T. slammed into it and hit his head. Partly dazed, McLaughlin stopped and rubbed his forehead. A noise that might have been a gasp of rage or a sob stuck halfway up his throat before he got a grip on the door handle and let himself out into the empty hallway. He leaned against the wall and wondered what to do next.

Nobby put his head around a corner and hurried toward him, loudly inquiring where the hell he'd been. McLaughlin told him to never mind that for now. Just find Cuttshaw. Get Cutty and send him here. Nalorian peered at him quizzically, but said only, "Will do," and retreated.

"What's up, buddy? You awright?" asked Cutty when he appeared. He reckoned that J.T. had poked back enough liquor to stun a rhinocerous, but he wasn't entirely sober himself, and wondered whether unspoken thoughts of Grimsby lay between them.

"I'm okay, yeah. Now listen, this is what I want you to do.

Give your car keys to Alice and tell her to drive Trish home. I'll wait for you here. Then we'll take my car. We're leaving."

"Why in hell are we leaving? Tell me what's happening."

"Later."

"Well, I'm not sure I'm ready to go anywhere unless you tell me what's going on."

McLaughlin lowered his voice. "Cutty, how long have we known each other?"

"Hah! Since Moby Dick was a guppy. What's that got to do with it?"

"Just that you'd better believe me when I say that in all those years I've never felt worse than I feel this minute. Never. Now go tell Alice. I'm asking you. Stow the questions. Go."

"Right. Gottcha. Shall I get our coats?"

"Doesn't matter. Just move. There's probably a back door here somewhere that we can get out."

"Back door?"

"I'm in no mood to wade through that party, understand? And I don't want to see Trish. We're getting out of this place by the most direct route, if we have to go out a window."

Cutty frowned, gave him another appraising look, then scuttled off.

23

Nalorian, not knowing what was wrong with J.T., but feeling the edge had been blunted on an already rather dull party, left the President's house minutes after he spoke to Cutty. Mildred wondered whether she should leave with him, but decided to stay on a while, relishing the attention of several tipsy men. Nalorian noticed Trish and Alice engaged in a conversation that seemed agitated. He concluded he might better steer clear of that, said his goodbyes to several colleagues, and slid out the door.

The autumn evening was so brisk and agreeable under a bright, full moon that he decided to walk south through Rosedale as far as Bloor Street. He chewed an unlit cigar and enjoyed the stroll. Crinkling leaves underfoot reminded him that the raw Canadian winter was coming, and that Grimsby had just gone. Unhappy old Bert. He quickened his pace and hummed to himself. From a half-remembered snatch of a Bach cantata, his humming made the glide to a J.P. Sousa marching tune, then on to a still more up-beat ditty as his spirits rose. "Dum dee dum do dum." How did it go? "Gold dust at my feet, on the sunny side of the street. Can't you hear that pitter-pat, and that happy tune is your step, dum de dum dum dum . . . ." He picked up a crimson leaf and, under a street lamp, marvelled at its flaming fine-veined beauty, then hurried on.

When he arrived at Bloor, he flagged a cab in order to reach Boffy's apartment with more dispatch.

When he arrived she was waiting for him, and embraced him avidly.

He said, "I don't know what it's all in aid of, but it certainly is wonderful."

"What is?"

"Nature."

"Aw, Nubby, I thought you might mean me."

"You, too, little golden one. But I've just had the most delightful walk through the leaves."

"Was it a good party?"

"Very pleasant. I enjoyed myself. I talked to some charming people and even engaged in some banter about economics before I got myself a rather plentiful internal glow on the President's quite excellent whisky. Favour me with another warming kiss."

She obliged with enthusiasm.

"Mo may be over later with some super stuff. Shall we whiff a little coke, Nubby?"

"Thank you, no, but I'd relish a finger of that cognac I left with you the other day if there's any left."

"Sure thing."

He watched her lithe movements with satisfaction as she searched for a snifter. While she poured the drink, he sang softly to himself: "And if I never had a cent, I'd be rich as Rockefeller; gold dust at my feet, dum dee dum dum side of the street."

Soon they were stretched out on her mattress and revelling in a passionate and anatomically imaginative dialectic.

"Ahhh, Boffy, my dear, you are sweet as maple syrup, warm as a buffalo robe. You are as consoling as an oasis to the parched tongue of a desert wanderer."

"Am I? You talk really nice, Nubby, you know that?"

"It is impossible not to speak with honey when tasting the supreme confections. I might even break my normal rule and have a cigarette."

She stretched for one, and lit it for him. "Tell me again what part of me you like best."

"Your nose, my dear."

Boffy giggled. "Kiss me on my nose."

He did. "There's a bit of poetry you should always remember:

'He who kisses the Joy as it flies
Lives in Eternity's sunrise.' "

"I like that. Where did you learn so much poetry? It can't have been from studying economics."

"From books and boudoirs, my orchid; life's greatest inspirations."

She laughed again, that low, enchanting chortle that he prized so much. "I wonder whether Professor Grimsby ever had much loving?" He shook his head. "Do you feel badly about him, Nubby?"

"Oh, yes. But also no. Bert was one of God's eternal duffers for whom two plus two never added up to more than three. He wouldn't let it, or didn't know how to. Possibly he's just as well out of it. The jagged little disappointments – what's that phrase? – 'can lacerate his heart no more.' Shall I get up and bring you a touch of cognac? I believe I'll have another."

"No, thanks. The truth is, I think I'm already a teensy bit tight. I drank a few tumblers of that Spanish wine while I was waiting for you to get here."

"Nonsense. You are only half drunk, which is the ideal state. It helps to reconcile you to the imponderables and the vicissitudes, and there seem to be rather a lot of those going around lately."

"So you really are a bit sad about Grimsby."

"Not a great deal. Tonight I feel full, full to overflowing with liquor and affection and contentment and even uxorious hope."

"What does 'uxorious' mean?"

"Never mind, my pet."

"If you're so full of everything tonight, maybe I should try again to spurt off more of your juices. Or are you too tired?"

"Never that tired."

And they enfolded each other again in the sweet, sweaty clutches of Venus.

At some later point in their languorous lovemaking, Boffy whispered, "Tell me another poem. I love it when you say poetry to me."

"Hmmmmm? My mind flits back to Shakespeare at such moments. Do you remember the lines–"

"Oooooooh."

"–the lines:

> 'Ruin hath taught me thus to ruminate,
> That Time will come and take my love away.' "

"I'm not sure I understand. Does it mean . . . ? It could mean–it's not specific."

"The wonder is in the delicate ambiguity. Just as in life."

"Wonder is all right with me."

"Wonder is the only thing."

She released from her throat a small sound, "Oooohaaaaahgrrrh."

Nobby smiled.

"Maybe I'm drunk, but I love you, Nubar."

"Don't say that."

"*In vino, veritas.* Isn't that what you say?"

"*Caritas. In vino caritas* is my preference. But wine is not real; it's magic. Love doesn't always survive the wine or the pleasures of the bed."

"I love you."

"Don't be silly, my dear, it's just a friendly foop."

She drew a few inches back from him, as far as the limitations of the mattress and their entwined position permitted. "Are you all right, Nubby?"

"Of course. It's just that I had . . . a strange sensation down my arm."

"Let's shift around."

"No, lie still. I think I'm all . . ."

But a fierce, crushing pain exploded in his chest and seized him.

"Nubby, tell me that you're all right!"

"Going grand, my poppet, going . . . ."

But with a burning sensation that seemed to come from his chest and scamper along his spine, his drumming heart ceased to beat and, leaning into a small wave of sperm, he smiled and expired.

Panic and horror fluttered through the mind of Boffy Bromley. Within a matter of seconds the man she grappled with had turned from ardent lover to chilly corpse. She was pinned under a dead body.

Suppressing a shriek of incredulous dismay, she extracted herself from the grasp of Nobby's lifeless form. Biting her knuckle did no good. She cried out to Nalorian and shook him. She attempted mouth-to-mouth resuscitation as well as chest massage to stimulate the heart, but nothing helped, nothing worked. When death's calling-card arrives on a silver tray it's too late to bar the door.

* * *

Cuttshaw and McLaughlin had been sitting in J.T.'s three-fendered car for more than an hour. When they left the party, Cuttshaw had had the presence of mind to liberate a bottle of the President's scotch on his way out. McLaughlin, driving aimlessly, had pulled up against the curb on Douglas Drive, overlooking Chorley Park, and it was here they sat passing the whisky back and forth while J.T. spilled his anguished guts. He told Cutty most of his fears and shock concerning Trish. It was all he could do to keep his moist eyes from brimming over. Cuttshaw couldn't find much to say, except that the situation seemed to him incredible. He asked where the letter was, and J.T. replied honestly that he had no idea whether he'd left it on the desk, dropped it in the scuffle, or whatthehell he'd done with it.

"But it doesn't matter. I saw it with my own eyes."

"You'd had a lot to drink, though. You could have misread it."

"Not bloody likely. I may have been naive, but I do know my own wife's writing, and I can read, for kristsake."

Cutty said nothing. He stared into the park.

"So my whole life is down the tube; my marriage, my job, probably my whole career. It's one helluva non-cheerful prospect." McLaughlin rested his forehead on the steering wheel. "It seems as though Naugle and the fates have my fortunes on the run."

"Now look, let's try to sort this out rationally. Seems to me, J.T., that if the President tries to lean on you, you could stand up and accuse him of, ah, messing with your wife. 'Alienation of affections' or whatever it's called. You could counter-attack and make Naugle look pretty bad."

"Thought of that. But if I made noises and accusations in public, I'd also be dragging Patricia through the sewer. Wouldn't that be charming? Nope, couldn't do it. Out of the question."

"Uh-huh. Well, on the other thing, the job bit, you've got tenure. He can't just send you down the road on the basis of some, ah, personality conflict. That's what the tenure lark is all about, after all. There would have to be proper procedures, formal hearings, and all that; he'd have to show cause. The Faculty Association would back you up. They'd have to."

"Oh, lovely. 'They'd have to!' Don't you see that I'd be forced to drag everything out in public just the same? Even if I could keep the whole thing focussed on academic matters, which I doubt, I'd be in the shameful position of pleading for my job, begging. At best I'd be one of those lurid *causes célèbres*. I'd be a laughing stock. And on what solid grounds could I defend myself? Ha! I can see it all now: 'Please don't fire me because I take hallucinogens before lectures. Please ignore that fender I tossed into the Dean's office; I just happened to be walking along with a fender and it slipped.'

Oh, it would go over real big. And I could spend weeks on my knees before a Tenure Tribunal saying that I take a swipe at the President only infrequently, and only in the privacy of his own home. It would be dandy great fun, all right. The lead on the newspaper stories would be: 'Junkie Prof Defends his Right to Kick the Piss Out of University President on Grounds of Academic Freedom.' Sweet suffering krist. In the end I'd have to change my name, like a hunted Nazi, and move to South America.''

Cutty reflected on this. Finally he said, "Do you know any Spanish?''

"I knew I could count on you to cheer me up.''

"Well, old buddy, when you run it by me the way you just did, I have to agree that things don't look too good. And there's also the consideration that your name isn't exactly aces and trumps with the Board of Governors these days, either. But at least they can't give you the shove before the end of the academic year.''

McLaughlin put his head back down on the steering wheel.

Cutty took a thoughtful pull at the whisky, noted that the bottle had suffered considerable evaporation, and passed it over. "Here, take another swig of this and then let's shove off. We can't sit here all night. Let's go home.''

"Home!" McLaughlin shuddered. "Not me." He sat up and squared his shoulders. He turned on the ignition key and threw the car into gear. "What I think we'll do, Cuttshaw me lad, is take a little drive.''

"Huh? Why?''

"It has been moved by the Hon. Member from Despair, and Seconded by the Hon. Member from the Slough of Despond, that we nip over to the university and say a fond farewell to the place. How do you vote?''

"I think I'd like to abstain.''

"Ahah! The Ayes have it." He accelerated down the road and blared a somewhat demented laugh. "Let's go and dynamite Naugle's computer. We could stage a cunning raid in–

burp! excuse me–retaliation. Wouldn't it be nice to repro-
gram that blipping bastard of a computer to reduce the salar-
ies of all administrators–except Wright–to one dollar per
month? And Naugle's salary to one dollar per year? I'd love it.
You know all about that sort of thing. Do you think we could?
We'll see whether we can break into the electronic inner sanctum and punch in a program that would pay a big bonus to all
the lowly Instructors and Teaching Assistants in grateful recognition of their superior contributions to university life,
compared with the asinine fumblings of the architects and the
fucking benighted bureaucrats. We might yet save the world.
We shall strike such a blow for freedom this night as shall be a
shot heard round the world. Or at least round the immediate
vicinity."

"Easy, boy. You're getting carried away."

"Who me? Pish-tosh and shitty-pies." J.T. laughed that
harsh, dangerous laugh again as he wheeled his battered
Camaro across the Rosedale viaduct and spun westward along
Bloor Street, heading for St. George and the campus. Luckily
they encountered little traffic and no police cruisers.

"What will we say if we get stopped by the cops?" Cutty
wondered aloud.

"We'll say, 'There was nobody driving, officer, we were all
in the back seat.' " He emitted another whoop. "And that's
me anyway; nobody. I've already been declared a non-person."
Thoughts of Grimsby filtered through his mind, but he fought
them off. "What I may have to do is leave town. The thing I
need is a stake, enough money to get myself set up somewhere
else. All I'd need would be about ten thou."

"Sure. Like all I'd need would be tits and I'd be Farah
Fawcett Majors."

"Don't be flippant, pal. I'm a desperate man."

Cutty scrunched down in the seat and tried not to think
about what was happening. When he tuned in again to the
manic voice of his friend, J.T. was still babbling almost as fast
as he was driving.

"You remember when we first came to Toronto, Cutty? A

252

couple of wide-eyed stubble-jumpers from the prairies. And gawd, boy, we were going to give it the old heavy shot, the real shitteroo, we were going to take the place by storm. The honchos from the last best west had roared into town like a pair of outriders from the Calgary Stampede. Hah! Maybe they thought we were just a pair of raggedy-jeaned jerks, but we knew, didn't we, we *knew* we could pop their corks and jangle their chandeliers and ravish their maidens and do-si-do their dossiers."

"Damn right," Cuttshaw agreed with only a small belch.

"Ah, shee-it, Cutty, we were gonna have it *all*. And we managed to cut a fair swath, right? We didn't do so badly at making them sit up and admit that the Western Wonders had what it takes to snaffle their scholarships and twiddle their little cliques and closed minds about where the balls really come from in this bloody country, and it wasn't from the stately homes of Old York, was it, boy, and we damned well–"

"Watch the centre line! You're over the centre of the road." They were by now, Cuttshaw saw, barrelling down St. George Street. "Easy, lad. The trick is only to stay on the road. Wait! You missed the turn-off into the college parking lot."

"No problem. We'll take this next turn."

"Stop! That's not a driveway. That's the archway!"

And sure enough, it was. It was the archway from the street that went beneath the cupola and through the Burke College student residence building into the west quadrangle. The passageway was eight feet wide, ten feet high; four deep steps led up to it from St. George Street. Cuttshaw let out a squawk of warning, but J.T. headed into the opening, broke a front shock absorber as the Camaro hit the curb, and geared down to mount the steps. The car hung over the third stair for a shuddering moment, then tore off its muffler and tail-pipe on the incline, and responded to McLaughlin's heavy foot by churning up the steps and roaring through the archway into the quadrangle.

The car burned rubber along the main footpath until J.T. got it under some semblance of control and parked it deftly on a bed of newly planted shrubbery. He opened the door and climbed out.

Cuttshaw gaped in disbelief.

"Come on," urged McLaughlin, "let's see whether we can find a computer to diddle."

* * *

Boffy was not at all clear how many minutes–hours?–later it was that Mildred Mott entered the apartment and called to her. No reply. Mildred found her roommate in a catatonic state of shock sitting on the floor of the bedroom, gazing in wonder at a cadaver that had been the most exhilarating force in her life, but had now departed.

It took half an hour and several cups of black coffee before Boffy could stop crying and they began to sort out what to do. Slowly, patiently, Mildred persuaded Boffy that it would not be acceptable to report a Professor dead in a student's apartment. Nalorian had, after all, a wife. There were social niceties to be considered, and possibly legal or even insurance implications which argued that the time and place of expiry might require alteration.

After long discussion, Boffy very reluctantly agreed that Nalorian's mortal remains should undergo a shift of venue. Preferably he should be taken to the university and deposited in his office. If a man must die, better he should expire where he belonged. Boffy could see that what her roommate urged was not merely socially or logistically desirable, but necessary.

With numb resignation and brimming eyes, Boffy conceded that Nobby could be wrapped in a sheet, or a blanket, and taken on the short journey. Too obvious, Mildred objected. Any passerby could detect what their burden was. After they got him dressed, it would be better to roll him into something more substantial. Like a rug. He could be rolled up in the bedroom rug and removed to the college. Boffy said that might do the trick and suggested that they telephone for a taxi to assist with the transfer. But Mott, keeping her head, pointed out that a taxi driver might make inconvenient inquiries as to why the rug was so heavy, or try to look into its rolled end, or generally become too helpful and over-curious.

The only thing for it was to take a walk. With Nalorian wrapped up like a wiener in a bun, they'd each take an end of the rug and, moving through the darker side streets with frequent stops to rest, they'd be able to transport their unfortunate burden the short distance from Spadina, over to Huron Street, along Wilcox, and up St. George to the north end of the college where, if fortune smiled, they might be able to gain entrance to the college. In her capacity as a Teaching Assistant, Mildred had a key to McLaughlin's office which might also unlock a rear door–she was pretty sure it would–and with any luck Nalorian's office might be unlocked or they might be able to deposit him in some more collegial setting. It was worth a try.

And so they set off into the night. The freighted rug was heavy, but they were sure they were doing the right thing, and with the extra rush of energy produced by desperation, they struggled along the empty streets toward Burke College, bearing their melancholy load.

* * *

The college quadrangle was deserted as the two ripped professors hurried through the shadows toward the back of the building. Cuttshaw failed to persuade his snorkered friend that trying to break into the computer room was a less than appealing proposition. He knew from long experience that once McLaughlin had his tiny mind focussed on a scheme there would be no holding him till he gave it a go. Dodging around some construction equipment that was being used for the reconstruction of the west wing in the college's renovation program, they approached a rear door.

"Funny," said McLaughlin, "my key doesn't seem to work, or else the door is stuck. Lemme try your key."

"Let's forget the whole caper and get out of here."

"No, I'll get this opened if–that's odd. Your bloody key doesn't seem to work any better than mine. Try it."

Cutty sighed and did as he was told. To his surprise he couldn't get the door to come open either. "I can get the lock to turn, but the door won't budge. You don't suppose that there are special night locks put on for extra security?"

"Nah, I've often come in or out very late. What time is it, anyway?"

Cutty consulted his watch. "Just after midnight. Let me try it again." He twisted at the key and yanked at the door several more times without result. Rubbing his chin and wrinkling his brow, he stared at the door. "You know, it's almost as though something was holding it after the key turns, almost like someone was pulling back against me."

"What? Don't be a clot. Next you'll be telling me that someone, maybe a caretaker, is in there trying to outsmart us. Sometimes, old buddy, you sound as far out as Nalorian."

Cuttshaw shook his head. "I dunno. It's just that it's most peculiar. I could have sworn–"

"Come on. Never let it be said that a couple of masterful break-and-enter boyos like us could be deterred by a mere sticky lock. We'll try another door. There's one to Stairway H right over this way."

But they couldn't seem to get that one open either.

After several further sweaty attempts they gave it up.

McLaughlin swore and gave the door a final kick. "I had my heart set on *doing* that computer. Have you got the bottle with you, Cutty?"

"Never fear. Supplies are to hand. It's my boy scout training."

J.T. took a deep slug of scotch and looked around for alternative routes or other diversions. "Say, come on over here. This steam-roller is what they must be using for the sidewalks on the renewal project. Wouldn't it be–*burp*! par'n me–be a hoot if we could bash it over Naugle and squash him like an envelope and slide him under his own door? Special delivery? Jeez. We're not having enough fun here. I have the notion to dynamite something. If I've got to be hurled out of this wonderful place, I want to go out with a blast. Some gesture of loving defiance, you know what I mean? Some token that I may have passed out, and I sure as hell got heaved out, but some indication that I was *here*. When I get the shove who will care? Who will remember? Did I give a decent lecture one day on McLuhan, when I should have been sticking to marginal cost curves? Fawk. Who's to care?"

He fumbled for a cigarette and flamed it. "I was not a great lecturer, Cutty; I know that. Lectures were made obsolete by Gutenberg, and still we straggle along, caring and trying, and not being good enough. Caring maybe too much, and pressing to get more interesting extra stuff wedged in between the orthodox bits on backward-sloping supply curves. Shee-it. It was a great time. It was a privilege. I'm going to miss it like hell. The university can be a lovely thing. Frustrating – all those closed minds, and all those rows and rows of good-hearted kids who want their biases reinforced, or want to be spoonfed and entertained. But sometimes we break through, don't we? Sometimes it works, and when it does it's just magic."

"I guess you're right. Yeah. But let's go home."

"Home? Whatthefuck. You keep saying that, don't you? I've just become an orphan. No home. I'm an aberration, an improper number that the big machine refuses to compute. Hey! Wait a minute. Let's go around to the front door. I've got an idea."

"I'd be quite conspicuously relieved if you didn't get any more ideas," Cutty moaned, but followed J.T. around to the south entrance to the college. He knew it too would be locked.

"There we are," McLaughlin chortled. "The way in. If you can't get through, you go over. You see it, don't you?"

"Can't say that I do."

"The tower. The workmen who are sandblasting and cleaning up the building have left their scaffolding over the main entrance. I'm pretty sure that the roof door to the top of the tower is always left open. I tell you, buddy, I'm going up and in through the top. It's the pinnacle or bust."

Cuttshaw considered this. "The 'scaffolding,' as you call it, is not fixed or steady. It's a 'stage,' on ropes, used for going up and down the face of the building where they're cleaning the stonework." He frowned uncertainly. "It's a slidy little platform they raise and lower by pulleys. I worked on a nasty thing like that as a window-washer when I was a student in Edmonton. The whole rig is suspended from the balustrade of the tower by a set of hooks and spaghettis that are very tricky, believe me. I wouldn't mess with the sucker."

"Did anybody ever tell you that you were timid? Nonetheless, I am ratiocinating fiercely. The rapier intellect of Professor J.T. McLaughlin, Ph.D., is poised to conquer all petty impediments to this caper. I'm about to scramble up this rope that's tied to the iron railing by the door–"

"That's the 'cable,' they call it, to steady the platform-stage thing."

"And rise through the air like the daring young man on the flying trapeze to the top of the tower. If I find some paint up there, or some whitewash or tar, I'll write my name for all eternity on the stones, or splash some uplifting message of social significance like 'Administrative Tyranny' or 'Naugle Sucks' or whatever. I'll think of something. I'm bound for the heights. Now, gimme a boost."

Cutty shook his head but cupped his hands and accepted McLaughlin's foot. With that leg-up, J.T. seized the cable rope and ascended like a starving monkey scaling a palm tree. He reached the stage, clambered aboard, and let out a demented whoop. "I've beaten the bastard, Cutty. It's onward and upward!"

Grabbing the ropes and fiddling with the mechanisms of the block and tackle, McLaughlin stood on the narrow board and began to pull and haul himself upward. Five sweaty minutes later he paused, looked down, and with a dizzy sensation realized that he was almost one hundred feet above the ground. The stage swayed with a dismaying motion, but he gulped and bellowed down to Cutty that all systems were 'go.' The top of the tower was only a few feet above. He pulled at a rope with an eager, frenetic jerk.

Something gave way. One end of the board dropped and fell. Clutching the rope in a desperate grip, he found his feet churning in empty air as though a trap door had sprung beneath him on a gallows. It was a moment when a lifetime might well flash before glazed eyes, but all he could think of as his hands tried to tighten on the rope and his feet thrashed in vacant air was that God was dead, and so were Santa Claus, Marshall McLuhan, the Tooth Fairy, John Lennon, and Grimsby. All dead. "But spare me," he begged. "Oh Lord, spare me." Still his feet touched nothing and his hands began to slide on the rope in a bloody ooze of lacerated flesh.

His heart leaped and jolted inside his chest like a salmon in a net. He was about to give it up, to let go and plummet to the concrete steps below.

But a blue light flashed beside him. An eerie light. Somehow a pulley creaked and the rope moved and his flailing feet found a board to stand on. The platform was level and firm beneath him, whether by his weight on the rope or by accident or by some mysterious intervention. He could not tell.

For a few moments he hung on where he was and simply gladdened to feel the rivulet of cold sweat trickling down his back. Sweat meant that he was alive.

Breathing deeply and reversing his efforts on the pulleys, he descended. The stage moved toward *terra firma* as though it had a mind of its own. When it reached the top of the doorway, within twenty feet of the ground, McLaughlin abandoned the board and slithered down the cable, hitting the ground with a reassuring plop. He rolled over and gasped with grateful incredulity. When he dared to reopen his eyes, he saw Cuttshaw bending over him and offering a swig from the bottle.

J.T. shook his head, delighted that it was still afixed to his neck.

"Hey," Cutty said, "did you blow a fuse or touch some wires when you were up there?"

"No wires," McLaughlin gasped. "No fuses."

"Then what was that peculiar burst of light up there when you were showing off and playing sillybuggers with your feet kicking in the air? It was like a huge short circuit. A sharp puff of blue light as though you'd turned to neon. What the hell happened?"

McLaughlin took another minute to find his voice. "I think," he said with a shiver, "either my mind registered 'Tilt' like an erratic pinball machine, or else I just met the ghost of the tower. Something grabbed me, Cutty, I swear. I was pretty sure I was a gonner. Something in that light put my feet under me. I think I just met Reznikoff."

"In one way, I think you're raving–but I did see that weird light."

"It was the ghost. No, I'm serious."

Cuttshaw considered this owlishly, peering at the tower and then at the shaken figure on the ground. "I don't know from spirits in towers, J.T., and I'm sure you're drank–I'm pretty sure we're both ripped–but I know I saw a light like I've never seen before." He shuddered. "Something tells me we're not in Kansas any longer, Toto. I need a drink."

"I've never been so terrified in my life."

"It's my opinion that we should get the hell out of here."

"Cutty, I've never agreed with you more." McLaughlin found his feet and lit out for his car as fast as a hungry hyena with a fire-cracker up its keester. Cuttshaw was not far behind him.

J.T. whipped the Camaro around and headed back down the pathway by which they'd entered the quadrangle. Without its muffler, the fractured Detroit iron roared demonically. He goosed it and decided against turning on the headlights.

"How are you going to get down those steps?" Cutty inquired.

"I'm not going down them, I'm going over them. We'll put her on the floor and shoot the rapids. Hang on!"

They sped through the archway and saw vague shapes ahead of them on the St. George Street sidewalk. It looked like two people carrying a long, heavy tube, but McLaughlin was going too fast to be sure. He let the car hurtle out the end of the archway and soar over the steps, and the dim figures scurried and separated in front of him as the Camaro rocketted into the street. He jammed both feet down on the brake pedal and screeched to a belated halt, then looked back and saw a body tumble out of an unfurling carpet onto the pavement.

"We've killed someone!" J.T. croaked in a pinched voice. "There's a body back there."

"I think it was just some kind of pipe that we high-jumped. There might have been people carrying it, but they got out of the way. Hit the throttle. Get us out of here," said Cutty.

McLaughlin didn't need much urging, and sent the car careening up the street. "Are you sure? I could have sworn I saw someone, a body, flop onto the sidewalk. Ohmygawd, I think I may be a murderer! What if–lovely leaping motherofgawd–what if we've *killed* somebody?"

Cutty hunkered down in the seat and mumbled, "Whadaya mean we? I'm just along for the ride."

* * *

On one side of the archway Mildred leaned against the iron railing, still shaking and struggling to compose herself. Boffy, on the other side, squatted on the curb, sobbing uncontrollably. The bedraggled form of Nalorian lay on the sidewalk between them. Mildred was screwing up her courage to try to ease the body back onto the rug to get it rerolled when she heard a voice beside her say, "Good evening."

"Oh! Zook. I mean, *Mr.* Zook. We were just—"

"Try to be calm, Miss, I'm here to help if I can."

"We were just passing by the archway, to come in from the north end of the college, you see, when a car came roaring through the arch right at us, and it jumped the steps, and Boffy ran one way and I ran another, and . . . ." Her voice trailed off as she looked from the Zook to Nobby to her friend blubbing on the curb.

Her eyes met the caretaker's even gaze. He explained that he had witnessed the entire incident. "And if I may be of assistance to you ladies, I will be pleased." Moving briskly, he got Nalorian rewrapped in the rug. Boffy made an effort to control herself and stood up. She watched him with amazement and gratitude.

"Perhaps you'd be good enough to explain to me how you came into possession of the mortal remains of Professor Nalorian, and why you were transporting him about the town in so unlikely a manner?"

As briefly and simply as she could, Mildred told him.

"I see. And now it is your intention to deposit him in his office?"

"We thought that would be best," Boffy managed to say. "Maybe we haven't been thinking very straight. It was such a shock, you know, such a horror. And now this."

"Just so. Death is the ultimate and icy surprise, but there's no help for it. Try to contain yourself, Miss Bromley. We can't leave bodies lying around the campus like this. It frightens the squirrels."

Mr. Zukowski loosened his huge black overcoat for greater freedom of movement and, with a strength that was remarkable in so elderly a man, picked up the rug and Nalorian, threw the whole bundle over his shoulder, told the girls to follow him, and set off toward the college with a measured pace.

They headed for the same door that McLaughlin and Cuttshaw had failed to open. Zook opened it easily and beckoned to the two young women to precede him in.

Within minutes they were in Nalorian's office and had him set up as nice as could be at his desk with an open copy of *The Canadian Journal of Economics* at his elbow. Boffy took a last fond look at Nobby and began to sob again. The old man escorted them back to the door and hurried them outside.

He said that he would arrange for the late professor to be discovered in the morning in the normal course of events, and his passing reported to the proper authorities.

Through her tears, Boffy tried to find the right words to thank the caretaker for his help and kindness. "I don't know whether we could have done it without you. We'll never be able to thank you enough, Mr. Zook. I just can't tell you how grateful I am. I want to buy you, I mean I want to send you some gift. Later, that is. You've been so good to us, Mr. Zook–and here, I don't even know your correct name. I'm sorry if we've been rude, but all I've ever heard is your nickname."

"It doesn't matter."

"But it does. Of course it does. Forgive me, but won't you please tell me your full name?"

He did so, but in such a soft, guttural voice, and with such a rattle of consonants through his accent, that the message did not entirely penetrate her saddened and still quite numb brain. Boffy then begged him to write it down. He produced a stub of pencil and Mildred found a scrap of paper in her wallet. The old man muttered something about people here always having got his name wrong, ever since he first arrived in Canada, and laboriously printed out the desired words. Boffy kissed him on a cold cheek and they parted.

Later, back in their apartment, Mildred asked to see what Zook had written. When Boffy produced the paper from the pocket of her jeans, they both looked at it, then looked at it again. In a childlike printed hand was revealed the words: "Ivan Zukowski-Reznikoff, stone carver."

24

Friday was not the most happy or perfect morning ever experienced by certain members of Chiliast University's Department of Economics. A good night often makes a bad day, as the old proverb has it, and the day began with a head-thumping endorsement of proverbial wisdom.

Alice Cuttshaw, listening to Cutty groan, remembered that he had a nine a.m. class. Somehow she managed to prod and coax him out of bed into a perpendicular if semi-comatose state. She got a muffin and a cup of coffee into him and propelled him out the door. Wives often have to work hard at this sort of thing. Having been up late listening to Trish's problems (after they had left the President's party in some confusion), Alice yawned and decided to go back to bed.

When McLaughlin woke up, he wished he hadn't. An affront of diabolical percussion instruments banged in his head like the hammers of Hades. His corroded throat and his tumultuous innards caused him only slightly more discomfort than the blazing strobe light which flashed with hard pulsations behind his itchy eyes. It was clear that little shitty-footed creatures had spent the night marching up and down his bacon-crisp tongue. If hangovers could enter competitions, his would sweep the prizes.

No less disconcerting was the fact that he had no idea where he was. Several of the events and most of the horrors of the previous night oozed through his gummy brain but did not reveal his present throbbing whereabouts or how he had got there.

He was on a couch. There was a telephone beside him. His watch, when brought near his face by a quivering wrist, indicated that the time was ten-fifteen. He decided to risk communication with the outside world, fumbled with the phone, and dialled Cuttshaw's number. It buzzed a busy signal. A second attempt, this time to reach his friend at the office, raised a slow and mournful response.

J.T. said, "Cutty? Jeez, where am I, Cutty?"

"How the hell should I know? Your plaintive bleat sounds as though you are in the pits of hell, but I didn't know Ma Bell had direct dialling from the Inferno."

"I'm not feeling my level best, and-"

"Believe me, I'm not feeling too swift myself."

"And I need to know where I am."

"You could try calling the police; they may have a bead on you by now."

"Please, Cutty, don't come on all funzies, all right? I'm a distressed and displaced person. Where was I last seen?"

"By me you were last seen in orbit over St. George Street, but my memory is mercifully blank after that. Tell you what. Is there a telephone near you?"

"I am not speaking to you via pony express."

"True. So look on the dial and tell me the telephone number you're calling from."

McLaughlin squinted, concentrated hard, and told him.

"Right. That's my home phone. You must be in my den in the basement. It's more than possible that I dumped you there in the frolicksome wee small morning hours. Got that? You're in my house. Say, is there a woman beside you?"

"Hunh? No."

"Thank God for that, at least. Now listen. I've just burped and gasped through what is laughingly called a lecture-or I got halfway through it, anyway, before I gave up-and when I crawled back to the office a few minutes ago, a secretary gave me some news. Unbelievable. Are you sitting down?"

"I am in no shape to sit up. I am horizontal. I await your glad tidings. So tell. My keen instincts lead me, through this dehydrated web of pain, to suspect you're about to inform me of an impending Nobel Prize. Or have I been nominated for a

Medal of Public Merit by the Women's Christian Temperance Union?"

"I'm being *serious*, dammit. Now listen! Nalorian – are you ready for this? – the secretary just told me that Nalorian is no longer with us. Dead. Apparently he was found at the college this morning."

"Nobby? But that's terrible! How did he . . .? Where?"

"Don't know. That's all I've heard so far. Maybe you should try to get down here. There's also been some mention of a car roaring through the archway – does that remind you of anything?"

"I have some dim recollection. You mean that really happened? Not a nightmare, but for real?"

"Bloody happened, you bet your butt. The Nalorian thing has me buffaloed, though. I can't seem to find out what the score is. Anyway, what are you going to do, J.T.?"

"Damned if I know. I may take my hangover for a walk. I may cut my wrists. Anything to beguile this joyous morning. Might go and throw myself under a passing truck, or maybe trundle out and rob a bank. You got any suggestions? For kristsake, can't you fill me in on Nobby?"

"I told you all I know. People are running around these halls like confused lemmings. If I knew – hold it! Gotta go. The Chairman is at my door. I'll call you back if I learn anything more." Cuttshaw hung up.

J.T. stared at the telephone for several moments before he replaced the humming receiver. He struggled to sit up. Found a crumpled cigarette. Lit it. Coughed. His numb mind simply could not absorb this new information. Surely it was Bert who had died, not Nobby. And yet, Cutty had shouted at him: Nalorian. Gone. He shook his head. What were Cuttshaw's words? 'At the college.' Why not *in* the college? Why at the college at all? Dammit, why dead at all? Was it possible that – the ding of a small warning bell penetrated his pounding head – that the person at the end of the archway, the glimpse he thought he'd caught of a body on the sidewalk when he shot the car through the archway? Was? Nobby??

He shuddered.

Through the heavy alcoholic fog of his memory there returned and persisted the image of a person, a body, on that sidewalk.

"I didn't mean to!" he cried aloud, choking. "Why me? Why Nobby?"

He sank back on the couch. Several minutes passed before he stirred again.

Contemporary scholarship in biology and neurology assures us that the human brain, if sufficiently assaulted and overloaded with the unacceptable, will snap like a dry pretzel. The brain may seize up and go into spasm. Certain intense degrees of stress may cause the despondent lump of grey matter in the noodle to call down the channels of the neck-bones to the resident noodlee: "I quit. The 'Do Not Disturb' sign has been hung out on the bottom knob of the cerebellum, announcing that the top-kick here on the apex of the spinal column will process no more information, attend to no more bad news, respond to no further stimuli till these matters are submitted to arbitration. No more messages will be sent leaping between the synapses. For the time being, the pilot light is snuffed; the body will have to jerk along on its own without conscious guidance. This encephalon has had it, and doesn't care bupkas whether you threaten or cajole, shit or steal third. A truce has been called in the battle for sanity here within the abused and abraded skull, and this cerebrum has downed tools and is off to nibble cool celery."

That, or something like it, was the last clear communication sent that morning by the beleaguered brain of Professor J.T. McLaughlin.

But the message, unfortunately, did not render him immobile. Lurching to his feet, he made it as far as the Cuttshaw's basement john. He did a half-gainer head first into the washbasin. He relieved his bladder, then stripped off his clothes and did two laps across the tin shower stall before the chilly onslaught of water drove him out. With eyes still shut against what reality might disclose, he leaned his head against the mocking mirror. His head felt like a leftover Hallo-ween pumpkin stuffed with balls of cotton batten. Can cotton batten throb? Evidently. Something was hurting, a lot. With a tentative finger he pushed one eyelid up and looked at the pupil. It seemed to be floating in a pool of strawberry jam. Trying hard to rally, he gave himself an encouraging grin and risked a major haemorrhage by opening the other eyelid. He looked again. "*There* you are, you handsome bright-eyed devil, you."

But attempts at good cheer were no use. His rebellious gut would not be denied, and he bent over the toilet and made his sacrifice to the porcelain god.

Minutes later he was back into his clothes and out the side door, so as not to disturb Alice. Lack of mental focus did not stop him from getting into his car and aiming it toward Bloor Street. While paused at a stop light, he did a rapid stock-taking of his circumstances. The debit side of the ledger loomed large and long. Thinking of Trish only made things seem worse.

He'd have to go away. Split. That would take dough. Which he didn't have.

Honking of cars behind him reminded him to move on. He shifted to grope a trousers' pocket and came to the not wholly exhilarating conclusion that he was possessed of twenty-two seventeen. Not a comfortable cash cushion for an escape to Mexico. He had a cheque-book and a couple of credit cards, but he was well over his limit of plastic liquidity, and not a few of his cheques had bounced recently like demons on pogo-sticks.

Money.

The solution was clear. He must rob a bank. Nalorian's for-mula for brisk robbery danced through his scrambled semi-consciousness. A bank heist, if quick and neat, might be the only thing. And what, after all, did a mug in his circumstances have to lose?

Laughing at the simplicity of it all, he then tried to figure out what bank to rob. Why not his own bank? He had a sub-stantial overdraft there, and might as well extend it. It's always nice to deal with people you know. McLaughlin began to operate on raw instinct and desperate spite. His switched-off, half-snapped mind gave him no help and, reeling without the stabilizing keel of reason, he began to formulate the dim outline of what he felt might be a plan, a simple and insouciant *modus operandum.*

He drove to a wig shop on Avenue Road and demanded a beard. The clerk looked at J.T.'s hirsute chin and asked, with pardonable puzzlement, what kind? J.T. requested a false beard to stick on, exactly like his own. Sort of an alternate, like a spare tire. After rummaging around in a big drawer, the clerk produced a reasonable facsimile, and offered to trim it and touch it up a bit to match the wild-eyed customer's own chin hairs. This done, McLaughlin paid for his purchase with a credit card, the financial soundness of which, luckily, was not checked by phone.

A gun, J.T. reminded himself. Every self-respecting robber should have a gun. At a nearby toy shop in Hazelton Lanes he selected a heavy black replica of a German Luger that looked appropriately fearsome. When the shop girl started to wrap it, he asked that it be put into a large plastic shopping bag in-stead. Next he drove over to the Park Plaza Hotel, went down the stairs to the barber shop, and asked for a shave. When his jaw had been scraped clean with only a minimal number of nicks, he got back into his car and drove to his bank at the cor-ner of Bay and Bloor. He cruised around the block a couple of times to survey the potential scene and fix his scheme in his aching head, then steered the battered car into the under-ground parking garage beneath the bank building. A parking space was available, around behind the stairway leading up to ground level, and he backed the Camaro into it. He removed his beige trench coat and tossed it into the back seat. Sunglasses might help his purpose of facial concealment; these he found in the glove compartment and slipped into a pocket.

Shopping bag in hand, up he went to the ground-floor lobby to reconnoitre. To the right was the inside rear entrance of the bank; to the left, Marika's Café. Sauntering into the café, he surveyed the coat-rack before ordering a cup of coffee, which he drank in three hot gulps. He paid for the coffee and chose a dark-blue raincoat from the rack, plus the biggest hat he could find. When the cashier looked at him quizzically he gave her a reassuring smile and walked out. The abstracted coat would be displaced only temporarily and, like the bank, the owner of the coat was doubtless insured.

The hat was too big, which was good. Turning down the brim, almost obscuring the sunglasses, further transformed his appearance. He caught a glimpse of himself in an interior shop window and gave the reflection his best attempt at a George Raft snarl. He barely recognized himself.

Through the lobby and onto Bloor Street, then a sharp turn brought him through the front door of the bank. He checked out the scene. Very few customers and no line-ups.

One thing McLaughlin did not notice was Mildred Mott. She was at the counter at the far end of the row of tellers, cashing her small Teaching Assistant's paycheque. Mildred, however, looked up and saw Professor McLaughlin, paused and looked again. She thought that he appeared very strange–clean shaven, which surprised her–but she'd know him anywhere. His behaviour was most peculiar.

Wanting to talk to him about Nalorian, Mildred thought she might wait till Professor McLaughlin had finished his business, then ask him to buy her a coffee or drive her back to the campus.

She watched him doing something odd with a plastic bag. Such a dear man, but all thumbs. Then he turned away from her and moved toward the counter.

McLaughlin tipped his hat still further down over his forehead. Cool, in the manner of the hardened criminal, calm as a sleepwalker enjoying a whimsical dream, he approached a teller whom he'd dealt with for years, but the woman didn't recognize him. She merely smiled and asked, "May I help you?"

"Yes, I hope you can. I need some money, but I don't have my cheque-book with me." Somehow it didn't seem quite the line that Raft or Bonnie and Clyde would have employed, but it would serve to break the ice.

"Do you have an account here, sir?"

"Certainly. That is, certainly not. But I do have a gun. I'd be grateful if you'd fill this plastic bag with money. Preferably large bills, please."

Her jaw dropped open. "You mean this is a hold up?"

"I'm afraid it is."

"Why didn't you say so?"

"Sorry. I'm rather new to the game. Just fill the bag, okay?" He waved the gun in a somewhat tentative manner.

She looked at the weapon and announced, "That's not a real gun."

"It damn well is."

"No, it's not. It's a water pistol."

"But it squirts acid, you see, which can be very messy."

"Oh." The teller decided that her minuscule salary didn't afford her enough to risk a slosh of acid. She plopped a handful of bills into the shopping bag.

"More, please."

She found another wad of fifties.

"Now," said J.T., "we'll both move along to the next wicket and invite your colleague to make a further contribution." The next teller glanced at the gun, looked at the first woman's rolling eyes, and concluded that co-operation was the wisest course. She scooped a very satisfactory quantity of bills into the bag.

McLaughlin nodded affably. "Thank you."

He then spun on his heel and dashed for the door. Turning to wave the toy Luger in such a way as to discourage pursuers, he stepped out onto Bloor Street, then veered immediately back into the next door leading to the lobby. His now shaking legs carried him pell-mell through the building at a fierce rate, showing a lot of early foot for one so hung over. A snappy left turn brought him back to the door leading to the garage. Down the stairs he bolted, and lost the hat on the way. At the bottom of the steps he hesitated, ears cocked for the sound of pursuing cries or footsteps, and smirked when he heard none. He plunged into the garage, ducking low behind a row of cars, and keeping out of sight as much as possible while he scuttled toward his own automobile.

Upstairs, Mildred Mott chewed a fretful knuckle, unable to believe what she had just seen. She ran over to the two quavering tellers and asked why they had given that man a bag of money. The reply was that they had a deep aversion to violence, especially when it involved their own persons. "Humpf," snorted Mott, and turned to a wide-eyed man who stood rivetted by the door. "Why didn't you grab that man with the shopping bag? Can't you see there's been a hold-up?" "Bloody right I saw," he replied. "But I make it a rule never to mess with a guy waving a gun. Chances are he wants to be alone."

Another man nodded agreement. "Any guy with a gun has the right of way."

The two bystanders made themselves scarce, not wanting to get involved.

Mildred glared after them and stood, wondering what to do.

Moments later, a police cruiser screamed up to the bank and a burly constable ran through the door. "Which way did he go?"

Being pretty sure the unlikely bandit had cut south, back into the next door, Mildred blurted: "Across Bloor and north up Bellair toward Yorkville."

The cop dashed to the cruiser's radio and sent his partner off to Bellair.

Fearful and amazed, Mildred decided to hang around a bit longer.

McLaughlin, meanwhile, had reached his car. He threw the shopping bag into the back seat; it landed with a pleasant plunk. The blue coat he stuffed through the open window of a car beside him, on the assumption that it would be turned in to the management as lost or strayed. He shoved the gun under the seat and gave the sunglasses an aimless toss. Now the beard. Breathing hard through a mouth gone dry, he fumbled with the sticky whiskers, then leaned toward the rear-view mirror to check the alignment, taking care to get the fringe on straight.

He had the beard affixed and was about to permit himself a small chortle over the apparent simplicity of it all when, suddenly, he saw his own eyes in the mirror. They were the eyes of a madman. Startled, he blinked and looked again. The mirror confirmed the message. Staring back at him were the wild, red, stricken eyes of a man demented. He clutched at his head, sagged in the seat, and wondered half-aloud whether those glowing lamps of madness could possibly be his. Would his own children recognize him?

Children. He gulped. For the first time visions of iron bars and striped clothing penetrated his head. A brittle explosion popped somewhere in his skull like the shattering of a flash bulb. Abruptly, McLaughlin reconnected with his brain with a terrifying cortical thud. He shook his head as his mental gears began to mesh and his interior wheels started to take hold and stop spinning.

Lucidity dawned, and panic was not far behind. Now what the *hell* could he do? He looked at the shopping bag in the back seat as though he'd never seen it before. Having reached the precipice, he needed to find a quick way back. His re-awakened conscience clawed for a handhold on the slippery slope to hell.

Keeping the money was out of the question, absurd. He'd have to act fast. Should he jettison the bag, simply abandon it, then start the car and make a run for it? But he might be stopped at the exit. Probably police outside. There'd be questions. And fingerprints? And how long had he been sitting here? Nothing was clear except that the money had to be returned and that the original plan was insane.

The original plan. Part of it was sufficiently bizarre that it might yet get him off the hook. Nobody around yet, and he was after all back in his own identity. Moving with a demonic speed bred of panic, he wrapped his beige trench coat around the shopping bag and nipped back through the garage to the stairway. His head ached, and with a resigned shrug he decided to take the elevator. Before the doors closed on him, two sweaty cops with drawn guns thundered out of the stairway and raced through the garage toward the exit ramp, but they gave him only a peripheral glance.

The elevator rose and disgorged him on the main floor. Mildred Mott, who was about to take a seat at the front of Marika's Café, saw him hurrying through the lobby toward the rear door of the bank. She deduced he'd come up from the basement, and decided to follow. Unaware of her, McLaughlin ambled back into the scene of the crime.

The place was in pandemonium, filled with police shouting into walkie-talkies, customers being questioned, and gibbering tellers. A patient detective was being bellowed at by the flushed bank manager, who gesticulated wildly at the farthest door while trying to explain that he'd seen nothing. J.T. braced himself, unfurled his coat, dropped it on the nearest desk, and started slowly toward the windmilling manager. McLaughlin's heart was jumping around near the top of his throat, his hands were shaking, and everything except his pounding pulse seemed to be moving in slow motion as he carried the shopping bag casually into the mêlée. He was about to deposit the bag quietly on a counter and scuttle out when an assistant credit manager recognized him and hurried over.

"Professor McLaughlin. We've just had a robbery! Maybe you should come back a bit later – you wouldn't want to get involved in this scene."

"Involved? Um, no. You're right. But the thing is, I seem to have something here which may belong to you."

"To me?"

"Well, to your bank, that is." As the man peered into the bundle and quickly waved the manager over, McLaughlin continued in a low, halting voice. "It, ah, the bag came into my possession in a, in an odd way. In the parking garage down below. There was, um, a bit of confusion. A scuffle, you might say."

"I'll be damned," said the manager.

The senior police detective, now at J.T.'s elbow, asked him to start over again and tell the story without haste from the beginning.

"Would you mind if I sat down?"

"Of course, of course," said the assistant credit manager, sliding a chair toward him as the manager danced around.

"Now if you'd just tell us," droned the detective, "what happened?"

"Well, I started to say. My car. It's down below. I was coming up the el–that is, up the stairs, I guess I'm a little shaken. And a man ran down the stairs toward me. I heard shouts, something about 'Robbery!' and 'Stop him!' So with this guy coming at me, I sort of blocked him."

"Did he have a gun?" inquired the detective.

"I guess he did, yeah."

"And you blocked him?"

"Or maybe tripped him. Just got in his way, you see? It all happened so fast. And when I dumped him, he dropped this bag.

"We both went for it," J.T. expatiated, warming to his subject. "I got to it first. There was a bit of a tussle. Gawd knows I was just reacting, rather on instinct. I might have given him a poke."

"You hit him," intoned the detective.

"Yes. Well, only one lucky punch. But enough to discourage him. I think he was more interested in getting away than he was in taking me on."

"You can describe this man?"

"Not sure that I could. Jeez, can you describe a six-second blur? What can I say? Hat down over the face. Blue coat. I don't know."

McLaughlin began to falter, at which point Mildred pushed through the edge of the group around him. "That's the man, officer!" J.T. looked at her uncertainly. "That's the man who stopped the robber and saved the money." Attention swung in her direction. "I saw the hold-up, and I thought the guy with the gun ran into Bloor Street, but when I went into the lobby next door, toward the coffee shop, there was the same man in the blue coat, looking around desperately. When I saw him go down the stairs, I followed, at a safe distance, and when I opened the door down to the parking area, there was this man – why I do believe it's one of my Professors from the university – this man here slugged the thief and rescued the cash. Oh he was dynamite, simply heroic. But I decided to hide in case the gun went off, and just backed up and got out of the way. And now here he is." She beamed at McLaughlin. "Isn't he magnificent?"

Everyone agreed he was. J.T. stared at his shoes and wrung his hands, scarcely able to believe his good fortune in the transformation from thief to crime-buster. The babble went on around him. Everyone wanted to talk at once, except J.T., who forced a wan smile to his bloodless lips every time he was spoken to, and only nodded in a suitably modest way. His clothes, which literally had been slept in, did look as though he'd been in some sort of a fight. The detective seemed more interested in Mildred than in him.

Someone fetched coffee, which was welcome enough, but J.T. felt emboldened to ask for something stiffer. A young accountant was dispatched to Marika's for brandy. "Make it a double," croaked McLaughlin. Soon, with a couple of belts in him, he began to feel better, almost human in fact. Mott continued to blither about how he had confronted a thug with a gun, how his bravery and daring had helped keep the world safe for capitalism. He found her thespian performance so compelling that he began to share in the general euphoria and half believe it all himself.

The bank manager talked loudly about a reward, perhaps a thousand dollars, and insisted that McLaughlin stay until T.V. reporters and photographers from the newspapers could arrive. J.T. did a little "aw shucks" number and allowed himself to be persuaded.

He took another small nip of brandy. From George Raft to Gary Cooper, he mused, and all within less than five minutes. Whatthehell. It felt sort of good, being a hero.

25

Over the weekend, the tipsy dominoes of McLaughlin's life finally began to fall into place. Media celebrity went to his head, if only temporarily. He was interviewed by every local radio station and local T.V. talk show on his role as a stalwart thwarter of crime, and the Toronto *Sunday Star* paid him a handsome sum to explain to its readers not only how he had gallantly tackled a thief, but the nature of his scholarly views on the relation between poverty, pillage, and the breakdown of civilized community relationships. The Canadian Broadcasting Corporation retained him as a consultant for a series of T.V. documentaries on capitalism, violence, and the disintegration of the social fabric.

Suddenly he was sniffing a lot of clover, and most of it was four-leafed. His total ignorance of the subjects he was expected to pontificate upon did not diminish his jaunty pleasure in the brief media attention.

At some point during that frenzied weekend, he was not sure when, he gave Trish the blue suit he'd worn to the President's party to take to the dry cleaners. As he went through the pockets, he discovered the crumpled note from Patricia which he'd expropriated from Naugle's desk. Reading it in full made him gasp and gulp and feel a lot better. So did dinner on Saturday night with the Cuttshaws at Gaston's when Alice gave him a patient explanation of how distraught Trish had been over the President's importunings and the necessity of writing the negative note. It was clear to J.T. that his wife had been trying to use Naugle's interest in her only as a means of advancing or protecting his career, and that she'd handled herself with her accustomed skill. No harm had been done. Their loving reconciliation was warm and complete. They even decided to get a babysitter for the following weekend so that they could be alone together for two nights at the rustic Millcroft Inn.

In fact, when McLaughlin arrived at his office on Monday morning, he was so high on life and Trish and the congratulations of his colleagues on the media-splashed accounts of his bold derring-do exploits that he scarcely cared whether the enmity of the President was about to undermine or revoke his tenure or not.

He sat for a while in the cafeteria, basking in the undeserved but head-turning felicitations and blandishments of colleagues, telling his story of how he'd preserved the sanctity of the banking system over and over again, enlarging on his intrepid deeds with each recounting of the twisted but appealing tale.

The Chairman came along and threw his arm over J.T.'s shoulder, then drew him aside and arm-in-armed him back to the departmental office. It was a pleasure to report, said Wright, that he'd just received a telephone communication from the President that all previous inconveniences had been forgiven and forgotten. "Naugle wanted me to tell you that he's delighted with the favourable publicity your dauntless exploits have brought to the credit of the university. Although he remains disappointed with the Innis lecture and, ah, certain other recent events with which you've been connected, the President wishes me to assure you that you are such a valued member of the faculty that a special sabbatical leave, with full pay, might be in order. I don't disagree, although I've never known him to recommend that sort of thing before. There was one thing he said that was curious, McLaughlin. Something about his deep approbation of, but his inability to find, some communication or other from your wife. He seems to admire her very much. Naugle expresses an interest in keeping any such correspondence confidential. He said you'd understand. Strange man, the President. Do you know what that's all about?"

"I think I do," said McLaughlin.

279

"Anyway, my boy, I'm delighted to tell you that in spite of some, what shall we say, some recent tensions and difficulties with which your name may have been involved, there appears to be a salutary thrust on the part of Naugle and his flunkies in Smyton Hall to give you every favourable consideration for upward mobility and preferment. Odd how the cookie cumulates, eh? Awrumph-umph-umph. I'm not entirely sure that I comprehend all the inwardness of the situation, but I might mention that my own modest effort of speaking at the opening of Korchinsky Hall seems to have skated over the thin ice of presidential scrutiny, possibly due to those who provided the liquid diversions with the firehose. At any rate, you seem to be out of the woods, or even regarded from on high as a most acceptable sheep in wolf's clothing. I'd be less than candid if I did not admit that it's sort of a from-the-gallows-to-the-gravy situation. Your skeleton may have won the dancing prize at the feast, don't you think? Awrumph-umph. And now you have a splendid sabbatical to look forward to. So I suggest that you get back to the main thing of the teaching; don't fret about any administrative tribulations. These days the proof of the pudding is in the posturing, I always say, and you seem to have managed to strut through the suet into the succotash."

McLaughlin floated out of the Chairman's office convinced that the world was a wonderful place, and that if you can't always be good you might still get by on blind, stupid luck.

En route to his own office, a secretary told him that Professor Nalorian's widow had telephoned. J.T. returned Mrs. Nalorian's call and agreed to drop by her apartment at four-thirty that afternoon for tea. Then he lit a cigarette and looked out of the window for a long time.

* * *

After he'd done his teaching stint for the day, he drove up St. George Street and found the address where Nobby had lived. Strange, he thought, that he'd never been there before. How long had he known Nalorian? Only two months? Less? It seemed much longer.

The elevator took him to the twelfth floor and he knocked. When the door opened he looked straight ahead into the living room, then lowered his eyes and found a small, fragile woman. In a wheelchair.

"I am Elzbieta Odgrżowski Nalorian."

Her hair was white. She reached up and offered him a hand to shake. The hand was frail and bony but the eyes were bright. She had a large, livid scar on her right cheek.

Although the room was simply furnished, the walls were crowded with paintings, apparently by Nobby, all of them bold and bright. The single black and white piece on a central wall was a representation of a city, thickly matted and under glass, which he later realized was an old etching of Warsaw.

"Thank you for coming, Professor McLaughlin. This is a melancholy time. I regret that we have not met prior to this. You may be surprised to find me in these circumstances, in this chair. Nubar always kept our domestic arrangements somewhat apart from his day-to-day work, but he spoke well of you and several of your colleagues. Yes, he spoke of Cuttshaw and Grimsby. Others, too, he mentioned, including Wright. But it was his view that you are an unusually good sort, and an honest man."

McLaughlin wanted to scream, Me? Honest? But he said only, "I'm glad of his good opinion. Your husband and I were becoming friends."

"Yes. He thought you were so charmingly–he meant it in the best possible sense–normal. Still, Nubar's views of normalcy were not entirely commonplace. He said you were a North American who might know better; do you see what I mean?"

"Not entirely."

"Well. It doesn't matter. The reason I called you was in the hope that you might advise me regarding funeral arrangements. My movements being limited, I'd value your assistance."

McLaughlin said he'd do anything possible, and they quietly worked out a few formal details over tea. The more she talked, the more impressed he became. Here was a woman of profound and remarkable interior resources.

At length, with most of the arrangements sorted out, J.T. blurted, "May I ask you a question?"

"Of course."

"I've been wondering, will you be all right now that Nubar is gone? Do you know whether there are benefits, pension, or insurance arrangements?"

"I appreciate your inquiry. Will you have more tea? These biscuits can be recommended. Nubar had them imported from England. But to answer your question, no, it is not at all clear to me whether I can expect financial benefits or support from Chiliast University. He'd been here only a short time, of course. One expects the minimum. Because of my imperfect health, the result of certain wartime experiences, I have been confined to this chair since 1945 and a burden to my husband since our marriage, or even before. Nubar was always attentive, and made sure that I was provided for in the short run, but he was not much of a hand at the 'forward planning,' as you economists call it, nor did he keep up with the various insurance policies he took out over the years. We moved a great deal, you see; largely because of his lack of complete qualifications."

"How do you mean?"

"His lack of the Ph.D. 'The union card,' as he called it. I had supported his studies, when we were both younger, with my work as a translator, but he was too impatient as well as too impecunious to complete the formal qualifications for the doctorate. For convenience, he assumed one, or perhaps I should say, forged one. It doesn't matter now. This fact, however, persisted in following him about and compelled him to move from one place of employment to another; this fact, plus the frequent discovery of his liaisons with students or with the wives of colleagues. Oh, yes, I was always fully aware of his physical propensities and emotional attachments, for he was not by nature monogamous, but excessively romantic, and I

282

have not been – by reason of infirmity – a social butterfly or a perfect partner. Still, we got on very well together. Very well. I would rewrite and edit his papers, and he would get them published under the aegis of the university at which he had arranged his next position.

"His publications made him employable, even gave him some reputation, but at no time did we spend longer than two years at any one institution. Not a man to sink roots, my husband. Yet I could not ask for better. Each morning he rose early and pushed me in my chair to a park or for a long walk. Each evening he would be with me to cook and look after my limited needs between seven and nine – unless of course he had to travel for professional reasons, in which case he would arrange a temporary nurse for me. Please do not think that I ever had any complaints against Nubar. I did not. I do not. And if there seems likely to be some trifling shortage of insurance or pension benefits, then so be it."

She paused and offered more tea. McLaughlin shook his head.

"Yes, when we were younger, I was able to help him, as much as my health permitted. Later he looked after me, most lovingly and assiduously, so far as his capabilities and temperament permitted, or beyond. Had it not been for him, my life would have been truncated. With him, my life was more than full and satisfying. He never let me down, you see, not in anything that mattered. Nubar was a man of strong loyalty. And he often assisted with my own publications. It is my hope that the royalties from the not inconsiderable number of my translations and books of poetry will afford me an income adequate to my plain needs. I shall miss Nubar much more than I shall ever miss an income."

"Mrs. Nalorian, I don't know what to say. Maybe if I were to press our Faculty Association there might be some way to be found around the normal rules of our pension scheme, and –"

"You are very kind. But I shouldn't trouble myself, if I were you, Professor McLaughlin. I will get by. I am a survivor, you see, and managed as a young girl to stay alive during the Resistance, even before I met Nubar. Nothing I have to face now will be as troublesome as those turbulent days. To be candid, I had often hoped to predecease my husband, so that I could make him more free. It's such a shame that he went before I did, but life is imperfect and irrational, is it not? Once I attempted suicide, mainly to relieve him of the burden, but he scolded me for that unmercifully, and I never tried it again. Life is short and in not a few ways unsatisfactory, but it is precious, or so I believe; so he taught me to believe. Yes, he was a good man. Not a prudent man, but good. When first we met, in Warsaw, I taught him to survive. Later, he taught me how to live. We reinforced each other."

"I'm sure you did."

"I count myself privileged to have been his wife. There was much joy he gave me. He was not, as I've said, sensible with money, yet he was always generous. His talents and energy kept it flowing in, and quite abundantly, but he also contrived to have it flow out with no less dispatch." She laughed. "I long ago concluded, however, that it would be useless to attempt to change him. He was eminently sensible about other things. Yes. He painted. He cooked. He did library work for me. He brought me stories and entertained me. Nubar showed me some aspects of life which my narrow upbringing and my restricted mobility might otherwise have left unknown to me.

"He even came to share my love of poetry. I well remember, when we were both struggling to master English as a new language-am I wearying you, Professor McLaughlin? No? Perhaps you'll indulge me in just this one vignette. I remember when he first brought me the poems of Emily Brontë, including a lovely thing titled 'Remembrance.' There was one bit of it which he liked most particularly, and frequently recited to me:

'Sweet Love of youth, forgive, if I forget thee,
While the world's tide is bearing me along;

Sterner desires and darker hopes beset me,
Hopes which obscure, but cannot do thee wrong.' "

She paused. McLaughlin looked away.

"You must pardon me if I am impaled by that memory," she continued. "Do you know the poem? No? Then you would not see the gentle irony, for the next stanza, which I dearly wish I had quoted to him more often or were able to let him hear today, is no less apposite.

'No other sun has lightened up my heaven,
No other star has ever shone for me;
All my life's bliss from thy dear life was given,
All my life's bliss is in the grave with thee.' "

McLaughlin rose and went over to the window. A clock ticked.

In a few moments her husky voice resumed. "I will mourn him, but I shall never regret him. He was not an orthodox person. No. Not an ordinary man. May I offer you another biscuit?"

"Thank you." He recrossed the room and made an impulsive decision. "Mrs. Nalorian, there is one thing you may not know about."

"What might that be?"

"Well, you know that Nobby, er, Nubar had prodigious energy. Did you know that he was helping our late colleague Bert Grimsby with a project? A textbook?"

"I don't recall that, no."

"Grimsby started it on his own, of course, some long while ago. But there were long gaps, and he couldn't seem to round it off, get it finished. Probably Nubar didn't want to make a big thing of it, at least not till it was done, but he began to collaborate with Bert and did a lot of work on it. Without Nubar, the book would never have been whipped into shape."

"Odd that he wouldn't have mentioned it to me."

"To him it was only a sideline. A bit of help to a colleague.

But the thing is, the manuscript has come into my, um, custody. Maybe because I'd known him longer, Grimsby left it to me. He and your husband had never gotten around to a contract. But Nubar had a real stake in it, sort of a co-author arrangement. I've read a bit, and I'm sure it has great commercial possibilities. So I hope you won't mind if I put some finishing touches on it – just a little editing here and there – and submit it to a publisher. Textbooks often make more money than other kinds of books."

"I've heard that."

"So you have no objection? Fine. I'll do what I can to see the book into print. Grimsby and Nalorian. *Principles of Economics*. I can't promise, of course, but I believe you may expect a very gratifying flow of income from it. If necessary, I'll undertake to revise it from time to time over the years, maybe for a small percentage when it gets to the second edition. But with Grimsby gone, the bulk of the royalties will be yours. As they should be. Does that sound acceptable to you?"

"Entirely acceptable. I'm surprised, but I thank you. And I trust I'm not depriving you of any source of revenue?"

"Not at all. I don't have many financial needs, and Nubar and Grimsby did the work, after all. My possession of the manuscript is purely accidental, and it will give me a lot of pleasure to see it succeed and be of some benefit to you."

When they parted, McLaughlin promised to drop in again, often, and to bring Trish. He smiled to himself as he went down the elevator. He felt better than he'd felt in weeks. It gave him a chuckle to think of Nobby and Grimsby as partners, and Mrs. Nalorian as the recipient of royalties. Even Sisyphus, he thought, got a reprieve on the downhill run. Easy come, easy go, and whatthehell.

For the first time in weeks he felt totally relieved – not guilty. Content. Confident. Even buoyant.

EPILOGUE

The university stood, solid and invulnerable, as institutions are and individuals are not. It was springtime, and as nature quickened her pulse the academic year, paradoxically, was coming to a close. The pressures of examinations had prevented most students from noticing that winter was gone and sunlit buds and grass beckoned. Undergraduates, only recently released from grim exam halls, still suffered from acute cases of end-of-term jitters and writer's cramp, while the faculty agonized over the scarcely perceptible differences on final scripts between C-plus and B-minus.

The annual graduation banquet of Burke College was an elaborate and happy occasion. Joyous youths congratulated each other on their triumphant B.A.s, little recognizing that they had barely reached the front porch of human knowledge, the introduction to long-term learning. Mrs. Nalorian smiled serenely as she sat among the distinguished guests at High Table. Dr. Wright addressed the graduating class and talked of opportunities yet to be seized, books yet to be read, and the importance of supporting the Alumni Fund. He surprised and relieved everyone by speaking only half an hour too long. Tributes were paid by the Principal to Grimsby and Nalorian, departed colleagues who would be missed, even though few students now remembered their names.

After the banquet, over coffee in the Senior Common Room, Wright recounted how he'd received word that, thanks to the efforts of the Faculty Association, a partial pension was to be paid to Mrs. Nalorian. Nobby's widow accepted the news with characteristic graciousness, and also thanked the officers of the college for having bought two of Nalorian's canvases as mementoes.

Inevitably the talk swung to matters of university politics. McLaughlin had been not in the least distressed to learn, several weeks earlier, that Naugle had resigned in order to accept the presidency of the Canadian Broadcasting Corporation – an impossible job if ever there was one, and J.T. wished him nothing but bad luck. Rumour had it that a search committee was about to announce the selection of Dr. Wright to succeed Naugle as President, which seemed to be a popular choice. It appeared likely that Cuttshaw had the inside track to become Chairman of the department if Wright moved up, and no one doubted that he would handle it well. In some ways it had been a very good year.

When the party broke up, McLaughlin drove Mrs. Nalorian home and then rejoined Trish and the Cuttshaws on the roof bar of the Park Plaza for nightcaps. Trish expressed keen delight over the forthcoming sabbatical. They'd decided to spend the year in London, where J.T. undoubtedly would write the definitive work on Innis or McLuhan or interest rates or whatever, while she made a close study of the fashion business.

They gossiped idly about friends and students. McLaughlin commented that he'd been glad to learn of Mildred Mott winning a scholarship to study with Giroux at the Sorbonne. In Paris she'd have a grand opportunity to hone her intellectual and social skills. Certainly she had done as well as or better than most of her colleagues, for Mohammed Zadran Khan had not finished this year but had run off with Boffy Bromley. Alice inquired whether they had gone to Afghanistan to uplift the poor? Not quite. The truth, as recounted by McLaughlin on the basis of several recent postcards, was that Mo had a relative, an uncle in California, who had set the lad up in business as the manager of a McDonald's hamburger franchise. Hopwood had talked of flying out to the coast to paint a mural for their walls, but the university had declined to pay the final instalment for his fountain and he was rather short of funds. Meanwhile, he continued to manage his nightclub on Bloor Street West. Trish insisted that J.T. take her to the Blue Venus some time. With Boffy and Mildred gone, Trish suggested archly, she might have a crack at winning the wet T-shirt contest. J.T. squeezed her thigh and allowed that she well might.

As the group left the bar and went out into the soft, warm night, McLaughlin commented how much he missed Nalorian, even though they hadn't known him long, but Cutty just smiled and nodded.

There were those who remarked that the ghost had not reappeared in the tower of Burke College all winter, not since the time of poor Grimsby's departure. Still, as Dr. Wright often observed, sensible people don't believe in ghosts anyway.